THE
DIGITAL
TRANSFORMER'S
DILEMMA

THE
DIGITAL
TRANSFORMER'S
DiLEMMA

How to Energize Your Core Business
While Building Disruptive Products and Services

Karolin Frankenberger, Hannah Mayer, Andreas Reiter,
and Markus Schmidt

WILEY

Library of Congress Cataloging-in-Publication Data:
Names: Frankenberger, Karolin, author.
Title: The digital transformer's dilemma : how to energize your core
    business while building disruptive products and services / Karolin
    Frankenberger, Hannah Mayer, Andreas Reiter, Markus Schmidt.
Description: Hoboken, New Jersey : John Wiley & Sons, Inc., [2021] |
    Includes index.
Identifiers: LCCN 2020025476 (print) | LCCN 2020025477 (ebook) | ISBN
    9781119701309 (paperback) | ISBN 9781119719472 (adobe pdf) | ISBN
    9781119719489 (epub)
Subjects: LCSH: Information technology—Management. | Organizational
    effectiveness. | Organizational change. | Strategic planning. | New
    products.
Classification: LCC HD30.2 .F727 2021 (print) | LCC HD30.2 (ebook) | DDC
    658.4/038—dc23
LC record available at https://lccn.loc.gov/2020025476
LC ebook record available at https://lccn.loc.gov/2020025477

Cover image: Wiley
Cover design: © sorbetto/Getty Images

Printed in the United States of America
SKY10020670_082520

TO ALL DIGITAL TRANSFORMERS

contents

Introduction

THE DIGITIZATION OF YOUR CORE BUSINESS IS NECESSARY, BUT THE FUTURE OF YOUR COMPANY LIES IN ITS NEW, DISRUPTIVE BUSINESS

YOUR BUSINESS MUST TRANSFORM TWICE TO SURVIVE

This book starts with a bit of bad news (which you already know) and some good news. The bad news, of course, is your legacy business is like a dinosaur, and threatened with the same fate—extinction. New start-ups, powerful tech companies, and other game changers are threatening the existence of every successful organization (see Figure 0.1). The good news is that firms (unlike literal dinosaurs) can prepare for drastic changes. This book is designed to help organizations prepare to meet the threat and succeed, by guiding them along the path of transformation.

The take-home message is, you actually have to transform twice: legacy firms need to transform their core, legacy-driven business while in parallel setting up new, disruptive (digital) businesses. That is, *all* firms. Irrespective of their industry, geography, or size, companies will need to strike that balance between two very different worlds. Large, well-known companies – like Michelin, Volkswagen, AB InBev, Nestlé, Novartis, and BNP Paribas – are just as much affected as smaller, hidden champions – such as Ohio-based manufacturer of precision instruments Mettler-Toledo, Swiss-based diversified tech conglomerate Bühler, or BTPN of Indonesia. We interviewed all of these – and many more – only to find that there is no safe haven for any particular kind of organization. Our apologies.

Figure 0.1 Dinosaur companies won't survive

Why is that, though? In essence, it's wrong to distinguish based on size or geography when it comes to digital transformation. Though some differentiation based on industry is possible due to differing sector maturity and the resulting differences in urgency to transform, the most relevant distinguishing factor is the age of the organization in question, making this a "start-up versus legacy firm" competition. Start-ups can launch disruptive innovations more easily than legacy firms because they are not bogged down by past (infra-) structural or mindset baggage. Legacy firms, on the other hand, cannot act as quickly because the organizational realities they face are more complex and harder to overcome. For them to continue to be successful in the old world while at the same time succeeding in a new world is a challenge no holistic consultant model captures – so far. We are trying to tackle the problem in this book.

The good news is, the digital world order that organizations need to brave is not as dystopian as one might think. On the contrary – it bears great potential that firms can tap into when they open their minds to disruptive innovations, including business model innovation paired with or based on the use of artificial intelligence, platform-based businesses, product-as-a-service, digitized customer journeys, and many more of those all-too-well-known buzzwords. We go beyond the buzzword hype, though, to illustrate how organizations not only can understand but can master the challenge of creating a radically new business which will rely on fundamentally different success factors than the core business.

Avid management literature readers will know that some books and concepts have addressed the necessity for disruptive innovations already. Think Blue Ocean Strategy, which talks about how companies can create new demand in previously untapped market spaces rather than fight over a shrinking profit pool with fierce competitors. Or think Three Horizons, which depicts innovation as occurring on three time horizons, with these time horizons gradually shortening, thus disadvantaging bureaucratic incumbents and advantaging nimble attackers well positioned to act swiftly. Yet one thing is missing: a concrete guide to the differing success factors in the core business versus those in the new disruptive business, particularly as relates to the implementation of such a transformation, and to how the tension inherent in the coexistence of these two businesses can best be managed. This is where we come in – the book at hand guides digital transformation practitioners from all sorts of organizations and across all career levels along the implementation of a holistic, two-tier digital transformation.

SOFTWARE IS EATING THE WORLD – AND COMPANIES STILL DON'T KNOW HOW TO ADAPT

Digitization is complicated and exciting and perilous. The possibility of autonomous cars has led automotive players to make huge investments in radically rethinking mobility – like Daimler and BMW, which have formed a joint venture covering new-generation services.[1] Now you can schedule a doctor's appointment via your phone while riding the subway to work. And don't we all value being able to search property listings online instead of having to drive to dozens of properties? On the more negative, perilous side of digitization, besides the much covered collapse of Nokia[2] and Kodak,[3] you may remember Nike halving the size of its digital unit, Lego defunding its Digital Designer virtual building program, and P&G not being able to achieve its ambition of becoming "the most digital company on the planet."[4] And, if nothing else, you have surely wondered how jobs, including your own, will be affected by digitization – especially given that 60% of occupations have at least 30% of constituent work activities that could be "automated away" and because significant skill shifts are expected as a result of automation and digitization.[5] It's understandable then that individuals and sometimes entire occupational groups fear digitization.

Digitization affects how we live, work, communicate, and consume products and services. It has enormous effects on how organizations operate – because established rules and best practices of doing business now have a rapidly approaching expiration date.[6] Also, established firms are being threatened by emerging start-ups and diversifying tech players, at the same time that traditional industry boundaries are falling. (Think about Google entering the healthcare and biosciences field by venturing into cancer detection and diabetes diagnosis.) Digitization also brings with it challenges like increased competition from China (Alibaba's possible expansion into North America and Europe), drastic shifts in customer preferences (TV's shift to streaming on demand), and new digital phenomena like ecosystems and platforms (can you think of a mobile operating system that is not a platform for thousands of third-party software developers?).

All these trends have gained momentum over the last few years. Nevertheless, we find that surprisingly few established firms have a clear view on how to best navigate the change brought about by digitization. All of them will, however, need to rethink their business if they want to ensure sustainable success. The bad news: sprinkling a bit of "digital glitter" over incumbents' core businesses does not suffice. Instead a fundamental overhaul of the business is necessary – a *digital transformation*.

It feels intimidating but transformation at this scale is actually nothing new. Think about the fundamental changes to ways of working as part of the industrial revolution in the 18th century. Digital transformation will have similarly wide-ranging effects. Arguably, transformations happen all the time across many organizations. But digital transformation is unprecedented in pace and impact, and thus drives profound changes in our economy and society.

From a fundamental economic and business perspective, the beauty and power of digitization comes from the fact that any digital representation can be perfectly replicated and transmitted at almost no marginal cost to a practically infinite number of globally dispersed customers.[7] Savor this slowly: virtually no marginal cost. This basic fact means that when a digital technology replaces an analog technology, the change it brings with it will be comprehensive, to say the least, thus fundamentally affecting the organizations and industries the technology touches. The organizations that can reap the most benefits from this are the digital pure players who lose any limit to scale and whose costs to scale are decimated. Meanwhile, some companies will continue to be bound by constraints rooted in the non-digital nature of their assets (for instance, physical constraints to cloud computing), though they may still be able to take advantage of the power of digitization (see the surge in demand for cloud computing).

It is this re-architecting of the nature of business that enables digital transformation to give rise to a wave of new opportunities for firms to take advantage of. And, generally speaking, it is exactly this fundamental disruption that makes a digital transformation structurally different from your typical plain-Jane business transformation, like cost-cutting transformations that have become commonplace for managers and employees alike.

In other words, a real digital transformation is not simply the deployment of information technology to aid traditional business models. Instead, a two-tier transformation is necessary: (a) careful thought needs to be given to how the traditional core of your organization can benefit from digitization and, at the same time, (b) you need to explore and capture new (digital) ways of creating value for your customers. This implies a fundamental re-architecture of an organization's business, which, post–digital transformation, needs to follow a dual business approach.

Historically, digitization has had an important, yet somewhat restrained impact on firms because it was introduced almost as a kind of "window dressing" on top of existing organizational systems, still reflecting typical processes. Most organizations did not drastically rethink their business model. By contrast, a business whose operations are founded on digital assets, structured around the ubiquity of data and information flows, would have profoundly different processes and constraints (this is a fundamentally new, digital business). While the former – the digitization of the core business – is vital for any digital transformation, the future of the business lies in the latter – the digital business. For instance, think of the extreme case of online pure players that operate solely in the digital space: there is no required human involvement when a price is changed at Amazon. Similarly, no human checks whether a new user should be allowed to join Facebook. The result: the absence of an organizational growth bottleneck and virtually no traditional limit to the scalability of these organizations. While we will not focus on such digital native companies or start-ups in this book, their business models and strategy certainly bear learnings and provide ample food for thought for established businesses, especially for how they may think about establishing their own digital business, thus venturing onto uncharted digital territory.

THE DIGITAL TRANSFORMER'S DILEMMA: ENERGIZING THE CORE BUSINESS WHILE BUILDING DISRUPTIVE NEW PRODUCTS AND SERVICES

Being the attentive reader that you are, you may wonder: none of this explains anything about a digital transformer's dilemma. Correct, the dilemma only arises once companies have understood there is a necessity to act across two businesses. Once they have embarked on their digital transformation journey, the dilemma they are all bound to face is: How can they maintain profitability in their legacy-based, core business activities (which we call the 1st S-curve) while reaping the full potential in a radically new, disruptive (digital) business (which we refer to as the 2nd S-curve)? In other words, how can the pursuit of the digitized 1st S-curve and the development of the innovative, digital 2nd S-curve best be reconciled in one organization, ensuring adequate links between the two? Put even more simply, how can firms digitize their core while reinventing their future (not just at the senior strategy-setting level but on the operational level as well)? That is the essence of the digital transformer's dilemma (see Figure 0.2).

The reality is that companies often struggle with striking that balance between 1st and 2nd S-curve efforts, often leading to animosities between the two.

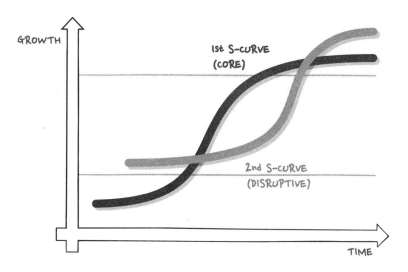

GROWTH

1st S-CURVE
(CORE)

2nd S-CURVE
(DISRUPTIVE)

TIME

Figure 0.2 Two S-curves

Source: Adapted from Gabriel Tarde. *The Laws of Imitation.* New York: Henry Holt and Company, 1903.

Think about it: the 1st S-curve will continue to generate the majority of the top line revenue for the time being and now also has to cover for the 2nd S-curve, which is bound to break even only later in the process. (It's a kind of sisterly rivalry, with a tendency of the 1st S-curve to be portrayed as the ugly stepchild.) Still, however, the 2nd S-curve will often be marketed both to the outside world and internally as a showpiece and token for visionary innovation. No wonder the 1st S-curve might feel undervalued and unjustly treated; similarly, no wonder that the 2nd S-curve might feel superior (many siblings would probably be able to attest to that). Managing the tensions between the two siblings . . . umm . . . S-curves is indispensable for the success of the digital transformation as a whole. The key to achieving that is for management and staff to internalize that the success factors on both S-curves differ significantly and that only through a well-orchestrated interplay between the two can the maximum digital transformation potential be realized.

If "The Digital Transformer's Dilemma" sounds familiar to you, you may have heard of Clayton Christensen's work. In his 1997 bestseller, *The Innovator's Dilemma,* he argued that successful companies can do everything right and still lose their market leadership position in the face of newly emerging competitors that pioneer disruptive technologies. Although his book dates from the 1990s, we believe a lot of the premises from *The Innovator's Dilemma* are experiencing a resurgence in importance today, including (and especially) in the digital transformation context. Decades of widely accepted principles of good management have become only situationally appropriate if not obsolete. Meanwhile a new set of rules and practices needs to be established to guide innovative (as Christensen argues) or transformational (as we argue) efforts.

WHAT OTHER DIGITAL TRANSFORMATION BOOKS DON'T TELL YOU

Many publications center around the "why" of digital transformation, convincing C-level executives of the role a digital overhaul plays for the continued success of a company and evangelizing there is a need to act to begin with. The "why" certainly is important because, arguably, knowledge is the first step to improvement – and admittedly it is also what we just dedicated the first few pages to and what we will dive into more in the next chapter as well. But we aspire to something more. To date there has been very limited guidance on the "how" of running a digital transformation. This book is the first practitioner-oriented roadmap on how to execute a digital transformation in real life. We present a set of actionable steps, highlighting how to avoid common pitfalls and address and overcome barriers along the way. This book is for all those who encounter digital transformation in their daily lives, not just the select few at the top but mid-level managers and staff as well. For the former, Parts 1 and 2 – where we describe the reasons for embarking on a digital transformation and how to go about strategy setting – will be particularly insightful. For the latter, the essence of our book – Part 3 describes in detail how to go about running a digital transformation and Part 4 is dedicated to success measurement – will be most relevant.

We want to entertain you, inspire you, and, most importantly, set you up for success when running *your* digital transformation with the tools you need to launch a digital transformation yourself. We introduce you to all facets of the dilemma, tell you how to manage the tension between the 1st and 2nd S-curves, and outline action plans for how to best address these challenges. To do that, we use an innovative format, showing a host of brand-new, in-depth case studies based on over 100 interviews with executives from a broad set of industries and geographies.

While the Alibabas and Amazons of the world may be prime examples for navigating the digital world, they never had to deal with the requirements of transforming a legacy business. Instead, we focus on those companies with a long legacy to showcase how they can transition into the digital age while keeping their core intact – maintaining their traditional business activities on the 1st S-curve while reaping the full digital potential on the 2nd S-curve. We explore how to best tackle the interaction between the two S-curves while making sure to strike a balance between maintaining profitability in the core and at the same time establishing the new, disruptive (digital) business. This holistic look at the two S-curves instead of just zeroing in on 2nd S-curve champions is a departure from what others have written. It would be grossly negligent to disregard growth opportunities in the core business that can be taken advantage of when digitization is introduced. In many industries and business lines, it is imaginable that the 2nd S-curve eventually becomes the 1st S-curve and the original 1st S-curve ceases to be a considerable top-line revenue contributor. But these are natural, longer-term developments. Even when that happens, though, a new 2nd S-curve will be waiting around the corner. Striking a balance between two very different worlds will remain a central topic for organizations even in the future.

To set you up for success, we also provide you with a load of practical tips and all the tools you need to succeed in real life. In the "Resources" section you will find interactive tools for guiding the strategizing and implementation of your own digital transformation alongside a set of actionable steps. On our website (www.thedigitaltransformersdilemma.com) you will find an even bigger repository of materials to make use of.

WHY AND HOW WE WROTE THIS BOOK

We hold ourselves to the same standards that we suggest companies follow, in keeping with the motto: You want to talk about transformation? You have to live transformation!

First, we saw the need to fill a gap: despite much literature on the "why," there's a lack of "how"-oriented digital transformation guides. We devised an initial experimentation phase: inspired by some of the textbook ways of working utilized in digital transformation, we first established a minimum viable product (MVP) of the book. We used that to test our vision with leading digital transformation minds (C-level executives, company owners, thought leaders, and scholars) and digital transformation practitioners (project managers, business unit heads, individual contributors). We incorporated their feedback, making frequent iterations before establishing a prototype of the book as early on as possible (following the motto "fail fast, fail cheap").

Eventually we needed some meat on the bone. A vision and an MVP are good and all, but you can't make something out of nothing. So, we assembled 100+ different corporate case studies based on interviews with leading executives and operational managers leading digital transformation initiatives in companies that managed to Uber themselves before they got Kodak'ed.[8] This informed our digital transformation how-to framework. We kept iterating this framework with various test audiences and made sure to incorporate their input.

Finally came the finishing touches, which, in author lingo, means writing up the whole thing. Well, as you can see, we did that, too.

But then something happened.

PANDEMIC MEETS DIGITAL TRANSFORMATION

Life – regular and business – around the globe changed abruptly and unexpectedly in spring 2020 with the outbreak of a novel Coronavirus, introducing new norms related to social distancing, reduced mobility, remote work, homeschooling, the (near-)shut-down of entire industries (and the sudden surge of others), expansive lay-offs, and haphazard stock markets. Companies found themselves in the field of fire, torn between the demands of radically new realities imposed by the virus and the deep-rooted necessity (and oftentimes, long-prepared ambition) to digitally transform. As COVID-19 brought with it a transformational impact on the nature of work, the structure of firms, and the economic realities of people, businesses, and countries, many questions emerged, some of which related to digital transformation: What does Coronavirus mean for digital transformation and how can the two be reconciled? Specifically, what are repercussions of the virus for the 1st S-curve, the 2nd S-curve, and their interplay? Who ends up a winner, and who ends up losing in this nexus of transformations?

We have no crystal ball to answer these questions and predict long-term effects of COVID-19 on digital transformation with certainty. This includes whether post-pandemic effects will reshape life fundamentally in the long run and alter the rules of the game completely, or whether it is only select parameters that will change and we'll largely be able to go back to business as usual. In the absence of such certainty, we would caution everyone to take our views with a grain of salt, as they reflect our latest thinking as of April 2020 based on the information available at the time and our own opinions. But one thing is undisputed: Coronavirus and digital transformation are intimately linked. Here's what this means.

One, the pandemic is like a benchmark to past digital transformation efforts and bears learnings on how well companies have digitally transformed

The COVID-19 pandemic is not unlike a stress test to a firm's digital transformation to date, able to unveil any flaws inherent in (digital) business models quicker than they would have otherwise surfaced. Those firms whose digital transformation across both S-curves was well underway before the COVID-19 outbreak are at an advantage in times of Coronavirus, as are firms that managed to swiftly rally digitization efforts at the onset of the crisis to rapidly bring about digital value propositions. Organizations that missed their ticket onto MS Digital Transformation (before and at the beginning of the crisis) are poised to be left behind. This means that companies whose value-add is generated and rendered through digital means (or that have managed to morph into this profile quickly) will, on average, weather the Corona storm better than those whose value generation lies purely offline. Though in a global recession, which economists agree we are headed into,[9] none are real but only relative winners. The question is not so much who ends up a winner but rather who will lose the least.

Naturally, digital pure players are well positioned to reap the benefits of a virtually powered economy, particularly when they don't rely on human involvement to complete transactions. Think, for instance, of ZOOM, which has managed to grab a large share of the delicious and oh-so-topical virtual conferencing pie, with shares surging 63% in three months.[10]

Foot traffic, unfortunately, is equal to a Corona-infested death bed: when there's no feet, there's no business. Companies that have adamantly focused only on their 1st S-curve operations hence are at a disadvantage. They will find themselves cash-strapped after the crisis. Traditional firms relying on in-person interaction to render services are thus hit the hardest, though if they manage to entertain or quickly set up a digital channel, they may be able to dampen negative effects.

One such example is Domino's, where delivery makes up 55% of total orders. Domino's is thus well positioned to thrive during Corona, as proven by its call to hire 10,000 workers due to increased demand[11] while millions of US workers file for unemployment.[12] It is one of the only big chains that refuses to work with outside delivery apps such as DoorDash or Grubhub, which promise to boost restaurant sales but take a cut of that money. Having its own delivery app, drivers, and pickup infrastructure – and thus full control over value chain and customer service – is a winning strategy for Domino's in times of social distancing. A focus on the Corona-minded customer who cares about contactless delivery[13] paired with increased profits thanks to cutting out middlemen proves a viable strategy to accelerate digital (2nd S-curve) as opposed to dining-in (1st S-curve) business.

Even among those entities that are system-critical, the digitally transformed ones will do best. One example is governments, which are center stage amidst the crisis, alongside select essential firms. Countries like South Korea were praised early on as flagship nations to have brought the spread of the virus under control, harnessing surveillance-camera footage, smartphone location data, and credit card purchase records to help trace the recent movements of coronavirus patients and establish virus transmission chains.[14] These countries have long been able to monitor and analyze such data, and may be expanding such tools, practices, and know-how into Western jurisdictions, though with adaptations to ease privacy concerns.[15] Known as digital frontrunners, some Asian countries have remarkable transparency over individual citizens' details, including not only their own whereabouts and movements but relationships to other patients. The widely hailed digital transformation of such administrations[16] serves their people well, now more than ever.

Two, while digitally transformed companies will, on average, weather the Corona storm better, some of the digital transformers will win more than others

Among the digitally transformed organizations, some will take away big chunks of the overall smaller pie that's being generated now, owing to their business model or industry.

For instance, subscription-related digital business models will likely fare better than ads-based ones because when a recession hits, companies typically reduce ad spending to a significant degree while individual consumers likely will still splurge on that US$9/month Netflix subscription.

Also, diversification away from the core product or service (particularly if that is eliminated in times of Corona) is a strategy worth aspiring to, if possible – and it's best combined with low fixed costs. Consider ride-hailing services. When people are staying home, they don't exactly need rides – a painful truth Uber, Lyft, and other ride-hailing companies know all too well. Uber, however, is in the position of being able to hedge some bets more favorable to a Corona-ridden economy. Think Uber Eats for food delivery, Uber Health for scheduling healthcare-related rides, or Uber Freight for shipping.

Industry-wise, the Corona crisis is summoning a bifurcation of economic sectors, where some are at a disadvantage because demand is eradicated and others are at an advantage because demand is relatively unaffected or even boosted. Among the losers is the travel and hospitality industry, with cruise ships and airlines taking the hardest hit. But even the digitally transformed players in that sector that even enjoy low fixed costs (such as Airbnb, which doesn't pay rent for its property listings) are hit hard because when travel is discouraged or altogether banned, demand and bookings plunge.[17] Among the winners are, for instance, grocery retailers, though sales of higher margin products (such as clothing) have declined sharply and been substituted for lower margin shopping (think toilet paper). Still, this is their moment. Walmart is doing particularly well, with investments in its ecommerce infrastructure paying off.[18] Besides the winners and losers, there are also some double-edged swords, where the pandemic is favoring one party of a typical two-party deal and adversely affecting the other. Consider the start-up scene and investing. This is not a terrific time for start-ups – at least, not for some. As a result of the overall economic downturn, start-up valuations dwindle and overvaluations are becoming a thing of a past.[19] While some start-ups struggle, this may just be the moment for PEs (private equity firms) and VCs (venture capital) who have ample dry powder[20] – unspent capital on their balance sheets ready to be invested[21] in ventures which they might be able to snap up at bargain prices. (And it is not just start-ups, but many industries hit hard by the crisis.) The relatively low valuations of entrepreneurial and other ventures paired with the availability of cash on the part of PEs and VCs will make for an interesting investing landscape, poised to favor the most disruptive, digital businesses. The Corona crisis may thus be a déjà-vu of the 2008 crisis, in the aftermath of which a number of now-unicorns hatched, including Uber, Dropbox, and Spotify.

Three, the pandemic spurs an increased push toward digital transformation for all firms

Efforts to accelerate both digital business and digital work will become more commonplace, following extended periods of time where all parties involved have become used to new practices and offerings.

On the digital business side, even beyond Corona, customers will appreciate the new digital value propositions and channels that are becoming standard. At the same time, organizations are well advised to continue to maintain and extend these digital offerings and sales channels, building on learnings from the Corona crisis and knowing that customers have morphed into digital aficionados. Think gym classes: luxury workout chain Barry's is keeping people engaged with free online gym classes (2nd S-curve) until in-person Barry's workouts return (1st S-curve).[22] But would there be a reason to discontinue online gym classes even when gyms have reopened? Probably not, given this is turning into everyone's daily routine.

Similarly, Walmart e-grocery delivery accounted for only a fraction of the turnover, but it's probably here to stay. Ping An's "Do It At Home" offering launched in February, allowing customers to access a series of financial and non-financial services on the Ping An Pocket Bank app, including lending, credit cards, FX, medical counselling, doctors' appointments, and auto services.[23] There's a good chance consumers will continue to value this well beyond Corona. If there was ever a time to digitize the core business or fast-track the disruptive digital business, then this is it.

On the digital work side, continuing to allow people to work remotely after extended periods of time where they have become accustomed to that will make sense. It stands to reason that we are at the onset of new work realities. With leading management consultants now advising their clients remotely, will strategy consulting as a whole become more accommodating to remote work? With the NYSE closing its trading floor,[24] will electronic trading become the new norm? With schools and universities bringing their curricula online in a matter of days,[25] will remote learning supersede (or be on par with) in-presence classes? With much experience in doing all of this in tow, businesses will likely hold on to these practices post-Corona, catapulting them all several years forward in their evolution toward digital transformation.

SUCCESS IS NOT SUCCESS – THE RULES ARE DIFFERENT IN THE OLD AND NEW WORLDS

Based on our research and practical experience consulting with many different firms, we found there are several success principles legacy companies must internalize as they navigate a minefield of digital transformation traps across the two S-curves. The key is understanding that the core business (1st S-curve) needs to be refined and digitized while a new, disruptive, digital business (2nd S-curve) is being established. The success factors for these two S-curves differ strongly, yet the two S-curves must be integrated with each other and not be operated as two standalone worlds. Particularly the success factors of the 2nd S-curve – and the 2nd S-curve business in general – will gain in importance, as disruptive digital products and services are key to making up for losses incurred in the traditional business in the aftermath of the Coronavirus pandemic.

Digital strategy needs to be part of a holistic company strategy – but the challenge, really, is not strategy; 2nd S-curve activities must not be based on lengthy analyses and philosophical deliberations; instead, quick-and-dirty implementation trumps extensive planning. The 1st S-curve should then take inspiration from the 2nd S-curve, using some of their principles where appropriate. Meanwhile the 2nd S-curve should rely on proven 1st S-curve success factors when it comes to scaling the new digital business. Both hard and soft factors matter for the success of the implementation, with soft factors revolving around talent and mindset and hard factors revolving around (infra-) structural elements. Once underway, performance needs to be measured on both S-curves, using different, S-curve-specific metrics, so as to keep track of the transformational progress.

To best illustrate how the success principles pan out holistically, we cast these insights into a four-part framework (see Figure 0.3). This framework lays out how the interplay of the two S-curves takes effect over the course of a digital transformation. Its dimensions (Why, What, How, Where) and sub-dimensions make up the structure of this book.

WHY: We investigate reasons for embarking on a digital transformation to begin with and explain why a dual business that allows exploiting traditional business activities (1st S-curve) and exploring ways of reaping the full digital potential (2nd S-curve) is necessary. We also look at why so many companies have failed to act timely and get it right.

WHAT: We describe how to develop an overarching strategy that includes a strategy for the core business, a strategy for the new, disruptive (digital) business and a plan for how to marry the two and adequately manage the interactions between the two. We also provide advice on how to develop a business model rooted in novel ways of value creation and value capture to bring the strategy to life and guide practitioners on how to go from strategy to business model.

HOW: While it's indispensable to go through the Why-What process, great thinking is only the beginning. The real challenge lies in the nuts and bolts

The Way Out of
The Digital Transformer's Dilemma

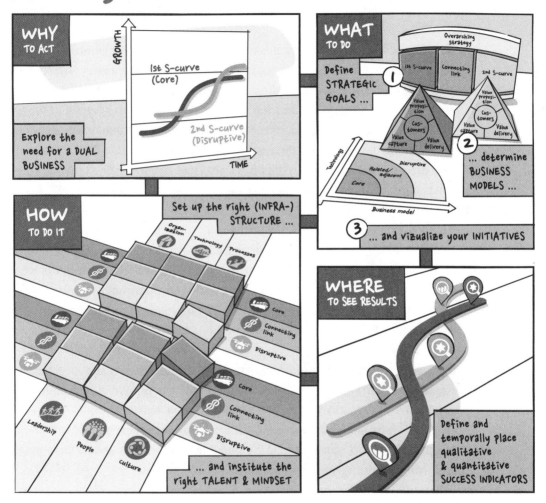

Figure 0.3 The Digital Transformer's Dilemma

Source: Business model components adapted from Oliver Gassmann, Karolin Frankenberger, Michaela Csik. *The Business Model Navigator*. 1st Edition. ©2014. Reprinted by permission of Pearson Education. S-curves adapted from Gabriel Tarde. *The Laws of Imitation*. New York: Henry Holt and Company, 1903.

of getting the transformation done – and this is what this book focuses on. To make sure the implementation goes smoothly, we explain how to set up the right (infra-) structure (organization, technology, processes) and institute the right talent and mindset (leadership, people, culture).

Organization: Adding digital roles to the organization is not enough. Instead, fundamental changes to the organizational setup are necessary. We start by outlining the different places the digital impetus can originate from both on the 1st and 2nd S-curves, and move on to portraying archetypes of where and how to best anchor the new (digital) business in the overall organizational setup, depending on the respective company's level of digital maturity and the similarity to the core business. We close by suggesting how to bridge the organizational gap between the two worlds.

Technology: Throwing around technology buzzwords like AI, machine learning, IoT, and big data is in vogue these days. Start-ups already combine the use of these trends with real business models. We tell incumbents what the most relevant technologies for them are and point out implementation success factors. We also deep dive into IT and explain to best combine the old and new IT architectures.

Processes: To run a digital transformation, it takes the right processes. We detail what an ideal stage gate development process looks like, following relevant best practices from the start-up scene and a lighthouse project-oriented approach. We also talk about the governance bodies it takes to support this processual setup, how budgetary allocation should take place, and where funding should come from.

Leadership: Leadership styles on the 1st and 2nd S-curves vary substantially. We talk about what specific leadership attributes are most conducive to digital transformation efforts on both curves, and how these attributes can be built. We also detail how the coexistence of these differing leadership styles in one company can best be managed.

People: The essence of a digital transformation is the people executing it. We showcase what the skills are that employees should be bringing to the digital transformation table and provide guidance on how the workforce of the future, contributing those skills, can be built.

Culture: Although the term "culture" may seem elusive to some, we define it quite strictly as the beliefs and behaviors determining how members of a company interact with each other. The question we then answer is, how can new beliefs and behaviors that are necessary for digital transformation be fostered in keeping with the organization's mission, vision, and values, which may remain unchanged. We speak about the kind of changes in beliefs and behaviors necessary and illustrate how to orchestrate this cultural change.

WHERE: Let's not forget that also in a digital transformation does the age-old saying hold: only what gets measured gets done. Measuring impact is therefore quintessential. We illustrate how to go about measurement across and specific to both S-curves, balancing qualitative and quantitative KPIs (key performance indicators). We also make sure to mention how to set objectives, assign account-ability, and ensure transparency vis-à-vis the relevant stakeholder group.

As you read this, we hope this appears logical and makes intuitive sense. Conceptual logic, however, does not always translate into real-life practice. Meaning, in reality, the individual dimensions of this framework are often not as clear-cut. Instead there is a multitude of interdependencies between them. For instance, a change in your **WHAT** will have game-changing influences on almost all of your **HOW** sub-dimensions; any impact you track in your **WHERE** may in turn have repercussions on your **WHAT**. This implies that the four framework dimensions are not typically passed through in a strictly consecutive order but that there can (and will and should) be loops. When was the last time you rode a rollercoaster? Well, time to get ready for some head-over-heels action again.

This is not to say that the framework presented here is not realistic, though. Simply what it means is that our framework is the depiction of the ideal state. Many (though, in this case, not all) roads lead to Rome. Companies can and have been successful with a variety of different approaches. But from our interviews, we have isolated the most promising ones and compiled them to form an ideal state framework. For those companies that have already begun their digital transformation, this means they can deep-dive into the elements and sub-dimensions that matter to them while sticking to their own strategy in others if they so wish. For those companies whose digital transformation journeys have yet to begin, we suggest following the ideal path we depict. It is based on the learnings of so many other enterprises and it may just save them a few gray hairs.

Even as the business world is changing in response to the COVID-19 pandemic, the guidelines for running a digital transformation remain just as relevant, with the only difference being that the importance of 2nd S-curve attributes is accelerated and those become the new norm more quickly. Firms not only need to manage the organizational ambidexterity of the 1st and 2nd S-curve but also need to balance the duality of having to manage the Corona crisis in the short term while preparing for a post-Corona world in the mid-term. New technologies are being introduced more quickly now than before. Think ZOOM, which has become the work-from-home communication medium of choice in no time, standing in for formal in-person meetings, informal catchups, watercooler chit-chat, and even superseding phone calls. Processes need to be expedited so as to take advantage of opportunities online – the new standard marketplace. 1st S-curve staff are being trained and repurposed to support on 2nd S-curve initiatives. Leaders need to demonstrate now more than ever their ability to lead within a VUCA (Volatility, Uncertainty, Complexity, and Ambiguity) world, demonstrating courage, resilience, entrepreneurial drive, and an aptitude for swift decision making. More networks, fewer hierarchies, more and quicker learning, fewer silos, and more agility are becoming the new cultural norms much quicker now than they would have if it weren't for Coronavirus. So, while COVID-19 goes down in the history books as a disastrous public health crisis, it did accelerate digital transformation significantly.

A real-life caveat to our ideal state framework is that there will be back-coupling effects between the two S-curves. Particularly, the 2nd S-curve will have implications on the 1st S-curve. Consider, for example, the **WHERE**: positive performance on your 2nd S-curve may lead to spill-over effects onto your 1st S-curve. Say the new (digital) business is achieving stellar growth rates and gets a lot of favorable press coverage. This will surely translate into increased investor confidence and potentially rising share prices, which are typical 2nd S-curve indicators. At the same time, the added speed the 2nd S-curve champions in their own business will likely spill over to the 1st S-curve, making operations and the use of resources in general more efficient, thus contributing to traditional 1st S-curve KPIs, such as Return on Assets (ROA). Remember the rollercoaster you were getting ready for earlier? We would imagine the rollercoaster to have multiple lanes such that, as you – a 1st S-curve rider – are sitting in your own seat in a carriage with your fellow 1st S-curve riders, other riders may be creeping up behind you on a separate lane headed toward the 2nd S-curve and giving your whole carriage a boost as you head further down your own path.

A final piece in our framework-rollercoaster logic is the inexorable truth that even if you have mastered the four elements and survived the ride, this is not the end. Eventually your 2nd S-curve might just become a 1st S-curve again as the original 1st S-curve ceases to represent any value to customers. And then the whole cycle starts anew. The conditions then may be different; the underlying technologies may have changed; your customers may have fundamentally new mindsets; or a global pandemic may have pushed you to introduce new digital products and services more rapidly than planned, with a resulting need to think about new frontiers beyond the original 2nd S-curve sooner than anticipated. But the reality of companies having to transform themselves yet again, and to do this in parallel to continuing to pursue what will have become their core business by then, remains unchanged. As Ginni Rometty, former CEO of IBM, correctly pointed out, "The only way to survive is to continuously transform."[26]

You will find this book to be lined with many more anecdotes from executives willingly riding that rollercoaster and owning it. Most are ruling select bits of the ride; a few have mastered them all. Certainly, all of them know the highs and lows associated with a rollercoaster. Let's turn to one thrilling example.

WASTE. TRASH. GARBAGE. SCRAP. RUBBISH. DEBRIS. REFUSE. JUNK.

When it comes to digital transformation, waste management may just feature some groundbreaking insights not only for the savvy environmentalists but also for the aspiring digital transformers among us.

SAUBERMACHER

Launched in 2016 in the quaint Austrian city of Graz by waste management company Saubermacher, "Wastebox" – an app-based waste disposal solution – announced in 2018 that globally leading resource management conglomerate Veolia of France had acquired a minority stake in the venture and would help facilitate its international expansion, beginning with Germany and France. Veolia joined to get access to a highly promising concept: a customer- and supplier-friendly solution for coordinating waste management via a digital platform, connecting construction companies with waste disposal firms to optimize construction waste logistics. A mere two years after its inception, Wastebox had garnered a significant valuation and Saubermacher was wooed by one of the global industry leaders to engage in a partnership with them. That's impressive by any account.

Let's rewind to see how they got there.

The notion to build a new digital business at Saubermacher was originally rooted in two senior executives', including Chief Market Officer Andreas Opelt, musings on where new (digital) industry entrants could potentially and most easily force their company out of the market. The waste management business basically consists of two sub-components: (1) logistics and (2) treatment. Treatment being a very capital-intensive business, logistics is more prone to offer room for digitization, and thus more threat for new entrants. The senior executives considered how their own waste logistics business – which can be seen as a web of taxi rides of large waste containers and skips between waste disposal firms and customers – was doing. Despite this in principle being a straightforward business, it was at the time characterized by low margins, opaque processes, and low customer satisfaction due to a poorly engineered business model. This is **why** they saw an opportunity to improve their own offering by proposing a radically new digital business model – preemptively before any new entrant could do so.

To determine the details of **what** to do, meaning of the digital strategy and underlying business model, they conducted an international screening in search of whether comparable solutions already existed. They found only one firm in North America with a similar idea that had attracted significant funding, which was a positive indication for them to assume that pursuing this path would present a viable business opportunity. Although they originally considered not building a product from scratch themselves, they couldn't find a suitable partner. So they sat together internally and conducted a textbook exercise on business model innovation: they used the Business Model Canvas[27] to think about the value proposition, cost structure, revenue streams, and so forth and hence developed a first proposal to become the "Uber of waste disposal logistics." They then had this challenged by an internal committee in a "Dragons' Den" style and made adjustments accordingly.

Once they had established the basics of the idea and stress-tested it with the "Dragons," several structural issues needed to be addressed. They opted to run the **organization** as a separate unit, quite disconnected from the parent company, which allowed them to operate very freely. In fact, they eventually formed a standalone legal entity called "Pink Robin," which continues to contain Wastebox and to be run as a 100% subsidiary of the parent company, Saubermacher. **Technology** was another key aspect of infrastructural decisions to be made. The key here was not to allow any requirements from the parent company. The only requirements were set by the new business itself: they wanted only what the "Googles and Facebooks" of this world would use, allowing for instant releases, native design, and so forth. Specifically, the **process** they followed entailed the following steps: in the first half year, a core team with around five members with cross-functional backgrounds was set up and jointly performed the Business Model Canvas exercise and developed the first mockups. At that time the entity was still embedded within the parent company but physically separate in their own co-working space. The following months saw more rapid prototyping and fast iterations of the product whose MVP launched about 15 months after the birth of the idea. This is when more sales associates were onboarded. About 21 months into the journey, the digital business was officially spun off from the parent company. Two years after inception, it had already turned into the largest construction waste disposal logistics provider in their home country, Austria. This is when the intent to internationalize kicked in. Following a number of partnership talks, including with a global waste management leader, a franchising model was agreed on according to which Veolia could use the model in exchange for a minority stake in the business. Three years after inception, the business is live in three markets across Europe and is steered by a team of 40 people.

At least as important as structural decisions were talent-related matters. For their **leadership** profiles, they were looking for people who would embrace a failure culture, who would have high risk tolerance, and who could be transformational leaders who inspire others to follow their vision. Most importantly, they were looking for people who, based on their expertise and experience, were able to relate to both the traditional business and the digital business world. In terms of the operational staff who were going to be part of the new digital business, they were looking for some **people** with a sales background to help the new product gain momentum quickly, some who had experience in the waste disposal supply chain and some with IT skills. Luckily, they were able find someone in-house who would later become the key IT mastermind of the new digital business. Others were hired and some redeployed. No retraining efforts were undertaken. For some specifics (for example, the app itself), they also relied on outsourcing to contractors (they worked with agile software development agency Denovo of Austria) although this was marked by an intense, very close cooperation given the centrality of the app itself to the business model and, ultimately, the success of the venture. Having assembled the team, a key point was to overthrow the traditional hierarchy-driven **culture**. In fact, the new digital business model has an official mandate to be a testing bed of new ways of working rooted in agility, cross-functional cooperation, and rapid prototyping. This was so successful that these ways of working have now been carried back into the core organization.

In terms of **where** to measure impact, transparency was considered key. It was ensured that the key performance indicators (KPIs) – for example, number of customers, number of transactions, number of participating partners – were transparently accessible to all key stakeholders. Learnings were obtained particularly with regard to objective setting. Initially, highly ambitious benchmarks were striven for. When it became clear that these were too ambitious to reach, they were adjusted to a reflect a more realistic, yet still ambitious aspiration level. That flexibility to reflect an updated knowledge of the market and its potential was deemed very important.

And it didn't stop there. In addition to developing a new digital business model, Saubermacher made sure to feed Wastebox learnings back into the core organization. Processes have been digitized using the Wastebox ways of working. Wastebox standards have started to be introduced as company-wide standards. Meanwhile, as Wastebox continues with its international expansion, it relies more and more on established ways of doing business during its scale-up phase. So not only are effects of the successful digital business now pervasive in the core but the new digital business is also starting to rely on proven success factors from the core. The two S-curves at Saubermacher thus do not live in isolation but cross-fertilize each other.[28]

The success Saubermacher experienced was not thanks to a lucky streak. You don't know it yet (and maybe they didn't know it at the time) but they followed the textbook recipe for running a digital transformation. Welcome to the recipe book.

Part 1
WHY TO ACT

chapter 1
ACT OR DIE, PRETTY SOON

n this chapter we investigate different reasons for embarking on a digital transformation and analyze why so many companies have failed to act timely and get it right. We also explain why a dual business that allows exploiting traditional business activities (1st S-curve) and exploring ways of reaping the full digital potential (2nd S-curve) is necessary (see Figure 1.1).

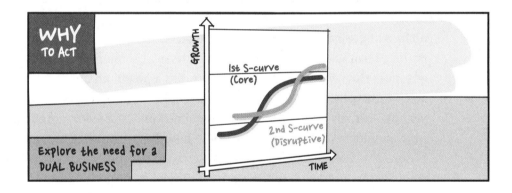

Figure 1.1 Key visual with focus on Why
Source: S-curve graph adapted from Gabriel Tarde. *The Laws of Imitation*. New York: Henry Holt and Company, 1903.

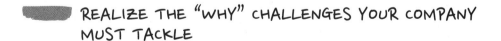 ## REALIZE THE "WHY" CHALLENGES YOUR COMPANY MUST TACKLE

Incumbents that aim to digitally transform their businesses face the dilemma of maintaining profitability in the core business and at the same time establishing a new (digital) business. What might sound trivial and like an intuitive approach is a challenge for many organizations, even before incumbents get to work on the transformation. Before they dive right in, they need to reach an agreement about the importance of a dual business approach. This requires them to build up awareness for the environmental factors that threaten their current business and any emerging opportunities for a new business model. Hence, incumbents need to ask themselves: How does digitization affect the core business in the short-, medium-, and long-term? Who are the players, and what are opportunities and threats that need to be considered?

While the need to act and transform the core business is often straightforward, things are not always so clear on the 2nd S-curve. Hence managers might also ask themselves: How can they reach alignment and clarity about the need to act on both S-curves? What needs to be done if management and supervisory boards do not agree on the importance of the new (digital) business? In fact, concerns around the current business often overwhelm other efforts that focus on new (digital) business opportunities. That's how numerous firms end up focusing most of their transformational efforts on the existing core business, putting insufficient emphasis on future growth opportunities. This begs the question: How can incumbents avoid ending up with an unbalanced approach and conflicts between the two S-curves? Prior to that, why should incumbents act at all if their core business is still doing well? And even more importantly, how should managers convince their boards to prioritize the new (digital) business, when their core business is struggling and requiring all available resources? And how does the urgency differ between industries? These questions should be answered at the very beginning of every digital transformation.

Once the organization has reached agreement about the need for a dual business approach, new questions emerge. For example, what are the common pitfalls that need to be considered in this phase? Why do so many organizations struggle to act timely and transform successfully? Lots of organizations have already tried to transform themselves, so is there something to be learned from past failures of others, and how can these mistakes be avoided? Many more could be asked and we are just at the very beginning of the transformation. But don't worry – we have you covered.

FIGURE OUT YOUR OWN "WHY" BEFORE YOU DO ANYTHING ELSE

"Self-awareness is the way to improve oneself," says an old proverb. The same holds true in the context of digital transformation. The first step is the realization that there is a need to act to begin with. The answer to the **WHY** question then forms the basis for all subsequent decisions. Understanding how digitization affects the industry and the business model is a good starting point to raise awareness about the necessity of a transformation and inform the required change in direction. Of course, realizing the need to act is first and foremost a responsibility of the top management. But this does not mean that this chapter is only relevant for them. In fact, it is often employees at lower levels who have an ear to the market and can therefore provide valuable answers to the starting question and initiate the transformation process in the first place. The **WHY** may be motivated by many different reasons. Based on our 100+ interviews, we have collected and sorted the reasons why incumbents felt the need to act and embark on a new, digital journey. Let's look into the various reasons.

Threat from new competitors

While incumbents are used to competitors of the same kind, digitization brings two new types of players to the table: big tech players and start-ups.

Companies such as Facebook, Amazon, Apple, Netflix, and Alphabet from the United States or Baidu, Alibaba, and Tencent from China are examples of so-called "big-tech" players that have radically changed the competitive landscape over the past few years. These firms, originally focused on the commercial internet (Apple being the exception), are now pushing into traditional industries, posing a real threat to the long-established business of many incumbents. They benefit from the fact that new technologies tear down barriers between established industries, allowing them to expand more easily into adjacent industries and domains. This leads to an unprecedented global competition between "old"-world companies and new digital players, as tech players are reshaping one industry after the other.

Big-tech players are not the only new threat in the competitive landscape. More and more start-ups try to break into established industries. Global hubs such as those located in Silicon Valley, Tel Aviv, Shenzhen, Berlin, Paris, and elsewhere form an ecosystem where new business ideas are born and raised. These start-ups enter into the traditional domains of incumbents and threaten their leading position, often with remarkable success. Just think about the large number of digital disruptors (or digital attackers) that we have seen in recent years. Online direct bank N26 or intercity coach service operator FlixBus are famous European examples of start-ups that have very successfully stolen substantial market share from incumbents in traditional industries. In the United States, Uber, Airbnb, and the like have started their triumph over established asset-heavy industries. Looking at the success of these start-ups, their compelling stories are often based on a relatively simple but smart combination of new technologies and business model innovation.

What large-tech players and start-ups have in common is their focus on the customers' end-to-end experience. Looking at customers' needs through a digital-first lens allows them to tap into unserved needs that have been ignored by established players.

Threat from existing competitors

While it's often new players that increase competition within established industries, forcing incumbents to react, the need for a digital transformation can also be triggered by other established players that set the tone for the entire industry. A global survey among 1,600 executives found that "reinvented incumbents" – established players competing in new and digital ways – are outperforming their traditional peers in terms of growth and returns.[1] The results of this study show that incumbents that truly embrace digital business opportunities in their investment and strategic decisions are just as big a threat to established players as digital native companies. Firms that act as leaders and shape the digital agenda put their counterparts under pressure to follow suit. Compared to their peers, the digital reinventors are more likely to make radical changes to their strategy and business models, to use new technologies at scale, and to make bolder investments into digitization efforts.

New or shifted industry and/or customer trends

In addition to competitive threats, the need to act can be propelled by new trends that fundamentally reshape the way businesses operate. The digital revolution is altering customer expectations and industry boundaries at a faster pace than ever before. Customer-centric value propositions connect previously separated industries and create new experiences that were unthinkable until recently. Just think about your smartphone, your smartwatch, your smart-home device, or the interactive control cockpit in your car, to name just a few examples. Blurring industry barriers lead to many incumbents facing competition from players they never considered before. Consequently, organizations have to define their business models not just in the light of industry peers, but they need to consider how effective these business models are in competing against rapidly emerging ecosystems, which can comprise a variety of businesses across different sectors. All of this has important consequences for incumbents' existing business models, as Onur Erdogan, former General Manager at Estée Lauder, the leading luxury and cosmetics company, tells us. He explains, "The digitization of our business is really driven by customers. Customers want personalized products, advertising, and communication. And if you want to deliver on this, you need to change the whole way you work and operate."[2] The trend toward customer-centric end-to-end solutions has a number of implications for incumbents. First, products and services need to become better, cheaper, more flexible, and more customized than ever before. Much of this development is driven by new technologies that allow for mass customization. Second, with the rise of ecosystems, incumbents are at risk of losing their direct customer access and becoming more of a component supplier or "white-label back office."[3] In such a situation, firms are at risk of earning low margins compared to (digital) players controlling the ecosystem and customer access. Third, changing customer expectations require incumbents to leverage digital technologies to give customers the convenient interaction they expect. Even in the health industry, digitization forces doctors, hospitals, and other institutions to consider how they interact with their patients, as Gieri Cathomas, an expert in the health management sector, explains. He tells us that young start-ups regularly come up with great ideas of how to connect patients and doctors directly and more conveniently. He sees this as a customer-driven development that can turn entire B2B (business to business) markets into B2C (business to customer) markets.[4] This means firms have to serve their customers on their preferred channels, with their preferred technology, and give them the seamless end-to-end experience they expect. What makes this even more complicated is that firms do not have much time to react, as Urs Kissling, CEO of Embassy Jewel, a Swiss retailer of luxury watches and jewelry, points out. Digitization and the underlying speed of change leads companies to having to act faster than ever before. "We need to act on trends even before we fully understand how they play out, otherwise we will be too late," he holds.[5] He would likely agree with Jean-Charles Deconninck, President of the Board of Directors of Generix Group, a global provider of supply chain solutions, who argues: "Today we live in a world of great fluidity. This fluid environment obviously requires organizations to become more elastic and flexible, much more than in the past. This need for elasticity and flexibility will affect the entire organization at all levels. It affects the elasticity of the production process as well as the elasticity of the minds of the individuals who work in these organizations."[6]

But the impact on incumbents does not stop there. The new digital era also has a profound impact on the role of suppliers, as Dirk Linzmeier, CEO of OSRAM Continental, a supplier for automotive lighting solutions, attests. While suppliers used to receive clear specifications from their customers – the OEMs – and had to develop accordingly, today they are asked for solutions at prototype status. This means that suppliers must build up new know-how and also anticipate what the market and the end customer need.[7] It is fair to say, however, that the urgency differs between industries. For most customer-facing industries, such as the retail industry, the need to act is hard to deny. In fact, digitization has become essential for survival. Much of this has to do with the fact that organizations in these industries are directly exposed to the mounting expectations of end-customers. Customers do not have different bars for different industries – they expect a smooth and simple customer experience, no matter whether they are ordering clothes online or applying for a loan. The experience they are used to from the top-notch digital champions sets the bar for all interactions with the corporate world. On the other hand, more traditional B2B industries, such as the mechanical engineering industry, have more time. They are not directly exposed to fast-moving customer trends and expectations and their core business is still booming (in most cases).

Nevertheless, change is emerging even in the most traditional B2B industries. The trends described above do not leave any industry untouched – in the long run, no one is safe. Many of the trends have long been regarded as B2C-specific, based on the common (but misguided) belief that traditional production and other asset-heavy industries will not be affected by digitization (soon). However, Airbnb, Uber, and others have shown that this is no longer true and that even asset-heavy industries can be disrupted.

Opportunity to improve and digitally expand existing core business (1st S-curve)

While digitization is mostly as seen as a threat, it is a huge opportunity, too, since it can help improve the existing core business along a number of dimensions. First and foremost, digitization of core processes allows for massive efficiency gains through optimizations along the value chain and more efficient use of resources, leading to substantial cost reductions. This reason is arguably the most important need to act for most incumbents, and legitimately so. If incumbents don't change the way they operate, they risk profitability in the long run. Second, digitization allows achieving unprecedented quality levels through higher precision in production. Third, it allows faster product development (leading to a faster time-to-market) and more flexibility in production (we talked mass customization already).

When looking for ways to improve the core business, digitization can be seen as an enabler or a problem-solving tool to solve challenges that have long existed. In other words, the problems solved are not new, but can be solved more easily or at lower costs using digital tools. And some companies have the foresight to know they need to revolutionize their core business model simply because their ways of value creation and value capture won't be viable in the long run.

▌▌ We looked at our own construction waste logistics business and saw low margins, non-transparent processes, and questionable customer satisfaction due to a poorly designed business process. This is where we saw an opportunity to improve our own offering by proposing a radically new business model before any new entrant would. **▌▌**

– Andreas Opelt, Chief Market Officer, Saubermacher
(the Austrian waste manager you met in the Introduction)[8]

Besides points centered around improvement of the existing business, digitization constitutes a big opportunity to digitally expand existing core products and services, increasing value for customers. Without a doubt, the digital expansion of core products and services is the second most important reason for incumbents, judging from our interviews. When combined with increased self-service engagement, digitization can help deliver a better customer experience while at the same reducing costs – this is a win-win for everyone. Fueled by changing customer expectations, incumbents feel pressured to serve customers with the same seamless experience they know from other products (kudos to Apple, Facebook, and the like).

But simply digitizing analog processes does not exhaust the whole potential in the core – more is possible. "Moving beyond the core" or "service beyond the core" are phrases that we came across quite often when we asked our interviewees how digitization can help them expand their business. Incumbents can enrich their core products (leaving the core functionalities unchanged) by adding digital product or service components on top, thereby adding value to customers. An example of this is the machines of Saurer, a technology group from Switzerland focusing on machinery and components for processing staple fiber. Saurer realized they can help their customers' production planning with data from their machines. No one knows Saurer machines better than Saurer, so it's their responsibility to provide their customers with the right data at the right time to support their planning processes.[9] This is where the new role of production companies and suppliers comes into play again.

A less prominent side-effect of digitization related to the more efficient use of resources is that it allows switching to a different use of assets, because organizations know much more about their equipment than ever before. Patrick Koller, CEO of French automotive supplier Faurecia, points out that organizations can outsource tasks, such as equipment maintenance, much more easily because such tasks become a predictive cost factor. Another example for the different use of assets would be to pay only for the effective use of equipment, reducing capex and leading to a more asset-light organization.[10] When the same idea is applied to products that are sold to customers, it opens up entirely new value pools and new ways of serving customers. Sounds like 2nd S-curve to us.

Opportunity to set up new (digital) business and new growth opportunities (2nd S-curve)

Besides the opportunities to improve and expand the core business, digital technologies are a great springboard for organizations to dive into new value pools. Initiatives from this category are mostly aimed at establishing new business models in an existing value pool, or at disruption altogether. Attempts to establish these new growth engines often require a lot of time and resources while the outcome is highly uncertain. However, these initiatives can yield huge impact if they prove successful. Zappos, Alibaba, and Netflix are examples of new business models that have successfully disrupted established industries.[11]

Firms' desire to search for new growth opportunities is often grounded in a declining core business. Some incumbents have concluded that further innovation of their core product is not possible or economically meaningful. Aesculap, a German-based market leader in surgery products, had a core product that was fully optimized, and larger innovations could not be expected.[12] Similarly, one of the largest manufacturers of forklifts worldwide realized that their R&D department was over-engineering their core product, and that adding a premium sound-system to the forklift probably would not help them reach their growth targets. For both firms, digitization was an enabler that allowed them to achieve completely new innovations and unleash new growth potential outside their core products.[13]

Similar to successful start-ups, most of these new growth engines are based on a combination of business model innovation and new technologies. Not surprisingly, more and more companies are experimenting with disruptive business models that include new technology components, pay-per-use models, or mass customization–based advanced analytics tools. No matter which new business model will build the foundation for your 2nd S-curve, getting there requires bold investments and a decisive strategy. We will talk about these topics in the **WHAT** chapter (Chapter 2).

Purpose of innovation and link to sustainability and social innovation

In addition to the reasons discussed so far, firms should consider the broader societal impact of a digital transformation, too. Considerations in this area should include, but not be limited to, the impact on organizations' workforce (how can the organization ensure the timely upskilling of employees to prepare them for the digital age, what will the workplace of the future look like?), the impact on sustainability (how can the organization use technology to reduce waste, how can circular business models be launched and scaled?), and trust in digital work practices (how does the organization deal with data privacy, security, and ethical use of data?).[14]

In order to reach transparency, prioritize initiatives, and streamline efforts, organizations should consider a "value-at-stake" analysis to calculate the potential impact of their digital initiatives not only on their business, but also on the wider society[15] (covered in the **WHERE** chapter, Chapter 9).

According to the World Economic Forum,[16] the key questions for businesses will be: Is your organization aware of the value multiplier for society from your digital initiatives? Is your organization able to measure and track the socio-economic impact of your future digital initiatives? How can your organization incubate digital initiatives that could deliver a high value to society and your business in the future? Is your organization's corporate affairs / social responsibility function suitably aligned with your corporate strategy team?

Clear answers are not just important from the viewpoint of corporate social responsibility. They are also critical to address younger generations' questions on this subject and to stay attractive for fresh talent. The purpose of (digital) innovation, and answers to the question, what does it mean for society, will only gain in importance for organizations that want to continue being attractive employers.

Over-indexing on the 1st S-curve is a commonplace problem

Figure 1.2 Imbalance between 1st and 2nd S-curve

We find that almost all companies work on the digitization of their core business, and most have already achieved substantial progress and results. While this is a reason to celebrate, it is unfortunate that many small and medium-sized enterprises (SMEs) think that digitization of the core is sufficient. This is a false assumption that poses a major risk to many SMEs. Almost all large companies have started working on initiatives to build up a 2nd S-curve. Unfortunately, many of them have failed to achieve their growth targets or the desired financial impact with the new business. While basically all firms are aware that digitization will change their industry and that they have to act, they often do not know what exactly will change and how exactly they should address these changes. This is why many of their digital initiatives are close to what they have already been doing in the past – they are not moving away from the core. Instead, they are working on the 1st S-curve, but not really setting up a new 2nd S-curve (see Figure 1.2). The need to act can vary from industry to industry, and it can even vary within organizations. For BASF, a large multinational chemicals company with more than 70 strategic business units and customers in more than 20 different industries, the digital era is not a general threat or opportunity – this can be very different depending on the industry. So, for large corporates like BASF, the need to act can be based on a variety of reasons.[17]

When talking about the need to act, a multinational conglomerate we interviewed illustrates how internal and external forces played out to motivate the firm's move into industrial IoT (Internet of Things).

US CONGLOMERATE

Before the firm started to invest in its industrial IoT (IIoT) platform, they realized digital transformation posed an immediate threat as well as a big opportunity.

The management noticed that the firm was slowly being disintermediated by third-party firms that started to build on its products. These firms tried to pull out machine data and leverage it to create new insights that could then be used to make production processes and interactions with other machines more efficient. The increasing digitization of machines, customer interfaces, and communication steadily reduced the importance of the company's own service employees. Management became aware that they were at risk of losing their direct customer contact as new players were trying to occupy the customer interface and that their own efforts to digitize applications and communications with clients were cannibalizing their customer service efforts.

Luckily, the same development that put the firm at risk of disintermediation held some opportunities. At the time, consumer platforms such as iOS and Android already existed, but there was nothing similar for B2B markets. This was when the management realized that the wave of disruption that was hitting one B2C industry after the other was soon to affect B2B industries as well. The management diagnosed that these digital trends were likely to impact how industrial assets are built, maintained, and repaired. To proactively address this development, the firm tried to better understand the factors that were driving those B2C disruptions and how they might apply in an industrial context. This marked the birth of the firm's own IIoT platform that could connect streams of machine data to powerful analytics, create new valuable insights for the firm and its customers, and more efficiently manage assets and operations (see Figure 1.3). Interesting to note that the point of departure was a consideration of how B2C trends could be transferred to a B2B setting.[18]

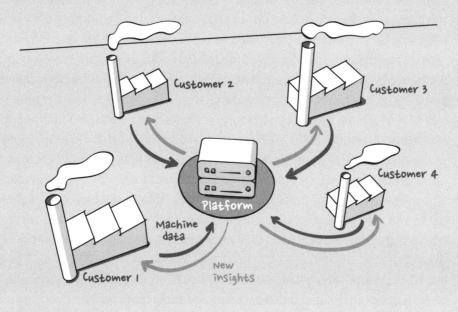

Figure 1.3 Platforms

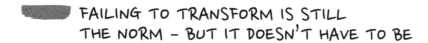 FAILING TO TRANSFORM IS STILL
THE NORM – BUT IT DOESN'T HAVE TO BE

Although it should be clear by now that digitization has a profound impact on all sectors, surprisingly few companies manage to act from a position of strength. This is confirmed by research which shows that only 20% of incumbents have adjusted to the digital era.[19] Unless management and supervisory boards around the world have kept their eyes and ears closed over the past two decades, they must have heard the warnings that digitization can significantly threaten their industry.

Despite these warnings, many incumbents fail to act timely. Jan Mrosik, COO of Digital Industries at Siemens, the multinational conglomerate, pointed out to us: "There's always a rather small number of leaders who decisively lead the development of new trends and business models, and digitization is no exception from the rule. Then there's usually a larger group of organizations that take the path in smaller steps. Last but not least, there's a large number of organizations that for the time being just want to see and observe."[20] This is confirmed by recent research: the small group of incumbents who successfully compete in the digital space make more investments and bolder moves than traditional incumbents.[21] It is important to embrace the change. The failure to react from a position of strength is a missed opportunity for many incumbents, as Julian Schubert, Managing Director at V-ZUG Services, a subsidiary of the V-ZUG group, the Swiss market leader for household appliances, notes.[22] As many incumbents miss this opportunity they have no other chance but to react from a position of weakness. However, acting under pressure does not make things any easier. For example, when you wait until your core business is writing losses, it gets difficult to justify uncertain investments to build up a totally new business model (more on this soon).

So, the crucial question is: What are the reasons that so many incumbents fail to act timely and in the right way – what is holding them back?

SELF-PLEASING MINDSET: Industry leaders often fall victim to their own success – enter hubris. A strong position might lead these companies to think "We are the leaders, nothing is going to happen to us." This conviction is often exacerbated by uncertainty about the success of new business models ("Who knows if this will take off . . .") and pressure to please investors with profits.

UNDERESTIMATION OF URGENCY: Even when incumbents realize the potential threat for their business, they often underestimate the urgency of the actions to be taken, because they think they have more time than they do. This is a common mistake because managers are used to the speed of business they know well, but not to the one that's about to disrupt them.[23]

FEAR OF CHANGE: Organizations don't like change. Managers and employees alike think that the change induced by digital transformation will lead to a less comfortable situation where they have to work more and undergo a stressful period of uncertainty, or that the change might even make their roles obsolete. The list of reasons why employees have a critical stance toward change could easily be extended. Julian Schubert from V-ZUG notes that while failing to change from a position of strength usually has adverse effects, sometimes you can also benefit from it. It can be easier to embrace change once the organization is under pressure, because a weak position makes it clear to everyone that the formerly comfortable spot is gone, and that the organization has to do something – even if they don't like it.[24]

IMPLEMENTATION DIFFICULTIES: Many digital transformations fail because firms often don't know how to go about implementation. While formulating the right digital strategy is already a difficult thing to do, as we will learn soon, executing a digital transformation can cause a whole array of problems leading to poorly implemented strategies or headwind from the organization, and eventually to unsatisfactory results.

HALF-HEARTED EFFORTS: Surprisingly many organizations think that digitization of the core business will be sufficient and forget about or ignore efforts to build up a 2nd S-curve. These organizations focus solely on making their core business more efficient or introducing a few digital add-ons to their core products. "Digitizing the core is fundamentally different from creating new opportunities," as a former senior manager from a large UK bank explains. In order to conceive new business models, organizations need to put on a digital lens. It's not sufficient to take an offline product and add some digital components.[25] As research shows, bold moves and decisive investments are important characteristics of successful digital businesses. Thus, those not ready to make fundamental changes and take risks fall short of the disruptive nature of a digital transformation.[26] Companies in this bucket often run a few digital initiatives that make their (core) business more digital but don't really trans-form the organization.[27]

DIFFICULTIES WITH STRATEGY DEVELOPMENT: Incumbents are often overwhelmed by the strategy development. Yes, incumbents know how to set up a strategy that helps them compete with industry peers (they have been doing this for decades). However, the new (digital) strategy has to address a new breed of competitors (that is, start-ups and tech firms), new business models (say, pay-per-use), and a range of new and unfamiliar technologies. Furthermore, the digital era requires traditional companies to be more agile and flexible than ever before, and they are required to formulate a strategy that supports this flexibility.

UNDERESTIMATING THE DIGITAL TRANSFORMATION: Many companies simply underestimate the breadth and depth of this transformation. The digital trans-formation is not just like any change project. It is unprecedented in pace and impact, and thus requires full attention of the entire management and super-visory board.

TO AVOID BANKRUPTCY, "DUAL BUSINESS" IS THE NEW BLACK

As we have learned from many digital transformation blunders, sprinkling a bit of "digital glitter" over incumbents' core businesses does not suffice. Instead, careful thought needs to be given to how the traditional core of the organization can benefit from digitization and, at the same time, new (digital) ways of value creation and capture ought to be explored. This is exactly the digital transformer's dilemma. The new operating model has to allow the continued pursuit of primary business activities, which will still yield the majority of revenues for the time being, while making way for the new (digital) business.

1st S-curve

To stay competitive in the core business, organizations need to reevaluate the current business model and make their core processes more efficient. That's exactly where the digitization of core processes and functions plays out. Efforts can range from supply chain, production, or sales processes, to marketing, R&D, or back office functions. The prioritization will depend on a number of factors, such as feasibility and impact. If incumbents want to reap the full digital potential in the core business, they will also need to consider initiatives that digitally enhance their core products (or services). Those are the digital "add-ons" or services "beyond-the-core" we talked about earlier.

However, focusing all digital transformation efforts solely on the 1st S-curve will not be enough. This could have severe consequences, because it leaves all new value pools and disruptive potential to competitors or new entrants. A risky strategy, as an executive at one of our conferences confirms:

companies that focus digital transformation only on the first S-curve could become very efficient in their core business today, yet create a problem for themselves in the long run. They could become the most efficient at making things nobody wants.

Max Costantini, Chief Strategy Officer, Mibelle Group,
part of the Swiss retail group MIGROS[28]

2nd S-curve

The new (digital) S-curve is more than a tiny rival on the side – it is the curve that will secure the long-term survival of the organization. A dual business approach is the only chance organizations can disrupt others before they get disrupted themselves.

Investments into new digital initiatives that are different from the core offering will expose incumbents to new risks, too. That's exactly why an imitation of Silicon Valley methods in traditional firms will not work. Throwing money at promising initiatives without a clear overarching strategy and link back to the core will not generate trust and support in the traditional core of the organization. Instead, incumbents would be well advised to leverage the strengths their legacy brings to the table.

Firms have to manage both S-curves simultaneously if they want to make their digital transformation a true success. Seeing them as separate from each other is the wrong approach. Instead, incumbents need to allow synergies and create organizational and procedural links between the two curves to reap the full potential. This is where we get to the heart of the digital transformer's dilemma, and it's why a digital transformation is not a classic change project. What makes it so challenging is that digital transformers have to manage three dimensions in parallel: the 1st S-curve, the 2nd S-curve, and the marriage between these two S-curves. Specifically, companies need to consider how to build the 2nd S-curve and maintain it in parallel with the 1st S-curve, move learnings from the 2nd S-curve over to the 1st S-curve, and ensure that 1st and 2nd S-curves are properly integrated with each other instead of establishing silos.

GET MOVING TO AVOID THE DINOSAUR FATE

When you go about finding the answers to the **WHY** of your digital transformation, we advise you to follow these best practices:

- Establish an understanding for the forces that influence your industry and your business and align on the need to act among the management team:
  - Consider potential threats from new competitors, especially large tech players (How could Google/Apple/Alibaba disrupt your business?).
  - Observe what start-ups are doing in your industry (Could they disrupt your value chain and/or serve unmet customer needs?).
  - Analyze threats from existing competitors that lead the digital revolution with bolder investments and more decisive moves.

- Evaluate how newly emerging customer trends impact your industry (What are digital-savvy customers doing differently?).
- Assess opportunities to digitally enhance your core business as well as opportunities to access new (digital) value pools.
- Reach clarity about the differentiation of your products/services from competitors.

● Beware of the most common pitfalls of a digital transformation:
  - Raise awareness for the importance and urgency of the transformation.
  - Make sure your organization does not shy away from change.
  - Be ready to revise your existing strategy and business models.
  - Prepare your organization for the breadth and depth of this transformation.

● Establish clarity and alignment about the need for a dual business approach:
  - Understand that the competitiveness of the core business still matters.
  - Make sure that all relevant stakeholders (especially the management and supervisory boards) are aligned about the importance of the 2nd S-curve to secure the organization's existence in the future.
  - Don't shy away from discussions about the possible coexistence of both S-curves (including synergies as well as possible conflicts, such as funding).

 GET INSPIRED (BY PICTURES)

CEWE
......

Since its inception in 1961, CEWE, the European-wide leading photo service company, had to make many corrective decisions and maneuver through uncertain times. The biggest shock was the invention of digital photography, which changed the market so profoundly that even the undisputed champion of the worldwide photography market, Kodak, went bankrupt in 2012. However,

CEWE managed to anticipate the required adjustments and was ready when two fundamental trends threatened their market and their business: increasing digitization of the photography industry, and the rapidly decreasing number of printed photos. To be equipped for the digital era, the company decided to turn their traditional business model upside down. As part of the new strategy, they introduced the CEWE photobook. This new product was a response to the increasing number of digital photographs and helped customers convert their digital images into a more durable, physical product. The photobook was a huge success and, as a result, CEWE is now the market leader for printing and manufacturing of photo books for digital images. In fact, it has grown even stronger and more profitable since digital photography hit the market.

But how can an industrial company like CEWE, one that has an impressive order backlog and solid profits, anticipate and execute needed transformation? At CEWE, the realization for the need to act and the motivation to come up with a digital business was rooted in an entrepreneurial company DNA and strong management support.

Entrepreneurial mindset: CEWE has always known that their market position was not to be taken for granted. They are well aware of the fact that their core products can quickly become obsolete. Because there is no guarantee for success, CEWE is constantly working on new ideas to improve existing products and invent new ones. Thanks to its innovations, CEWE feels well prepared to fight off potential new competitors or disruptions, not least because they try to disrupt and attack themselves every single day – and that's how they stay agile and proactively drive new developments as industry leaders.

Management support: CEWE's digital transformation was fully supported and driven by its top management. Their former CTO knew that developing a shiny website would not do the trick. Instead CEWE was willing to invest heavily into new competencies, building up IT expertise to support the development of digital products and services. What's more, the board was ready to give new ideas the necessary freedom and flexibility, even when it meant cannibalizing the existing business. CEWE's board was ready to fight against internal opposition, too, especially from middle managers who feared that their dominant market position was about to be eliminated by the new digital unit.

While the digital transformation was a necessity – not an option – for CEWE, other companies and other industries have more time. But when a digital transformation does not seem essential, many companies wait far too long, as Reiner Fageth, CTO and head of R&D at CEWE, tells us. Companies then lose time and their transformation takes longer and becomes more difficult and costly. All of this typically results in poor acceptance among employees and other stakeholders. CEWE's management realized in time that some disruptive change was headed their way and that they needed to confront it head-on instead of hoping for it to bypass them.[29]

KEY TAKEAWAYS:

- **Support is crucial** – Transformation needs strong management support to be successful, especially when initiatives cannibalize the core, and when large investments into new capabilities are needed.

- **Don't wait too long** – If you wait to see how certain developments play out in your industry, things normally don't get any easier: you lose a lot of time and your transformation will become more difficult and costly.

- **Disrupt yourself before someone else does** – Proactively push the development of radically new ideas. Remember the best defense is a good offense.

Part 2
WHAT TO DO

chapter 2

HOW TO MAKE YOUR STRATEGY, BUSINESS MODEL, AND DIGITAL INITIATIVES STOP FIGHTING EACH OTHER AND WORK TOGETHER

I n this chapter, we describe how to develop a strategy that includes (a) a strategy for the core business, focusing on how digitization can help safeguard and increase the competitiveness of the core, (b) a strategy for the new (digital) business to generate additional growth, and (c) a plan for how to marry the two. We advise on how to develop new business models, and guide practitioners on how to use a strategic initiatives portfolio to go from strategy to business model (see Figure 2.1).

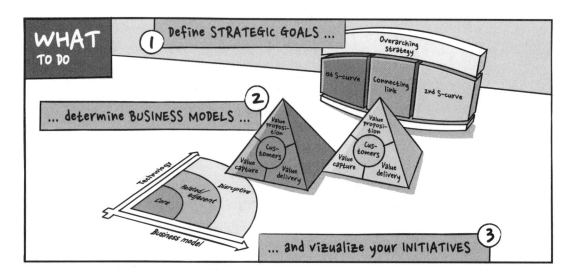

Figure 2.1 Key visual with focus on What

Source: Business model components adapted from Oliver Gassmann, Karolin Frankenberger, Michaela Csik. *The Business Model Navigator*. 1st Edition. ©2014. Reprinted by permission of Pearson Education.

REALIZE THE "WHAT" CHALLENGES YOUR COMPANY MUST TACKLE

A key challenge in defining a digital strategy and the right business model to support it is the discussion on how to pay for it, since the core business will initially have to fund efforts on both S-curves. Some 2nd S-curve initiatives might even cannibalize the core business. Digital transformers tend to lose sleep over such conflicts. The question then is whether there is a way to circumvent such conflicts. If not, how can incumbents deal with such issues? How can a sound strategy and clear guidelines facilitate this discussion?

What makes strategy development so difficult is that incumbents need to conceive a strategy that covers not one but three dimensions:

1. Organizations need a sound strategy for the core business as they need to digitize their core processes (1st S-curve).

2. Organizations need a strategy for the inception of a new (digital) business, which is often totally different from the core business (2nd S-curve).

3. Organizations need to consider and plan for possible interactions between the core and the new (digital) business.

Especially the definition of a strategy for the 2nd S-curve is a difficult task for many incumbents because competing against a new breed of competitors is new to most of them. The central question then is, what's the best way to approach this? Are there any best practices to start the strategy development, and what exactly constitutes a good strategy? How can managers of legacy organizations reach clarity of the overarching strategy and how can the two S-curves complement each other? Answering these questions will prove important for the future success of the transformation, as having two unaligned strategies within the organization is a recipe for digital disaster.

Another challenge relates to the overall speed of strategy development and decision making in the boardroom, which tends to be much slower in legacy companies compared to the new breed of competitors (especially start-ups). To what extent does this have to change in the context of a digital transformation? What needs to be adjusted so that incumbents' strategic decision making becomes faster and more iterative, considering competitors' moves as well as market reactions and trends? As strategy development is no longer a top-down planning and execution exercise, managers might also ask themselves, to what extent should the strategic thinking at the top be accompanied by an involvement of lower-level managers? And what should be the role of project managers, department heads, team leaders, mid-level executives, and other managers tasked with running a digital transformation?

While most incumbents employ a professional portfolio management for their initiatives in the core business, something like a professional portfolio steering of transformational initiatives, like those on the 2nd S-curve, rarely exists. Should incumbents develop a similar approach for the 2nd S-curve? How can this best be arranged so the organization ends up with a perfect mix of strategic initiatives on both S-curves?

Taking a step back, how should these strategic initiatives be found and designed in the first place? How should incumbents reevaluate their existing business model in the core and think about a new (digital) business model rooted in novel ways of value creation? The key questions that incumbents should ask themselves with regard to their business models need to encompass strategizing along four dimensions: Who are the customers that will be served? What is the value proposition that is being tendered to these customers? How, and using whose support, will this value be generated? How will value be captured and revenue generated from this?[1]

DON'T STRATEGIZE IN SILOS: CREATE A HOLISTIC STRATEGY ACROSS BOTH BUSINESSES

The term "strategy" is used excessively nowadays, especially the term "digital strategy." It has been used to describe a plethora of different things – from digital marketing strategy to corporate strategy. The way we define digital strategy in this book is to describe the plan that incumbents need to design and implement in order to steer their digital activities on the 1st and 2nd S-curve, respectively.

This plan is not just a rigid top-down strategy development and implementation process. It's an organization-wide undertaking that should also involve lower-level managers and staff, as we will explain in more detail.

In general, strategy can be understood as the plan that describes the course of action an organization is taking in order to reach its objectives. A clear strategy is not just important to avoid uncoordinated efforts and a waste of resources, it's also critical for success. Digitally maturing companies (that is, companies that use digital technology and capabilities to improve processes, engage talent, and drive new value-generating business models) are five times more likely than companies at an early stage of their transformation to have a clear digital strategy in place. In fact, a lack of strategy was identified as the most critical obstacle for companies in the early stage of a digital transformation.[2] And that's exactly what makes strategy so important, especially in the context of a digital transformation. Embarking on the digital transformation journey without a clear plan is a risky endeavor that is likely to fail. "It is important to establish a clear digital strategy and decide in advance: what do we actually want to do, where do we want to end up," Thomas Pirlein, CIO of Müller Group, a food corporation, points out. He says that companies should also address related key questions, such as the most relevant areas for digitization and the prioritization of topics.[3] This will set important boundaries for the identification of use cases to digitize the core business as well as for the search for opportunities to set up new (digital) business models. We will detail what's needed to define a strategy that guides the way through the transformation.

Understand your starting point

At the beginning of strategy development, the organization should have a clear understanding of where it stands, including the challenges it faces, or they are unlikely to find the right strategy to move forward.[4] A thorough analysis is needed to understand the firm's competitive environment and how it's likely to change. But the thinking should not stop there. Incumbents should also consider how new technology and customer trends might influence their current or future position. New digital technologies or changing customer preferences can fundamentally impact the economics of the current business model – make sure you understand the implications it will have on your business and the likely impact it will have on the competitive landscape of the future, for example, which players it will empower, how it will shift market power and control. Be explicit about the most likely scenarios as it is on their basis that new strategy will be built.[5]

The previous chapter addressed similar questions, as motives to embark on the digital transformation journey are also based on a reflection of environmental factors that trigger a need to act. Indeed, the need to act forms an excellent basis for your strategic thinking. However, while the need to act might be based on a single or a small number of factors that threaten the incumbent's future, the strategy development should be based on a thorough understanding of all factors in a firm's environment, even when they do not appear to be immediately relevant. We highlight this because many companies wait too long to take digital opportunities or threats seriously. Before new business models take off, they seem negligible and it's unclear whether they will ever materialize. Often incumbents only wake up once sales shift and new business models take off.[6] But it's too late then.

To make this whole brainstorming activity a successful exercise, it's crucial to think broadly. The analysis should cover as many potential opportunities and risks as possible. And this exercise is not something that should take place in the boardroom only. Top management should leverage the collective brain power of project managers, department heads, team leaders, mid-level executives, and staff. If organizations restrict their thinking in this phase, they risk excluding from consideration something that could hit them hard.

Paralleling this effort, organizations need to undergo an assessment of their current digital maturity. This analysis should cover multiple dimensions ranging from culture, strategy, and capabilities to organization and talent.[7] An honest evaluation of the status quo will be helpful to identify the gaps that need to be filled, which can guide future investment efforts.

Develop a strong vision and ambition

Once organizations know where they are starting from, they should develop an understanding of where they are heading. Or better: where they want to be headed. Organizations should define an ambitious but achievable vision that describes the target-state where they want to end up. A vision or ambition can thus be understood as the potential end result of strategy.[8] Important to note in this respect is that the overall guiding vision and values that incumbents have determined to be key in their organization and that guided their activities in the past do not have to change (read more about this in the **Culture** chapter; Chapter 8). Rather than throwing overboard all historic values and guiding principles, incumbents should define and add a digital vision and ambition. Digital strategies fail more often because of too little ambition rather than too much.[9] Incumbents should develop bold strategic visions when it comes to the future target state. The vision should act as a north star for the entire organization and can guide recruiting efforts, development activities, as well as management meetings. "Digitization is such a broad field and there's a large number of external providers that reach out and offer support with all sorts of digital services. The process can easily get confusing. It's therefore important to stay focused, to define a specific purpose and be clear about the road ahead," Safer Mourad, Vice President of the Saurer Technology Centre, told us.[10]

Apply a nimble approach to strategy

The overall speed of strategy formulation and decision making in the boardroom has to change as well. The time has passed when companies could engage in classic corporate strategy planning processes every three years. Organizations should regularly revisit their strategy to check if it is still configured most conducively for the path ahead. Rapidly changing environments and a continuous stream of new technology and customer trends requires companies to make little adjustments more often than before. This requires the strategy development to become faster and more iterative.[11]

Every strategy review should consider new moves of competitors, new market trends, as well as new information gained through customer feedback and testing. Of course, the required frequency and importance of reformulation depends on the market dynamics and pace of technological change in a given industry. Rapid changes in technologies and trends require a more iterative and nimble approach to strategy making, especially in fast-moving industries.[12]

This does not mean that companies should no longer engage in long-term planning. They should revisit their strategies, test the validity of the assumptions they have made, and adjust their course of action based on new learnings and insights.[13]

Although this strategy discussion is primarily relevant for top management, it does not mean that it's not important for practitioners managing the day-to-day operations of digital transformations. This does not mean that the board loses control over the organization and employees at lower levels take over. It becomes an organization-wide undertaking that involves multiple departments and levels of the organization. While the top management defines and sets the strategic boundaries, the overall direction, and the priorities going forward, employees at lower levels are the ones who ideate and propose the concrete actions to be taken. If you are a project manager, department head, or mid-level executive tasked with running digital activities, it is likely your responsibility to think what the new (digital) business model could look like, or which process of the core business could be digitized. This also means that senior leadership should allow and listen in an unbiased manner to strategy-related ideas and thoughts that were triggered bottom-up. Employees at lower levels often have an ear to the market and to the customer. They know much better what customers really think and can add valuable information to inform the future strategy.

Implement a balanced strategy

Organizations must have a strategy that helps them manage the present and execute on the current business models. They also need a strategy that guides them along a path toward new growth engines. Research has shown that many companies focus too narrowly on just one element of the digital transformation and miss unleashing the full potential of both S-curves. It has also become apparent that the companies that made bold moves typically outperform their peers.[14] Clearly, a "wait-and-see" approach will likely be an unsuccessful strategy. Companies should act decisively and proactively tackle both S-curves in parallel. What does all of this mean for the existing strategy, and when does the new strategy come in? Three things need to happen:

1. To allow for the full benefits of digitization in the core (1st S-curve), the existing strategy for the core business needs to be reviewed and adjusted where necessary.

2. To guide efforts that aim to establish a new (digital) business (2nd S-curve), the company needs to expand its strategy to plan for and incorporate these new activities (the strategy for new (digital) business). This means incumbents will have a more broadened strategy that will then cover not just one, but two S-curves.

3. To support the digital activities on both S-curves, incumbents need a new overarching strategy that combines and bridges the respective digital strategies for the 1st and 2nd S-curve accordingly (the overarching digital strategy).

Let's have a closer look at each of these steps.

Strategy for core business (1st S-curve) When it comes to the review and adjustment of the existing strategy for the core business, incumbents should follow two goals. First, incumbents should use digital technologies to increase the efficiency and improve the competitiveness of their existing business. Second, incumbents should make the digital enhancement of the core business a strategic goal.

Several of the companies we interviewed started their digital transformation journey with a focus on the 1st S-curve because they found there was a huge potential for efficiency improvements. However, organizations should not just throw digital technologies at core processes to see where they stick. They should follow a well-structured approach by mapping out their entire value chain and identifying the activities that constitute the biggest challenges and/or opportunities. Many firms ask each business unit to identify the biggest pain points and prioritize the cases based on the savings potential. This approach had two major advantages: First, the savings free up capital that can be used somewhere else (for example, to build up the 2nd S-curve). Second, it allows testing approaches that are later applied and sold to clients (for example, predictive maintenance solutions).

One of the key goals that Schindler – a global manufacturer of escalators, moving walkways, and elevators – pursued as part of its digital strategy has been the efficiency improvements in its core processes. In addition, digitized core processes have built the basis for new products and services, Christian Schulz, head of Operations at Schindler, explained.[15] In a similar vein, the executives of WACKER Chemie AG, a global chemical company from Germany, told us that one key element of their new digital strategy was the improved customer-orientation and customer focus by means of digital tools and technologies, which unlocked entirely new growth potentials for the core business.[16]

As these examples illustrate, incumbents should also make the digital enhancement of their core business a strategic goal. Using digital technologies and tools, incumbents can substantially improve the customer experience related to existing core products or services. Aesculap, the German producer of medical surgery products, found an appropriate name for that, labeling their strategic efforts in this area "digital services beyond the product." It allowed them to improve the customer experience in ways that would have been impossible to achieve with yet another incremental innovation of an already highly engineered core product. Hence, digitization did not only allow them to make core products and processes more efficient, it also enabled them to expand their core offering.[17]

Compared to the strategy for the 2nd S-curve, the strategy of the 1st S-curve will not encounter much opposition. Business unit heads of the core will not complain about additional cost savings and improved processes as long as they are not left alone with the savings target. When it comes to digitally enhanced core products and services, the resistance might increase. The reason for that is not that the business units refuse additional growth but that the origin of innovation often lies outside the traditional R&D and product departments, which don't give up their territory easily. Nevertheless, the real hitches come with the new (digital) business model and the alignment between the two S-curves.

Strategy for new (digital) business (2nd S-curve) Incumbents need to develop a sound strategy for their 2nd S-curve. The new, disruptive (digital) business that resides here will be the future growth engine for the organization. While almost all companies developed a more-or-less structured approach to digitally transforming their core business, not all firms understood the importance of the new (digital) business. Clear strategies and ambitions for the 2nd S-curves are often missing, as an example from one of our interview partners reveals. When a healthcare company started its digital transformation journey, it established several digital teams and asked them to ideate and develop a digital proof-of-concept. It turned out the board was overwhelmed by the unprecedented speed and creative output produced within a short period of time. Board members could not decide on the top three ideas to push further and realized that they were not willing to invest in these uncertain ideas while their core product was still successful.[18] Truth be told, this is not an uncommon problem.

Organizations tend to underestimate the potential for new business models and do not pay enough attention to new opportunities,[19] failing to make bold moves on the 2nd S-curve. This can have lethal consequences. Winning firms will act before they are forced to – or as Gisbert Rühl, CEO of Klöckner & Co, the globally operating steel distributor, put it, "We have to disrupt ourselves, or someone else will."[20]

The new rules of the game will have important implications for the strategy as well. Compared to the 1st S-curve, incumbents must be more patient and disciplined when it comes to entirely new (digital) business models. It can take years for them to take off. Until then, companies have to invest without expecting short-term returns – something they are not used to. An organization's motivation can take a hit and they might even lose faith in the new business model.[21] Incumbents have more to lose than start-ups in this respect. Those that are cash-constrained might even have to exit existing positive revenue streams to free up the capital needed to invest in new ideas – a predicament start-ups will never find themselves in.

While aiming for disruptions is the right thing to do, it involves a level of risk that incumbents are often unfamiliar (and uncomfortable) with. The further the level of risk increases, the further the initiatives stray from the core business. Although the required risk-taking is a topic that should be discussed openly at the top management level, it is something that often falls short in the strategic discourse, Thomas Gutzwiller, a platform and business transformation expert, identified.[22] Similarly, Samy Jandali, Vice President Digital Business Empowerment at BASF, points out that the scope of the digital transformation, especially the scope of the 2nd S-curve, should be discussed early on. "The organization should develop a clear understanding for what's allowed and what's not allowed. If management fails to do that, they might end up with business models that are too far off and run against the purpose of the whole organization. Having this discussion early on and establishing a clear direction can save a lot of time, resources as well as cumbersome conflicts." He goes on to explain that it is also fine to initially leave this open in the beginning and to discuss it on a case-by-case basis. Sooner or later, however, incumbents need a clear take on this and to align their selection criteria of digital initiatives.[23]

OVERARCHING DIGITAL STRATEGY

Both the strategy to digitize the core business and the strategy to develop new (digital) business should be linked together by an overarching digital strategy. The most successful firms develop a clear perspective on potential synergies and conflicts between the two S-curves. There are a multitude of potential synergies between the two S-curves, and we will discuss many of them in more detail in the **HOW** chapters (Part 3). What is important from a strategic point of view is that these synergies rarely come about by chance. Successful companies devise a clear plan of how to foster and manage synergies and actively pursue activities to realize them. This includes a discussion of the role that the 2nd S-curve can play for the digitization of the core business and how assets of the core business can be made available to the 2nd S-curve. Successful firms anticipate the potential conflicts that may result as a consequence of the activities on the 2nd S-curve and define principles to deal with them.

Interestingly, it's not always the ideas that are completely different from the core business that cause the most trouble, Markus Brokhof, former head of Digital & Commerce at Alpiq, a leading energy service provider in Switzerland, illustrates. Often more problematic are new business models that are somehow related to and potentially cannibalizing the core. According to Brokhof, the core needs to understand that the new strategy supports internal competition and that it is better for the firm to cannibalize itself before others do it.[24]

Bernard Leong, former head of Post Office Network & Digital Services at Sing-Post, Singapore's public postal service, argues similarly, "It's important to discuss how the 1st and the 2nd S-curve go together and to talk about how the incumbent deals with the disruptive force that exists within the same organization. Lots of CEOs talk about that topic but they rarely put the two heads [the core business head and the head of the new digital business unit] in the same room to have that kind of conversation."[25]

But does a dual business always end up in conflict? The ugly truth is that this is likely to happen. The 2nd S-curve will almost inevitably stumble into conflicts with the new digital business as long as it's allowed to spend resources generated by the core. According to Markus Brokhof, former head of Digital & Commerce at Alpiq, this conflict requires a lot of management attention. The new direction and strategy of the company needs to be clearly communicated by the top management team, he explained.[26]

And yet again, this involves a strategic discussion around the question, how far shall we stray from the core? At the very center, this question deals with the diversification and risk appetite of the firm. While most activities on the 1st S-curve do not normally change the fundamental economics of the existing business model, firms often break new ground with digital business models. Depending on the rules that the company sets for itself, the resulting ideas and business models might be close to or far from the existing core business. The outcome of this strategic discussion will also have implications for the further direction of 2nd S-curve activities as well as potential for synergies and conflicts between the two S-curves.

Olaf Frank, head of Business Technology at Munich Re, a globally leading reinsurance company, confirms top management and board alignment on risk appetite, collaboration between business units, and the future direction of the organization is key for success.

I think, at the end of the day, the success of the transformation really depends on the alignment of managers from different organizational units. If we all pull together at the management-level, we can make a lot of things work. But if not all managers are fully committed, they will get in the way of each other. Someone who does not want to act, will find their reasons. And someone who does want to act, will find their way, too.

Olaf Frank, Head of Business Technology, Munich Re[27]

Most of the firms we interviewed pursued a diversified strategy. The digitization strategy of Deutsche Bahn, the German federal railway company, is based on three pillars. The first pillar relates to the digitization of business processes and work-flow functions. The second pillar of its digitization strategy focuses on enhancing the core business by providing better products and services, which ultimately improve the customer experience. The third pillar focuses on iterating and pivoting new digital business models, for example, shared mobility concepts.[28] Note that the first and the second pillar address the digitization and enhancement of the 1st S-curve while the third pillar addresses the attempts to set up a 2nd S-curve. Similarly, BASF's digital strategy focuses on the use of digitalization[29] to become more efficient and improve their production and operations processes wherever possible (1st S-curve). Additionally, they focus on the creation of new, exciting customer interfaces and an improved customer experience through digital elements ("modern, faster, better") in the core business (1st S-curve). Furthermore, they address new growth potentials for the firm based on the use of digital technologies and tools (2nd S-curve).[30]

Another case in point for a comprehensive digital strategy is Deutsche Pfand-briefbank (pbb), a German bank that specializes in real estate financing.

DEUTSCHE PFANDBRIEFBANK (PBB)

Before the bank embarked on its digital transformation journey, management clarified what digital actually meant for the organization. The bank focused on three main themes. The first was efficiency, including improved processes and cost savings (1st S-curve). The second was customers, including customer satis-faction, engagement, and interaction (1st S-curve). The third theme was business models, encompassing digital products or services that could be built on top of the existing core products, or entirely new business models (2nd S-curve).

Additionally, pbb broke down digital transformation into four layers. The bottom layer was what they called "foundation" and included digital ways of working and mindset as well as a new digital culture. The next layer focused on the transfer of non-digital data elements to digital data-formats. The third layer was the digitization of processes, making use of digital data-formats, directly leading to efficiency gains and cost savings. The fourth and top layer was called "digital transformation layer" and focused on new digital products or services as well as totally new business models on the bases of new digital technologies.

Based on that, pbb combined the four layers with its three main themes to span a broad digital matrix. This digital matrix helped structure strategic dis-cussions and provided the strategic boundaries for initiatives on the 1st and 2nd S-curve respectively.

As for the prioritization of initiatives, pbb categorized all initiatives into two buckets: the first had to do with efficiency gains and required a business case. The second was seen as long-term investments into the future, such as R&D investments. These initiatives did not have to meet strong financial return requirements.[31]

While it's important to do all the strategic thinking discussed so far, this is not where the strategy development process ends. Strategy development should encompass a bottom-up ideation of strategic initiatives to digitize the core and build up new business models. The resulting portfolio of strategic initiatives is then the direct, visible result of strategy.

ONE THING COMPANIES FORGET WHEN THEY MOVE FROM STRATEGY TO STRATEGIC INITIATIVES

Many companies struggle with the variety of potential use cases and places to start the digital transformation. They do not know where and how much to invest, leading to a suboptimal allocation of resources and time. The overarching digital strategy should guide the prioritization of budgets and other resources. Companies that poorly execute their strategy often do not link strategy to budgets and execution and are more likely to fail.[32] Companies that allocate 70% of their activities to core initiatives, 20% to adjacent ones, and 10% to transformational activities are most successful. Firms that used this 70–20–10 formula had a significantly better performance in terms of share price performance than their peers.[33] Although this seems like the magic recipe, it isn't. The required allocation of resources to support innovation activities will depend on the ambition level that the company has defined.[34] Again, it all comes back to the strategy and ambition that the company set out earlier. While the top-down strategic guidelines will provide direction and guide the selection and prioritization of initiatives, it's the bottom-up initiation of concrete strategic initiatives that defines how strategy plays out in practice.

To visualize the set of strategic decisions taken and the initiatives currently underway, the advantages of a structured strategic initiatives portfolio play out (see Figure 2.2.). While you can choose from a number of reasonable axis labels (for instance, financial impact, time-to-market, ease of implementation, and so on), using business models and technology as the axes proves most useful. It allows you to easily visualize your strategic initiatives along the most important dimensions for your transformation. This helps you visualize how far your strategic initiatives stray from the core. The initiatives can be either close to the existing business model, adjacent to it, or fairly unconnected to the existing business model and have a more disruptive character. It also helps you plot how explorative your organization is with regard to technologies employed. Does the strategic initiative rely on existing technological capabilities that are well-known within the organization? Does it experiment with related technological capabilities (which might be new to your organization, but not new to the sector)? Or does it explore an entirely new, disruptive technology that has not been firmly established?

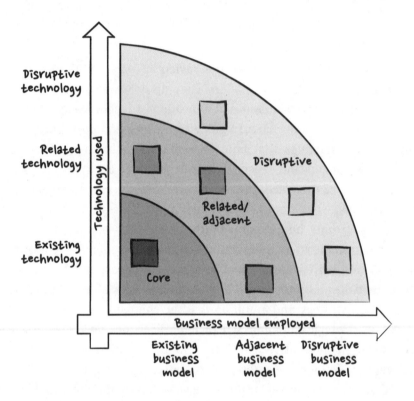

Figure 2.2 Business model–technology matrix

A strategic initiative portfolio is an easy and powerful tool that helps you connect the top-down priorities with the strategic initiatives that were initiated bottom-up. Successful digital transformers will strike the right balance between initiatives to digitize the core, initiatives to digitally enhance the core, and initiatives that aim to establish new business models. The successful portfolio steering of innovation and growth initiatives is key for any digital transformation to succeed.

Most incumbents have a fairly unstructured approach at the beginning of their digital transformation journey. It's not uncommon that digital initiatives are spread all over the place. This is where a structured mapping can prove useful. If done right, the strategic initiatives portfolio is simply a visualization of the strategy. If you prioritized new, disruptive (digital) business models over the digitization of your core business, the portfolio matrix should make this visible. That means we would expect to find the majority of strategic initiatives on the 2nd S-curve. If you want to focus on the digitization of your core business, you should make sure that the majority of strategic initiatives resides on the 1st S-curve. A portfolio approach – accompanied by practical visualization tools – is thus a great means to check if your initiatives are (still) in line with your overall strategic direction and ambition, or if you should shift your focus and resources.

Another advantage is that a strategic initiatives portfolio helps identify the initiatives that do not deliver on your strategy. While stopping initiatives is no easy task – every initiative is run by people who really care about them and who easily find arguments to keep them up and running – it is critical to do so because it will free up funds and other resources. Finally, a portfolio approach is a great way to visualize, discuss, and communicate progress to key stakeholders, such as board members, investors, and the entire organization.[35]

Most incumbents run a regular evaluation of initiatives for all projects that they have in the core. However, the strategic initiatives portfolio should become an overview that includes all strategic initiatives: those in the core business as well as those aiming to develop new (digital) business models.

A good example is Munich Re. When the company started its digital transformation, the management defined a list of domains that were considered important for the future and that were also related to the digital transformation. Topics such as risk management, sales support, predictive maintenance, and IoT were on top of this list. For each of these domains, Munich Re identified and invested in a certain set of basic competencies and skills that were needed to operate in that area (for example, analytics skills). In addition to that, the firm ran a number of initiatives to test and learn from concrete uses cases. Starting from the digital direction defined by the board, Munich Re defined critical domains to be pursued and started initiatives to make progress in areas that were strategically important. Olaf Frank, head of Business Technology at Munich Re, points out, "The final and most important test for an idea is always 'is anyone actually willing to pay money for it?' Firms should use market criteria whenever possible. Only what proves to be successful on the market will prove to be valuable for the firm."[36]

The selection of certain priority topics, domains, or "search fields" builds a bridge between strategically relevant topics and concrete strategic initiatives. The strategic initiatives portfolio should then include a fair number of digital initiatives in each prioritized domain. This will allow incumbents to follow a systematic approach to innovation. One example to illustrate this is a diversified technology company we interviewed. For each dimension of its strategy, the firm defined important "search fields" through ideation sprints. The resulting priority search fields (for example, smart factory) were backed up by ideas to explore each of these fields. In another sprint session, management prioritized the ideas based on the criteria impact and feasibility. The outcome was the first tranche of strategic initiatives for each search field, which then became part of the new strategy. This resulted in a well-structured strategic initiatives portfolio that could be tracked and managed by the board.[37]

We can also learn from a multinational manufacturer of materials handling equipment.

FORKLIFT MANUFACTURER

Whenever organizations decide to revise their strategy, it should be based on a well-structured approach, explains Harald Brodbeck, innovation expert at the consulting firm Horváth & Partners, who supported the forklift manufacturer on its journey. "To avoid chaos later on, the top management has to be aligned on why they are doing this and where they want to end up – this sets the boundaries for what has to be done."

Following the best practice, the company first identified all relevant technology trends and environmental factors that directly or indirectly impacted the organization. Based on a sound understanding for the trends and technologies that affected the organization, they gathered key people from middle management positions of all units. Managers identified the priority topics or "search fields" for the future.

Since the company's overall corporate strategy demanded initiatives with short-term, mid-term, and long-term impact, the selection and success criteria for these were very different. Short-term initiatives needed to have fast success and excite employees (1st S-curve). The mid-term initiatives should be business model innovations (1st or 2nd S-curve), and the long-term initiatives had to be ideas for a new 2nd S-curve, in case the core business changed dramatically. Having prioritized key topics, the firm was able to span an "innovation matrix architecture."

The organization then reevaluated all existing innovation activities and checked if they aligned with one of the prioritized innovation fields. If not, they were stopped, and the allocated money was channeled elsewhere. The company also started an ideation process to identify new ideas. The ideas were evaluated based on short fact sheets and those prioritized went into an execution funnel.

One important mistake to avoid at this stage was to be overly technology-driven, Brodbeck tells us. The identification of initiatives within a certain search field should always be problem-driven, never technology-driven. Too many companies have a technology bias that leads to situations where "technologies search use case or applications" while it should be the other way a round.[38]

Managing a strategic initiatives portfolio will require management to develop a higher tolerance for ambiguity and risk than incumbents are used to. The first trial to establish a new business model will likely not be successful. Digital transformation is not a one-time effort. Successful digital transformers manage a continuous stream of strategic initiatives with a well-structured portfolio.

GAIN A COMPETITIVE EDGE THROUGH BUSINESS MODEL INNOVATION

Before we dive into the conversation on business model innovation and possible techniques, let's clarify what we mean when we talk about business models.[39]

In simple terms, a business model describes how the business of a firm works.[40] It is the overarching concept that describes the different components of business and how they are put together to create and deliver value for the company and its stakeholders.[41] A company's business model consists of four key dimensions:[42]

- **Customers**: describes the target customer segment(s) the company is trying to serve.

- **Value proposition**: describes what the company offers to its customers.

- **Value delivery**: describes the activities and processes that need to be in place to bring the value proposition to life.

- **Value capture**: describes the value-generating mechanisms of the business model.

Every digital transformation should involve not only the setup of new (digital) business models, but also a reevaluation of the existing business model. Business model innovations have clear benefits from a growth perspective. Fundamental business model innovations can unlock an entirely new value creation potential for incumbents, much more than is possible through continuous stream of product innovations or process changes. Business model innovation can deliver a 6–7% premium on the total shareholder return compared to peers that focus on product and process innovation only.[43] Digitization of the core business is not only an opportunity to prolong the life of your core business, it is also an opportunity to unlock entirely new value pools in the core. Faurecia, the French automotive supplier, collects tons of machine and customer data. These insights help them devise new business models, such as pay-per-use models. In addition, predictive maintenance requirements allow them to outsource maintenance and servicing tasks as the need to own that knowledge internally becomes obsolete.[44]

In reality, 90% of all business model innovations are recombinations of existing business models. In fact, these business models go back to one of 55 business model patterns.[45] The good news is that managers can make use of a range of systematic approaches that make business model innovation a much easier exercise. Tools and frameworks such as the "Business Model Canvas,"[46] "Blue Ocean Strategy,"[47] or the "Business Model Navigator"[48] (see Figure 2.3) can help overcome the aforementioned challenges and renew an existing business model systematically. A systematic approach also comes in handy when organizations try to ideate new business ideas.

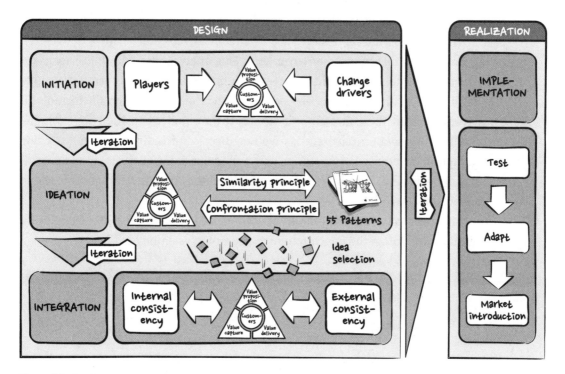

Figure 2.3 The Business Model Navigator
Source: Adapted from Oliver Gassmann, Karolin Frankenberger, Michaela Csik. *The Business Model Navigator.* 1st Edition. ©2014. Reprinted by permission of Pearson Education.

The left-hand side of the framework is the design stage, which should be closely interlinked with your strategy and ambition. The right-hand side of the framework is the realization stage, where concrete ideas are developed and tested in an iterative fashion before they are launched in the market. Let's have a closer look.

Initiation phase

Similar to strategy development in general, business model innovation should start with a clear understanding of the company environment, including other players, partners, customers, and other drivers of change, such as technology trends. At this stage, a clear understanding of customer needs is key. If the customer is not in the center of value creation, the risk of failure is high.

The business model design process should always start with a 360-degree analysis of the incumbent's environment. This analysis should not just focus on existing customer groups, but also create an understanding for customer groups that are currently not being served. Similarly, the analysis should include all players that contribute directly or indirectly to the value proposition (for example, suppliers, innovation partners) as well as direct and indirect competitors (for example, from adjacent industries). Last but not least, the analysis should take all kind of trends into account (for example, regulatory trends, demographic shifts, technological trends).[49]

Eissmann, a German automotive supplier, demonstrates the importance of a sound evaluation of the environment the company is embedded in.

EISSMANN
. . . .

Being an automotive supplier, it's hard, if not impossible, to bring about disruptive business models, Norman Willich (former CFO) and Alexander Maute (Director IT & Business Services) explain. Suppliers are usually involved only in a later stage, when decisions have already been made by OEMs. Receiving detailed product specifications from OEMs, suppliers often function more as executors rather than as strategists. Thus, automotive suppliers – as most suppliers in any industry – are by definition followers, as most changes are dictated by the commissioning parties (in this case, OEMs).

Of course, the entire automotive industry, including suppliers, is affected by digitization (for example, more displays in a car's interior), but these are merely applications, and thus part of the digitization of the 1st S-Curve. There's not much room for fundamentally new business models – at least not from the supplier's point of view. The further we go down in the "automotive food chain," the less disruption there is. While the large OEMs dominate with disruptive business models (for example, shared mobility), there is already less disruption in Tier 1, and even less in Tier 2.

There are still things that smaller suppliers can do, as Willich and Maute point out. If small suppliers want to make it on their own, they need a lot of courage, and be willing to step outside their comfort zone and aim to inspire the broader industry based on a niche that small suppliers excel in. "If, in the future, cars are shared, then it might make sense for cars to have multiple interior equipment configurations depending on the driver – this is called 'second skin.' The development of this 'second skin' interior equipment is something that automotive interior equipment suppliers can pursue independently from OEMs, at least to a certain extent." Another way to initiate change from the supplier side is to generate more data (for example, by measuring, regulating, steering more of the interior of the vehicle) and provide it to OEMs so they can act on it. However, the harsh truth is, OEMs still need to be willing to listen for all of this to take effect.

The environment that companies face, and the network of players they are embedded in and depend on, is a crucial driver for the boundaries of what's possible. Not having a solid understanding for – or, even worse, ignoring – the reality that a company is facing could lead to failed innovation attempts – something that Willich and Maute do their best to avoid.[50]

Here's another example of a firm that radically changed its business model based on an analysis of its environment and the effects on its business model.

OSRAM

Founded in 1919, Osram is one of the largest global players in the lighting business. Lamps formed the core of its portfolio for several decades. But things changed quite radically for Osram. They analyzed industry trends and came to the conclusion that their lightbulb business was likely go from a multibillion-dollar opportunity to close to zero within a short period of time. The reasons for that were two-fold: first, traditional lightbulbs were being replaced by LED bulbs. This alone would not have been dramatic, since this development could have been countered simply by making a shift toward LED-based bulbs. The second reason was more severe: where traditional lightbulbs last only several thousands of operating hours, LED bulbs will last 50k, 100k, 200k hours – and LED can be built directly into the luminaires. Hence, selling lightbulbs individually was a dead-end street. Recognizing these two factors, Osram had a strong incentive to radically innovate their business model. In fact, they not only reinvented their business model – they also sold their lightbulbs business to a Chinese consortium.

Another insight they gained during the initiation phase guided the way for their new setup. A study by Gartner explored the role that connected products play in the future, and while lightbulbs were not connected at all, LED products led the way. "Light is a central topic in buildings, and this will not change any time soon," says Thorsten Müller, former Group SVP of Innovation at Osram. "Alongside electrical distribution, HVAC [heating, ventilation, air conditioning] and so forth – lighting is one of the key trades you will want to monitor – and remote control – in a building," Müller explains. Following this logic, Osram made the move from being a pure production company to providing digital services, answering customer questions such as "How can I lower the energy costs in my building using smarter lighting solutions?" The value proposition changed from pure product business toward helping clients solve their problems based on extensive expertise in the domain of lighting.[51]

Equipped with a thorough understanding of future trends, industry developments, and new opportunities, incumbents can spot dead-ends and emerging opportunities more easily.

Apart from the analysis of influencing factors in the firm's environment, the initiation phase should also include a description of the existing core business model. This will shed light on the weaknesses of the existing business model that can potentially be solved through digital elements. This analysis alone can be a powerful source for new ideas, and thus a perfect starting point for the next phase.

Ideation phase

Especially during the ideation phase of the design stage, using a systematic approach will be decisive for success. Tools such as the "Business Model Navigator"[52] provide a well-structured method to brainstorm new ideas while at the same time fostering creative thinking. The method makes use of the 55 business model patterns that can be applied to the existing business model to identify ideas for improvements. To facilitate the ideation process, organizations can use one of two principles. The first one, called similarity principle, creates new ideas by searching for analogies in patterns from other industries or companies that face a similar challenge. The second principle, called confrontation principle, confronts the existing business model with patterns that are completely unrelated to the model. Both principles are helpful in identifying weaknesses in the existing business model but can also be applied to brainstorm ideas for entirely new business models.[53] (Find more information about the business model innovation patterns on www.businessmodelnavigator.com or our website www.thedigitaltransformersdilemma.com.)

A good example to illustrate how one can launch a new business model based on an industry analysis and inspiration from other players is Klöckner & Co, the German steel distributor. Klöckner & Co's moves were triggered by the existing industry environment and potential threats from other industries. Klöckner & Co came to the conclusion that the highly opaque steel market and inefficient industry processes offered opportunities for improved steel distribution processes. Inspired by disruption that the likes of Amazon brought to the B2C market, Klöckner & Co adopted the platform idea to the steel industry and set up a new distribution platform for its products.[54]

Whenever incumbents try to detect weaknesses of their existing business model and when they try to generate ideas for new (digital) business, they should bear in mind that digitization can change the nature of supply, demand, or both.[55] During the ideation process, incumbents should try to challenge their existing business with as many weaknesses as they can find; they should also look for as many opportunities for their existing and new business as possible. One approach is to assume the position of an attacker to try to find disruption potential within a given industry. Incumbents should also probe how competitors within their own industry and from adjacent industries could affect them.[56] This exercise should focus not only on the risk of getting disrupted, but also on opportunities to disrupt others. Whenever incumbents identify an indicator of potential disruption risk, it is also an opportunity they can exploit themselves.

The more structured the approach, the more likely it is that the organization does not miss opportunities. One approach is to systematically scan and evaluate the demand and supply side as well as market dynamics for indicators of disruption potential and opportunities. As far as the demand side is concerned, new (digital) business models often serve an unmet demand by unbundling or tailoring or by offering a better customer experience (for example, digital add-ons). Whenever the customer experience does not match the best practices of other industries, there are likely opportunities and risks related to the business model. Where the supply side is concerned, digitization offers the opportunity to organize production capacity in new ways, for example, easier access to supply and increased utilization of capacity. Digitization can also function as the basis for overhauling the entire value chain, for example, by taking out redundant steps or automating certain activities, thereby changing cost structures and economics of supply.[57]

When we analyze the dynamics between supply and demand, there will be opportunities to intermediate the market whenever there's a possibility to connect the two sides of the market in new, more efficient ways. Such a market-maker function (acting as connecting point between supply and demand) can create new customer value by offering highly transparent and efficient matching-services, for example (we have seen this happen with several new aggregators that disrupted established markets such as insurance). A more extreme version of this are platform- and ecosystem-based business models that span across multiple product categories, customer segments, and even industries. They offer unprecedent opportunities for up-selling and cross-selling, create valuable insights based on massive amounts of customer and transaction data, and often involve high barriers-of-entry due to scale effects. By using such a systematic supply-and-demand analysis, incumbents will get a much better understanding for nature and type of digital threats they are facing and for digital opportunities.[58]

Schindler, the manufacturer of escalators, moving walkways, and elevators, is a great example to illustrate how firms can identify opportunities for business model innovation when they systematically explore their environment.

SCHINDLER

When the Swiss multinational started to digitize its core business, the initial goal was simply to achieve efficiency improvements. However, the company soon realized there was much more to gain from digitization and decided to also exploit the potential of adding digital products and services to its core offering.

This transformation allowed the company to drastically improve its value proposition. End-to-end connectivity between the elevator, the Technical Operation Centre (TOC), and the service technician allows customers to access real-time status updates while ensuring the service technician receives an alert when something goes wrong. Also, the TOC, supported by machine learning algorithms, delivers additional information about which spare parts are needed on location. This all reduces downtime of the transportation system, majorly benefiting customers and passengers.

Additionally, digitization of the core builds the basis for entirely new business models, as connected elevators make way for a totally new user experience in vertical mobility, Christian Schulz, head of Operations, says. For example, the display in the elevator can be used for entertainment and advertisement and this even in a personalized way, as the passenger is identified automatically by his mobile phone or key card. Receiving individual ads or news while riding an elevator could become a standard soon. So, transit management in larger buildings is no longer reduced to the speed of getting to the required floor.[59]

A relentless customer focus is indispensable for successful business model innovation, as the following example also illustrates.

MICHELIN
· · · · · · · · · ·

The French firm, well-known for the production of tires and its restaurant guides, is a good example to illustrate the innovation potential that comes from moving away from a pure product perspective and instead toward a focus on the customer journey and related pain points.

In certain industrial segments, Michelin has changed its business model from the pure production and sales of tires to a concept of connected tires where only the actual usage of tires is sold. They have, for instance, launched connected tires for trucks, mining equipment, farm tractors, and passenger cars. And they are planning to apply this to the airplane industry as well, where they intend to move to a pay-per-landing scheme, working together with Safran Landing Systems to make this happen. The new value proposition will have great advantages for airlines. Laws require pilots to check the condition of the tires before take-off as part of regular safety procedures. But whenever a plane lands, its tires are exposed to such high pressure that they overheat and need, on average, two hours to cool down to their normal temperature. During that time, tires cannot be checked by the pilots. But having a plane sit around in an airport is expensive and undesirable. Anything that Michelin can do to support airlines with the review process and reduce the downtime of their planes is of high value. Based on this customer-first perspective, Michelin is working to build connected tires that include sensors that check the condition of the tires just before landing. This will effectively eliminate the need to have the plane parked idle for so long before its next departure.

Michelin approached the mining industry – another of its customers – similarly. They installed sensors on tires for mining equipment, which allows them to collect and analyze tire data. Michelin can then make recommendations that help optimize production efficiency (imagine messages along the lines of "you can increase the speed of the mining vehicle by 5% without the tire suffering"). Another use case is rooted in their ability to help with predictive maintenance. The tires can measure the water content in the air and predict the weather based on that information. Maintenance can then be scheduled at a time when the weather will be bad and mining vehicles cannot be used. This helps reduce the downtime of the mining vehicles during good-weather conditions – a scenario that leads to productivity loss.[60]

Integration phase

In the last phase of the design stage, the most promising ideas should be refined further and tested for internal and external consistency. Internal consistency refers to a coherent design of all business model dimensions. External consistency refers to consistency with the external company environment. This is also the point where all new or refined business models have to be tested for effects on stakeholders (for example, regulators, distribution partners). Consistency of relevant trends and competitive factors needs to be considered as well. Whenever the business model is not fully consistent, incumbents should change dimensions of the business model iteratively.[61]

Julian Schubert, Managing Director at V-ZUG Services, can tell a thing or two about the importance of this last phase. Before he was given the approval to realize a new business model idea in parallel to the existing core business, he had to go through each and every step of the value chain over and over again. Especially when the new business model has negative implications for the existing business model, an analysis of possible contingencies is critical for success, he says. So, Schubert and his team analyzed all possible effects on the current business model. This included estimates about the likely profit impact, customer reactions, suppliers' feedback, and so forth. Schubert explained that, being embedded in the context of a traditional organization, the heads of the new business model need to be able to provide good answers to the consistency questions and possible implications for the core business. If the new model can't pass the consistency test, it's likely not going to get the approval of the supervisory board.[62]

So be careful not to fall in love with your new business model idea too soon. Especially in large traditional firms, consistency will be one of the main concerns of the supervisory board, which tends to be cautious, trying to avoid reputational risks.

V-Zug's perspective on new business model innovation resonates well with that of polymer business REHAU. An active player in the construction sector, REHAU knows the industry well, and knows how to run construction projects. A common problem of the industry is that construction projects are often over budget and over time because they are hard to manage and the industry as a whole can hardly be standardized. So, REHAU came up with a licensing-software for construction management. Because both the revenue model based on licensing and the development of software instead of engineered hardware were completely new terrain for the firm, REHAU was naturally critical about the new model. The company tested and challenged its ideas from all angles, remembers Martin Watzlawek, now head of Strategy & Innovation at REHAU Automotive and former head of Strategic Development at REHAU Group and thus responsible for the project. "When defining a new business model, the leading question always has to be 'Why REHAU?' Why should a customer buy the product or service from us rather than from anyone else, and why should REHAU even pursue this new product or service? The whole story has to fit or else there will be neither internal nor external acceptance of the new business."[63]

Once incumbents have designed a business model idea that is fully consistent, they can start to bring the new business model idea to life. We call this process the realization stage, which is shown on the right side of the framework in Figure 2.3. The business model should not be implemented with "one big bang." Instead, small prototypes of the new model should be developed and tested following a highly iterative process. Such prototypes can be developed at relatively low costs and with minimal effort – even tests with a small group of target customers can reveal valuable insights that help improve the idea.[64] There are plenty of approaches that organizations can use to test their business model in order to identify likely-to-fail ones and improve the most promising models further so that they turn into real growth engines. The best way to do this is to use a structured approach, such as the "BMI Testing Cards" that provide 22 tips on how to stress-test a new business model idea, making the overall business model innovation process more effective.[65]

All phases (design-prototype-test) are done multiple times before the business model ultimately hits the market. Over time, the uncertainty related to the new business model is massively reduced and the level of detail increases gradually. Thus, both design and realization are not fully linear but rather iterative processes. When business models are tested and new learnings are created, the designers will have to go back to the drawing board and check where they have to make adjustments and corrections. Of course, every adjustment will have to be checked for internal and external consistency again.[66]

As a general rule: when it comes to the realization of new business models, it's more about testing than about detailed business plans. Instead of calculating very detailed business cases that are based on dozens of shaky assumptions, companies should spend more time thinking qualitatively about the potential of ideas and testing their assumptions with prototypes. Rapid testing helps verify assumptions and increases the speed of knowledge development.

Of course, the analysis of the existing business model does not always have to end in a complete overhaul of the business model (note: we call it a business model innovation when at least two dimensions of the business model are changed). Many of the companies we have interviewed kept the existing business model more or less unchanged, but gradually digitized their core business by running a number of digital initiatives.

Over time, these strategic initiatives can also lead to a gradual overhaul of the existing business model, especially since further initiatives will likely focus on other dimensions of the business model. For example, the next digital initiative might lead to the introduction of new digital services or add-ons, which affects the value proposition of the business model.

When we compare strategic initiatives that aim to digitize or enhance the core and strategic initiatives that aim to establish entirely new (digitally based) business models, the steps are not that different. In the design stage, a thorough understanding of the environmental factors and the reality that the incumbent is facing will of course be relevant for both S-curves. Similarly, in the ideation phase, organizations should follow a well-structured approach, no matter whether they try to identify the most promising use cases to digitize the core or ideas for entirely new business models. However, compared to the generation of entirely new business model ideas, the ideation of strategic initiatives for the core business will often be more problem-driven. That means incumbents will try to identify pain points along the entire value chain and evaluate ways to solve them by using digital technologies or tools. Last but not least, the integration phase will also be relevant for strategic initiatives on both S-curves, because only in the rarest of cases are activities happening in a vacuum. Whenever a strategic initiative has implications for other dimensions of the business model, or for relevant stakeholders, the organization should reevaluate the internal and external consistency of the model.

GET MOVING TO AVOID THE DINOSAUR FATE

When you go about designing the **WHAT** of your digital transformation, keep in mind these best practices:

- Define clear strategic guidelines that lead your way forward on both S-curves:
  — Establish a clear understanding for your starting point based on an analysis of the firm's competitive environment, current and emerging customer and technology trends, as well as economic and regulatory trends.
  — Think broadly about possible opportunities and risks; consider all threats, regardless of estimated importance.
  — Develop a strong vision and ambition to define where you want to end up.
  — Realize the need for a balanced strategy to support your dual business: the strategy for your 1st S-curve should focus on the digitization of the core business and enhancement of the existing offering; the strategy for your 2nd S-curve should focus on the development of new (digital) business models.
  — Align the two S-curves through an overarching digital strategy – consider potential synergies and proactively address potential conflicts; discuss "how far you want to move from the core".
  — Decide on the right balance between 1st and 2nd S-curve initiatives and link your strategy to budgets and resources.

- Establish a strategic initiatives portfolio as a matching layer between strategic guidelines and concrete strategic initiatives:
  — Review and evaluate all existing strategic initiatives in your organization.
  — Define priority topics or domains based on the strategic direction.
  — Map all existing and new strategic initiatives to get an overview of the strategic activities underway.
  — Use this portfolio to track the innovation pipeline, manage strategic initiatives, and communicate your strategic and transformational activities.

- Use a structured roadmap and established tools to ideate and develop strategic initiatives:
  — Involve lower-level managers in the bottom-up definition of concrete strategic initiatives.
  — Before you think about new strategic initiatives, make sure you understand the company environment and your current business model.

- To ideate new strategic initiatives, build on structured tools and approaches such as the "Business Model Navigator."
- Refine your ideas until they are internally and externally consistent.
- Use an iterative development and testing approach to realize strategic initiatives.

 GET INSPIRED (BY PRINTING PRESSES)

HEIDELBERGER DRUCKMASCHINEN

Heidelberg is the world's largest manufacturer of offset printing presses with a 40% share of the global market. Their traditional business model is based on selling offset printing presses and related supplies ("consumables") and providing maintenance services to B2B customers.

In the course of their strategy development, Heidelberg realized they could grow their business not by selling more printing presses but by taking a share of the utilization of the installed machine, following a subscription-based business model. To understand the mechanics behind this logic one must understand the most important driver of profitability of the printing press industry: overall equipment effectiveness (OEE), which is a utilization degree of resources employed. The print industry today is transforming from typically small handcraft print shops to highly industrialized factories. The potential for productivity increases across the entire industry is thus enormous. Just so you get a feeling for the numbers, OEE in the printing industry is approximately 30%; in the automotive industry it is approximately 70%. Meanwhile the print production volume of the total industry will not grow considerably but the effect of having to distribute industry profits among fewer competitors will offset the limited growth. These will use fewer but much more productive and thus better utilized machines to produce the same outcome, which brings the machine sales model of Heidelberg under pressure. On the other hand, compared to a small handcraft print shop, a highly industrialized print shop consumes much more software, services, and higher volume of consumables (ink, etc.) per machine.

Despite this growth opportunity in service and consumables even with industrialized customers to compensate for the limited machine unit growth, Heidelberg's consumables business was also under threat. Heidelberg does not produce the consumables themselves, but is a leading authorized dealer. The larger the end print company is, the more likely they were to buy directly ex-works from OEMs and not from an authorized dealer like Heidelberg. As a consequence of the industry's consolidation, Heidelberg's consumables business was at risk as well because buying ex-works became more commonplace. As Heidelberg struggled to grow and compete on a product-by-product basis, the solution to counter such problems was to combine all such "products" required to print a sheet (machine, software, consumables, and performance services) into one single solution. Such a product system solution would generate more value to the customer than its single parts sold per unit. The "Smart Print Shop" was born. A key capability of Heidelberg was to manage such a product system to its optimum through its access to big data enabled by IoT connectivity of the machines. Such data allows Heidelberg to understand the performance of a print shop even better than its customers.

As a consequence, Heidelberg has started to transform its business model from a traditional "sell more units"-oriented business to an "outcome-oriented" business model. Revenue growth comes from higher utilization of machine units installed. In this new business model, customers basically pay for the printed sheet, including a monthly fee with a guaranteed outcome of printed sheets. Here Heidelberg provides the whole "Smart Print Shop" at its own cost and generates revenue when the system starts to print. The price per sheet for the customer assumes a relatively high level of productivity of the "Smart Print Shop," which is attractive for the customer, who can focus more on marketing than production issues. It is also attractive to Heidelberg, of course. If Heidelberg manages to exceed such productivity levels (meaning if more sheets are printed on top of the plan based on better utilization), the company receives a profit share from its customers as a premium. All products become an integral part of a single connected smart solution.

Heidelberg basically introduced the "Nespresso principle" to the printing industry. One kilo of Nespresso coffee costs 70 EUR but you are willing to pay that premium because of significantly less coffee waste and/or better utilization per cup, and more importantly because of the convenience it affords you (no more messy coffee filters that produce a liter of coffee when you only need a cup, no more being bound to the kitchen to do all that, and so forth). Thanks to the better utilization of the resources required to produce a printed sheet Heidelberg is able to charge a lower price per sheet compared to the current cost per sheet of its customer. At the same time, the price per liter of ink may be much higher compared to what customers pay today, but better utilized. On top of that, customers don't have to worry about setting up the machine, maintaining it, and so forth, which creates time to focus on product innovation and customer acquisition instead of spending time on production issues. In addition to this new model, Heidelberg continues to remain in business with its traditional transactional sales approach while driving the new model more and more to rely on a less cyclical, more recurring, thus more stable, more easily plannable, and more profitable business.[67]

KEY TAKEAWAYS:

- **Get inspired by business models from other industries** – Heidelberg was the first company to bring the "Nespresso principle" to the printing industry.

- **Align the business model with your (target) customer group** – Heidelberg successfully paired a novel business model for those customers who changed their focus from traditional print production to print sales and marketing.

- **Anticipate changes and act proactively** – Heidelberg, by anticipating several trends that threatened traditional business models, was able to act proactively and ward off negative hits.

Part 3

HOW TO DO IT

—

While it is indispensable to go through strategy development, great thinking is only the beginning. The real challenge lies in the nuts and bolts of digital transformation. The key differentiating factor for a successful digital transformation is a company's ability to implement what they set out to do. Surprisingly few companies have a clear view on how to best navigate the change and execute the digital transformation; only 16% of companies that try to digitally transform their organization are successful.[1]

Why is it so hard to digitally transform a legacy organization? The answer is simple: it's the digital transformer's dilemma. Incumbents need to maintain the profitability in their core business (the 1st S-curve), while reaping the full potential in new (digital) business (the 2nd S-curve). The reconciliation of both S-curves in one organization as well as adequate links between the two are at the very heart of the digital transformer's dilemma and are also the reason why so many organizations do not succeed.

We compiled a six-part roadmap on how to approach the execution of a digital transformation and succeed on both S-curves. This "transformation engine" breaks down the problem into smaller buckets that touch upon the most important dimensions of a digital transformation: set up the right (infra-) structure (organization, technology, processes) and institute the right mindset and talent (leadership, people, culture) across the whole company (see Figure 3.0). For each of the six dimensions, the digital transformer's dilemma takes different shapes and forms. We walk you through the challenges for each dimension and explain how to tackle them.

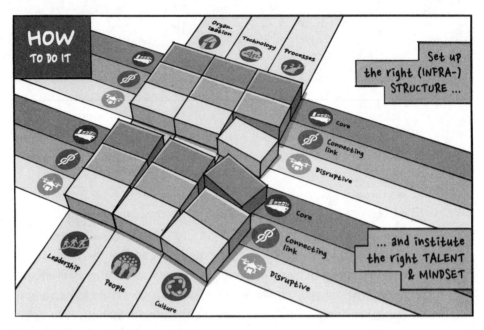

Figure 3.0 Key visual with focus on How

GET A GRIP ON THOSE "HARD" FACTORS OF YOUR DIGITAL TRANSFORMATION

Let's start with the first three dimensions of our transformation engine, which are related to the (infra-) structure that needs to be in place for the transformation to succeed.

In the **Organization** chapter (Chapter 3), we start by outlining why a dual business requires a certain degree of separation to become ambidextrous. We explain the different places digital initiatives originate and move on to archetypes that show where and how to best anchor the digital business in the overall organizational setup. Further, we explain how this is dependent on the digital maturity of the organization and the similarity between new business models and the core business. We outline why ties beyond the boundaries of the organization become increasingly important.

In the **Technology** chapter (Chapter 4), we start by analyzing why and which new technologies have become increasingly relevant for traditional organizations. We describe how incumbents should best approach the build-up of technology-related know-how and point out common pitfalls and key success factors for the implementation. We discuss the importance of technology as a driver for the digital transformation. We also look into the problems of legacy IT and explain how to best approach challenges related to IT architecture (that is, how old and new systems can be integrated). While we discuss many technology-related topics in the context of the transformation, it will neither be a content-related introduction to these topics nor a guide for IT transformations.

We close the discussion of (infra-) structure–related elements with the **Processes** chapter (Chapter 5). Here, we dive into the details of how to run a digital transformation and tell you what an ideal stage gate development process looks like. We also tell you how to best manage the links to the core business and prepare your initiatives for growth and scaling. We touch upon processes at a higher level and discuss the governance bodies it takes to manage the transformation engine, and how you can solve budget and funding-related challenges and discussions during the transformation.

Let's get started.

chapter 3
ORGANIZATION: HOW TO DEVELOP A FLEXIBLE ORGANIZATION

I n the first chapter related to the (infra-) structure, we explain why achieving a flexible organization is far from easy. The structure of incumbents is usually tailored toward stability and efficiency while new business models require flexibility and freedom. Digital transformers need to consider separation as a means to overcome this challenge. We also discuss where digital initiatives can and should reside (and when) within the organization. In addition, we discuss how to bridge the organizational gap between the two S-curves and why incumbents should consider partnerships with other players (see Figure 3.1).

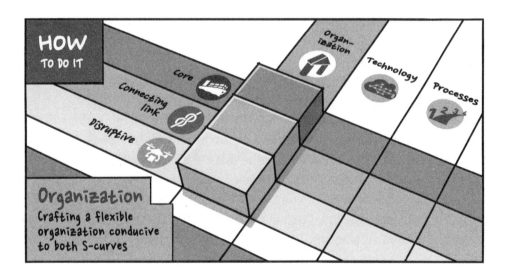

Figure 3.1 Key visual with focus on How/Organization

REALIZE THE ORGANIZATIONAL CHALLENGES YOUR COMPANY MUST TACKLE

Early on, thought needs to be given to how the digital transformation, and particularly the new (digital) business, will be embedded in the broader organizational context. The most fundamental question in this regard will be: What is the right organizational setup to support parallel efforts on both S-curves?

What sounds trivial often requires fundamental changes to the existing organizational structure, as a dual business approach requires more than adding a few digital roles to the incumbents' core businesses. Note that the current success of the core business is the result of a structure tailored to the needs and requirements of the 1st S-curve, but is this still the right setup for the future? How do you install an organizational structure that allows for the flexibility and freedom that the 2nd S-curve needs? And prior to that, you need to ask yourself, how does the organizational setup depend on the overall strategy and the aspiration you set yourself for the 2nd S-curve? The broader the scope of the 2nd S-curve (the more disruptive and further away from the core), the more separation is needed to avoid conflicts with the organization's legacy. This begs the question: How can you support the coexistence and alignment of two differing organizational setups within a single company? The link back to the core organization will make or break the success of that separate unit. But how can you ensure a solid integration of the two S-curves so as to minimize siloes? And which integrating mechanisms are necessary to unleash synergies?

Besides the right organizational structure for new (digital) business ideas, think about the digitization of the core as well. Where do you locate the digital resources and capabilities that drive the digitization of your core business and how do you manage them? What do the responsibilities and tasks of core business unit heads need to look like? What is the ideal role of dedicated digital leaders (for example, Chief Digital Officer)? You also need to consider how the organizational setup fits the digital maturity level of the organization.

BECOME AMBIDEX-WHAT?

The digital era has prompted many firms to add new digital roles or to extend traditional roles by adding a digital touch. More than likely you have come across one or even all of the following roles: digital strategist, chief digital officer, digital project manager, digital transformation officer. While adding dedicated resources to take care of the digital transformation is a good thing, this alone is not sufficient. Incumbents face new requirements in the digital era that do not go together with the hierarchical management structure that traditional firms bring to the table. The desire to work on new (digital) business ideas often leads to opposing interests and potential conflicts between the two S-curves.

Let's illustrate this with Kollibri, a hybrid between cab and public transport. The low-cost shared shuttle bridges people's last mile from their homes to public transportation hubs (or vice versa). It was a mobility venture tested by PostAuto, the transportation services arm of the Swiss federal postal services.

KOLLIBRI (MOBILITY VENTURE OF PostAuto)

The Swiss Post, like most incumbents, has fairly strict corporate governance rules and procedures in place that need to be followed whenever new suppliers or other external partners are involved. These rules guarantee that any new partner is fully compliant with internal processes and structures so that the efficient operations in the core business are not endangered and a smooth integration is possible. As you can imagine, in a large corporation, the onboarding procedure can be a lengthy and cumbersome process, involving multiple departments. However, that's usually the exact opposite of what a venture on the 2nd S-curve needs, Mirco Mäder, former Manager of Kollibri and project manager at PostAuto, explains.

New businesses need the flexibility and freedom to try out new things quickly, without all the red tape. Because the corporate compliance rules of the mothership would only thwart the efforts of the new ventures, the Post decided to accept less rigorous criteria for these initiatives. Mäder explains, "Our holding has a network of really capable external partners. But usually it requires a 100 percent solution. Senior management at the holding has meanwhile realized that Kollibri – and other internal ventures – need a healthy 80/20 approach. So the holding is now officially recognizing "early label" ventures that they lower their criteria for external cooperations for. This has made fast decision-making and establishing partnerships quickly much easier for us. The trade-off pro agility and quick results and contra long processes really made a difference."[1]

The digital natives that keep incumbents up at night subscribe to rapid product development and testing. Incumbents need to adopt some of these traits, too. Established firms have to be quicker to react to market and customer demands, to reallocate resources swiftly, and to change the course of action based on customer feedback when needed. However, this is exactly where traditional firms run into problems.

The problem that comes with legacy structures and processes becomes particularly apparent when we look at examples of highly regulated markets. Erbe, a producer of high-frequency surgical systems, confirms that their existing company structures would form a deadly environment for new ventures. First, new businesses founded within the mother organization would be bogged down with cumbersome processes and structures that are commonplace in historically grown companies. Second, operating in the medical industry, Erbe has to fit into a tight regulatory corset imposed by the legislator. "The list of requirements and standards you have to meet to be able to operate in the medical space is huge. However, the many medtechs out there, like start-ups in general, need more freedom in how they conduct business, especially as long as they don't have a market-ready product," says Reiner Thede, President & Co-CEO of Erbe.[2]

Nevertheless, moving the entire organization from a traditional setup to a flat start-up-like structure is a risky approach, as this change will likely be too radical and the cultural shock too big for most traditional firms.[3] We are not saying this is not possible – depending on the digital maturity of your organization, the gap might not even be too big. Generally speaking, incumbents will feel more comfortable with a step-wise approach. To get there, managers should evaluate which elements of successful digital natives' operating models they can incorporate into their organization. The best solution for incumbents is often to set up a new unit with flat hierarchies that's kept somewhat separate from the rest of the organization.[4]

Conflicts between the core business and new digital initiatives are the second reason to organizationally separate the two S-curves. How much separation is needed mainly depends on the similarity of new ideas and the existing (core) business. Depending on how far you loosen the reins, efforts to set up the 2nd S-curve might result in new initiatives that are in opposition to your current core offering. That's when managers of the core business will raise their hands and fight against the cannibalization of their own business. Truly disruptive ideas get killed easily when they are being held too close to the core. Surveys show that almost 50% of managers are aware that internal policies slow down the development of new business ideas while only less than 10% of firms give their new ventures the freedom to operate fully independently.[5]

The view that a certain degree of separation is necessary to become ambidextrous was not uncommon in the interviews we conducted, with many managers stating that their digital transformation benefited from the speed and effectiveness of separated teams.

We see a stark negative correlation between the size of an organization and its ability to act quickly and innovate. This is because large corporates tend to kill new ideas quickly. I fundamentally believe that you need to separate units working on radical innovations from the mothership. Large organizations like ours can never act like a start-up, it's just not possible. Decisions and processes take too long, everything holds you back. In order to be fast and agile like a start-up, separation is indispensable.

Former Chief Digital Officer, chemical and consumer goods company[6]

"We first tried to do it internally, but it did not succeed, because every new idea was immediately opposed with ten counterarguments why something can't succeed. We were just stuck in old thinking. That's why we decided to separate our digital initiatives and set up a digital innovation hub in Berlin. The new location allowed us to attract the right people and move things fast."

Gisbert Rühl, CEO of Klöckner & Co[7]

"We found that a certain degree of separation from the mothership was important for our digital lab because the legacy and governance of our core would just adversely affect the effectiveness of our digital lab. So, to ensure the required level of freedom, flexibility, as well as short decision cycles in your digital lab, you need to separate it."

Markus Brokhof, former head of Digital & Commerce at Alpiq[8]

Thus, without a certain degree of separation to get the drone off the ground, new business-building activities are commonly inhibited by legacy processes, structures, and mindset (see Figure 3.2). Another company that faced this challenge and successfully solved it through spatial separation is an internationally leading fashion retailer we interviewed.

FASHION RETAILER

The fashion wholesaler was one of the first companies in the industry to set up an online channel for its products. For their former CIO, it was clear that a certain degree of separation was a precondition for being fast. "The two channels had nothing in common, except the supply chain and the products. The whole presentation of products, the pricing, the interaction with customers, and so forth was completely different. Back in the day, an online channel was a completely new world that required new skills and new ways of thinking. This was nothing that our core employees who only knew the brick-and-mortar business could do in addition to their daily business."

That's why the company started a separate corporate unit to work on the new digital channel. The physical separation set the ground for fast development and implementation of new processes and structures that were necessary to break with the company's legacy. The new unit, which was still located at the corporate headquarters to facilitate communication and alignment, received more freedom than the average core unit. However, the separation from the core also required integration efforts, as the former CIO points out. "That's why it's crucial to align on the process and have a discussion early on about the division of revenues and costs, and the interplay of processes, especially when two worlds somehow overlap, as in the case of the online sales channel."[9]

Figure 3.2 Cargo ship versus drone

Unless you already have a flexible organization structure and have found a way to nurture even disruptive ideas within the core, you need to be prepared to make fundamental changes to your existing organizational setup.

SAY GOODBYE TO ONE HOLY GRAIL OF INNOVATION AND EMBRACE DISPERSED INNOVATION EFFORTS

It's almost impossible to know in advance which innovations will prove successful. That's why organizations should not rely on a single approach to digital innovation. Instead, they should rather try a variety of approaches, that is, they should place several bets. This requires that firms develop a clear perspective on the organizational setting and direction of strategic initiatives. Incumbents need a clear understanding of where digital innovation takes place in the organization (that is, where the digital impetus is located) and how this differs depending on the type of innovation. What we have seen is that firms that take digital transformation seriously have a diversified portfolio of digital investments and a broad approach to the development of new opportunities.

Depending on whether you prioritized the 1st or the 2nd S-curve in your strategy, you should cultivate more strategic initiatives in the core business or in a dedicated digital unit. But there are even different approaches to drive initiatives for a given S-curve: for example, you can push the digitization of your core business through fully internal initiatives, or you could bring in external start-ups to work on pilots together. How you balance initiatives between different approaches and how much emphasis you put on each one will depend on your strategy and the internal competencies and resources you bring to the table. We will talk more about this at the end of this chapter. Before that, we want to give you an idea of what's possible.[10]

As far as the digitization of the 1st S-curve is concerned, incumbents have to decide if they want to run digital initiatives internally and/or with external support (see Figure 3.3). Internal initiatives are usually run by line managers as part of their efforts to digitize their core business units or located in some kind of (digital) innovation lab, which serves as a creative environment to work on initiatives. In such labs, employees from the core business work in cross-functional teams, often bundled with external expertise (for example, agile coaches or consultants) to bring in an external impetus and avoid organizational blindness. Corporations can also use hackathon formats to organize the collaboration of diverse teams. In terms of agenda and scope, these formats normally have a clear strategic focus and address specific business problems (for example, digitization of core value chain activities). These formats are thus not completely unfamiliar to incumbents, because in essence, they solve core business problems. What's new is that this happens often in a new environment, using digital problem-solving techniques (such as design thinking, rapid prototyping, and so forth – more about these in the **Processes** and **Culture** chapters, Chapters 5 and 8). Whenever the lab format is used, some additional caveats apply. Because digital innovation labs, which are often separated from the core, support the digitization efforts of the core and act as an impetus to bring new ways of working into the core, close collaboration and partnership with the traditional business units is necessary. Depending on the agenda and scope of these digital labs, some ideas might extend beyond the boundaries of the core business and eventually result in a new business model. If the lab is allowed to or even asked to explore ideas that are on the edge of the current business (stretching the 1st S-curve or merging into a 2nd S-curve), the labs will need more autonomy and freedom.[11]

Approach	1st S-curve	2nd S-curve
internal	○ Digital projects within business units ○ Digital innovation labs	○ Corporate incubator/ corporate venture building/start-up factory
external	○ Open innovation/collaboration programs	○ External company builders ○ Corporate accelerator programs ○ Corporate venture capital

Figure 3.3 Matrix of origin of digital impetus

Besides the fully internal approach, incumbents can also choose to drive the digitization of their core with external support. Common approaches are open innovation and collaboration programs and other corporate accelerator–like formats in which start-ups are invited to co-innovate and work with a large corporation. They can serve as a vehicle for incumbents to identify and select external start-ups and collaborate with them to work on core business problems (potentially also to develop new business ideas). From an incumbent's perspective, collaborations are a relatively easy and fast way to tap into innovative external solutions at low costs (compared to often time-consuming, costly, and uncertain in-house development) and bring in an outside digital impetus to the organization.[12] Start-ups, on the other hand, can benefit from corporate assets (for example, customer access, infrastructure) and know-how (for example, market or regulatory expertise). Depending on how the collaboration is set up, corporations can also learn more about the range of possible solutions to their business problem, for example, when they interact with multiple start-ups during the selection phase.[13] This setup will be particularly useful when your organization can identify start-ups that provide exactly the solution you are looking for, or if they can support or speed up the process. To find the right collaboration partner, incumbents can launch a competition or proactively screen and approach relevant start-ups. Very often such an approach will be the preferred option when the organization knows it will not be able to develop a use case independently, or if it would take too long (for example, to build up the expertise).

The interaction with external start-ups can come in all shapes and forms, depending on what makes strategic sense and is most useful. The collaboration can range from a simple project collaboration or joint projects to more formal agreements, including investments and equity shares. Arrangements might also culminate in a joint venture or full acquisition.[14] As the bonds between incumbents and start-ups get closer, the required investment increases as well (as in the case of a joint venture or acquisition). If it's not an independent start-up but a mature company that is looking for guidance and access to resources, the collaboration will resemble a typical buyer–supplier relationship. In any case, incumbents can use such collaboration interfaces to bring in external support and accelerate the digitization of the core.

By using one of the above formats, established firms can create the necessary environment for new ideas to flourish. Although these initiatives will be relatively close to the core business (in fact, they must be because they aim at digitizing the core), keeping them at a certain distance from the core is still needed to protect them from legacy thinking, structures, and processes. A key success factor for this type of setup is for them to be led by managers who can manage both the traditional core business environment as well as the non-hierarchical digital environment (more on that in the **Leadership** chapter, Chapter 6).

As far as the 2nd S-curve is concerned, incumbents often choose a balanced approach between internal and external venture building. In the first case, incumbents run their own corporate start-ups and try to grow them into full-fledged businesses. You could call this approach (internal) corporate incubator, corporate venture building, or start-up factory. Even more than ideas for the 1st S-curve, these internal start-ups normally require substantial funding and support. The ideas for such new ventures can come from a variety of sources, for example, from innovation labs or from incubator programs in which firms run ideation sprints (learn more about this in the **Process** chapter, Chapter 5). Those corporate ventures, once started, can be located in or close to the digital innovation lab – to leverage resources and create synergies – or separated completely.

If the start-up factory is set up with a certain distance from the core, it can protect new business ideas from red tape and cumbersome legacy processes of the incumbents' core business. Separating the start-up factory from the core is also helpful to give the unit more autonomy and freedom.[15] To avoid ending up with "old problems with a new look," these units should be staffed with external experts who have business-building expertise and bring in the right mindset and attitude. Thus, such corporate incubators, corporate venture building units, or start-up factories (it's up to you to choose the label) provide a structured environment to develop non-core business innovations and support them on their path to market.[16]

In the second case, incumbents can choose to directly or indirectly invest in new business ideas. For example, they can decide to directly invest into a promising start-up that's working on a disruptive business model. You will find many examples where traditional firms have done exactly that (for example, Toyota's investment into self-driving car start-up Pony.ai or Microsoft's investments into data preparation software Paxata and other promising tech start-ups). Most large traditional firms that we interviewed have multiple direct start-up investments. Alternatively, firms can use an indirect investment, for example, investments into company builders or VC funds. In doing so, incumbents can get a foot in the door without the struggles related to company building (as this is taken care of by externals). Most traditional firms choose this approach if they want to stay active in new technologies or trends but it's too soon to fully evaluate their potential. Hence, (external) corporate venture activities help incumbents to engage in new innovation activities and bring in new insights from non-core markets as well as new technologies and capabilities.[17]

While both, internal and external venturing, have their merits, it makes sense to implement a balanced approach, primarily to hedge one's bets and increase the likelihood of success. Internal venture activities require substantial resources and long-term commitment, especially compared to investments into external company builders (where an external provider takes care of infrastructure and support). The resources and time commitment that come with an internal approach limit the number of start-ups than can be looked after and supported at the same time. Moreover, given that the internal expertise and capabilities will unlikely cover the full breadth of ideas for new business models, some ideas will have their natural home within the company while others should be pursued more indirectly and through a team of dedicated experts (that is, external company builders and VCs).

One incumbent that successfully set up such a build-and-buy portfolio is Deutsche Bahn (DB), the German railway company.

DEUTSCHE BAHN
. . . .

Imagine you are a board member of a railway company and have to prepare the organization for the future of mobility. To make it even more challenging, you have to address the increasing cost pressure in your existing core business and make your current offering more attractive to customers. This is the situation Deutsche Bahn (DB) (and possibly many other railway companies) found itself in.

Stefan Stroh, Chief Digital Officer, describes their setup as "build-and-buy portfolio" with several parallel approaches. As far as the existing business is concerned, DB uses what they call "Innovation Labs" to work on core business problems. These labs are located next to the core business units and work on products or services and on solutions to existing problems that are close to the core business. Due to the proximity to the core business, these initiatives are mostly profit-oriented (for example, focusing on efficiency improvements) and are funded by the core business units directly. The labs employ digital experts who work together with employees from the core business and help the core business apply new ways of working (for example, agile methods and tools). In addition to these labs, DB established a collaboration vehicle that they call Mindbox. Whenever the core faces a challenge that can be better addressed with the help of external start-ups, Mindbox helps approach, select, and collaborate with these start-ups. Once they completed a successful pilot, DB decides how they want to proceed (often in the form of a standard buyer-supplier relationship with the start-up).

As far as new business models are concerned, DB separates them more clearly from the core business. These initiatives are usually funded directly by the board and have a longer investment horizon compared to the initiatives that aim to improve the core. Initiatives are split into ventures that are built internally and those that are built externally (for example, through company builders or ideas accessed through venture capital investments). Compared to the ideas that are developed within the Innovation Lab or Mindbox, these initiatives require a certain degree of flexibility and separation from the core to function. That's why DB set up less stringent governance and compliance requirements for their internal ventures program. However, all initiatives are regularly monitored, and further funding is only granted after previously defined milestones are reached. The ventures get access to assets of the core, whenever that is useful (for example, to test and scale ideas). Given the nature of these new business models, these investments have a longer funding horizon and tend to be riskier.

While initiatives to improve the core business are not new to incumbents, it's this new type of venture investments that incumbents have to get used to – they require a longer investment horizon and a different organizational approach, too.[18]

As you can see, there are plenty of approaches to structure your organization to pursue digital activities. While they differ in terms of focus (that is, internal versus external, 1st S-curve versus 2nd S-curve), they have one thing in common: they are a tool to deliver on the strategy, rather than an end in itself.

ANCHOR FIRST, THEN SET SAIL – THINK ABOUT WHERE TO POSITION YOUR DIGITAL EFFORTS NOW AND LATER

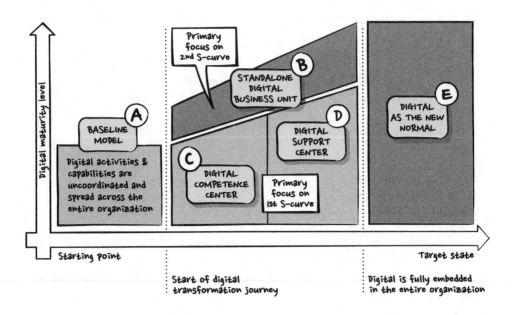

Figure 3.4 Common organizational archetypes

Now that we have discussed different formats to create and develop digital innovation, we have done the groundwork to look more closely at how digital topics can be anchored within the broader organizational structure. The anchoring within the organization deals with two important organizational questions: first, who is responsible for driving the digital transformation; and second, which digital capabilities should be centralized and what can or should be integrated within business units. Given the nature of these questions, the answers will have important governance implications, too.

Comparing the different approaches our various interview partners have used, and contrasting them with the commonly known patterns,[19] we find that digital transformations are commonly organized following one of five broad archetypes: baseline model, standalone digital business unit, digital competence center, digital support center, and digital as the new normal. These archetypes differ in the degree of centralization and the degree of digital maturity the organization exhibits.

Reflecting on these archetypes, we find that the common pathway toward "digital as the new normal" usually looks like Figure 3.4.

Baseline model (A)

We find the digital journey starts most often as a rather turbulent voyage until firms find the right setup that works for them. Asking our interview partners how they ended up with their ideal setup, we discovered that most of them started from a position where digital initiatives were fairly uncoordinated across business units (as shown in Figure 3.5). Even organizations that were at an early stage of their digital transformation pursued at least some digital efforts somewhere in their organization. Although little is better than nothing, these digital initiatives normally fail to produce large-scale impact and are usually rather insular product- or business unit–related digital initiatives. These siloed efforts

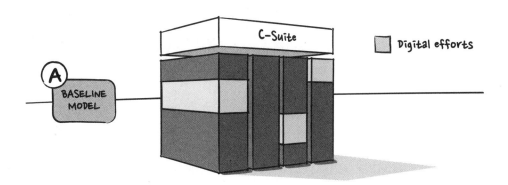

Figure 3.5 Baseline model (A)

lack a holistic digital perspective. While companies employing such approaches do become more digital over time, an overarching digital strategy and central coordination of digitization efforts across the entire organization is missing in this approach.[20] Firms in this position are most often traditional organizations that are at the very start of their journey. It is not surprising that such uncoordinated efforts normally only lead to incremental innovations and limited success.

Standalone Digital Business Unit (B)

The standalone digital business unit structure boasts the highest degree of separation from the core business of all archetypes (see Figure 3.6). Organizations following this archetype set up a completely separated digital business unit that has the freedom to run digital initiatives independently from the rest of the organization. Quite often these units are physically separated and have an entirely different (that is, flat) hierarchical structure with networked, self-learning teams focused on a specific business problem or idea. The prime goal of these units is most often not the digitization of the 1st S-curve, but the build-up of new, disruptive businesses (2nd S-curve).[21] An advantage of this structure allows the new business unit to break with old legacy systems, processes, and structures. That's why it's handy to have 2nd S-curve initiatives reside here.[22] Quite naturally, a unit that focuses on 2nd S-curve activities is also

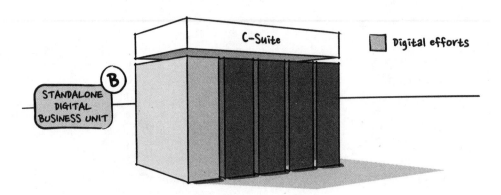

Figure 3.6 Standalone Digital Business Unit (B)

well-positioned to host potential business building and corporate venture activities we discussed earlier.

Setting up a fully separate digital business unit makes sense when the incumbent's strategy prioritizes the 2nd S-curve. When the initiatives to digitize or digitally enhance the 1st S-curve conflict with the core business, it often becomes necessary to shield them from the rest of the organization, too. When it seems impossible for the core business to accept and support new ways of thinking and digital activities, a fully separated unit is likely the only way out.[23]

The disadvantage of such a standalone digital business unit is the potential frictions with the rest of the organization, particularly if it's seen as an ivory tower that is completely disconnected from the core organization. Often core employees see themselves as the ones who actually earn the money and don't understand why they should share the budget with the standalone unit.

The importance of a standalone digital unit as compared to a normal division within the mothership is something that an expert in the automotive industry, particularly in the areas of urban mobility and autonomous driving, we spoke to highlights. He points out that a division that is too close to the core organization often tends to focus too much on incremental and evolutionary innovations.

//The typical car maker focusing on driving assistance systems usually makes small steps. That means they start with an ultrasound sensor, then they improve and adapt them and so on. It takes ages until they can use this as a basis for autonomous driving. If you look at Waymo owned by Google, on the other hand, they were founded as a standalone entity, completely separated from the mothership. Different from OEMS, they focused on their end-goal of autonomous driving right from the start, and didn't waste time with evolutionary innovations and intermediate steps. Elon Musk and The Boring company are doing the exact same thing. Without this separation from the mothership, OEMS easily fall into an evolutionary trap.//

Automotive expert, automotive supplier[24]

Digital Competence Center (C)

The digital competence center is a specialized central unit that is responsible for the overall direction of the digital transformation and acts as a catalyst between the board and the business units (see Figure 3.7). This organizational structure often comes with a dedicated Chief Digital Officer (CDO), who reports directly to the CEO.[25]

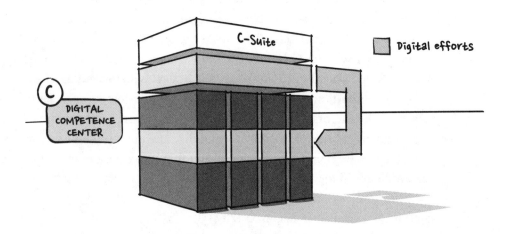

Figure 3.7 Digital Competence Center (C)

Such a central unit is especially useful when the organization has already defined a digital vision and strategy but wants to centralize the digital expertise and establish formal governance and coordination to drive the transformation of the core. The central team can set up a unified roadmap to implement the strategy, set clear guidelines and rules for the execution, and foster collaboration across business units and functions to avoid uncoordinated efforts.[26] The unit will also host digital assets and capabilities for the entire organization. This is most helpful when the digital maturity is low (that is, when the business lines do not have sufficient digital capabilities) as the central team can then sharpen the focus and help build up digital assets in a more coordinated fashion. Central digital units are commonly the host of digital innovation labs and oversee collaboration activities with externals that aim to digitize the core.

Since the digital competence center will be the key driving force behind the execution of all digital activities in the core business, it requires close collaboration and support of core business units. This setup requires that business units have a say in the identification, development, and implementation of use cases. Without the support and buy-in of core business units, the centralized unit will find it difficult to build up acceptance in the broader organization.

One firm that followed this approach and installed a central digital unit is Deutsche Pfandbriefbank (pbb), the German bank that specializes in real estate financing.

DEUTSCHE PFANDBRIEFBANK (PBB)

When we interviewed Michael Spiegel, head of Digitalization at pbb, he had a dual role within his organization. In addition to his responsibility to digitize the core organization, he was also CEO of a newly founded subsidiary for a specific digital business. The subsidiary focuses on an entirely new business model with a fairly disruptive character (broker platform for public sector financing).

The digitization of the 1st S-curve is driven by a new digital unit which is part of the core organization (acting as digital competence center for the core business). This unit holds the digital capabilities within the core organization and its main responsibility is to digitize the core. As part of this activity, the digital unit sets up and leads new digital initiatives together with employees from the core business units. "It's important to find and integrate the digital-savvy employees acting as multipliers and catalysts to drive digitization," Spiegel explains. But it's not just a one-way street – these employees communicate pain points and potential use cases to the digital unit and are thus crucial to the identification of new initiatives. The digital unit also interacts with the HR department to organize digital education and training sessions. Mutual projects with the core business units and regular education and training efforts provide a continuous digitization impetus to the core. "We think it's important that employees receive this training on digital methods and tools. The first-hand experience they can acquire through mutual projects with the digital unit is the best way to convince them. Once they are aware of the benefits, using such methods – even without support of our digital unit – will become a no-brainer," Spiegel points out.[27]

Digital Support Center (D)

The support center is similar to the digital competence center with the important difference that more digital competences and responsibilities reside within the core business units (see Figure 3.8). Thus, with increasing digital maturity of the organization, the central digital unit has a smaller field of duty while responsibilities and tasks for core business units increase. This setup can thus be seen as a hybrid approach, where the core starts to own digital topics and core business units are in the driver seat, pushing digital initiatives forward. Although core business units run the digital activities now, they can still fall

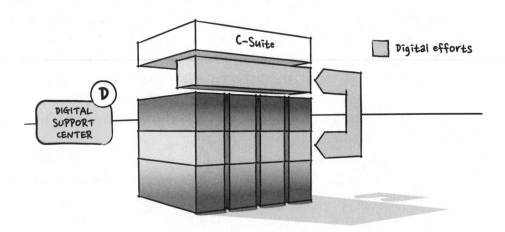

Figure 3.8 Digital Support Center (D)

back on the support center to receive guidance on best practices, tools, and so on. Thus, the emphasis of the central digital unit moves from driving and injecting digital initiatives to knowledge sharing and support. The ultimate goal is to educate and enable the business units so that they become independent.[28] Thus, when the digital maturity increases, digital capabilities move from the centralized unit to the business units, and the organization adapts a more decentralized structure. The transition from a competence center to a support center will only work when the organization is well aligned with the strategy. The responsibility to drive digital topics within the core resides within the business units, so they must have sufficient understanding and a firm belief in the way forward.

However, not all capabilities are transferred to the business unit. Some digital capabilities will still reside in the central digital unit. For example, it often makes more sense to keep data analytics skills centralized, since this makes it easier to leverage synergies. It might also be economically unfeasible to build up such expertise separately in each business unit. In other cases, the resources might not be fully utilized if they are located within a particular business unit, so that it makes more sense to keep them in some form of competence center or cluster.

In short, the central team reduces its activities to best practice setting and support of business units. It acts as a digital advisory and support unit in the organization, while the business units drive the implementation of the digital agenda.[29]

A great example to illustrate this setup is an American conglomerate we interviewed. Their digital transformation is accelerated by a central digital unit that offers support to all traditional business units undertaking digital initiatives. While the responsibility for the digital initiatives also resides with the core business units, the central digital unit supports employees of the core business by providing the digital expertise and skills the core business units are still missing. Once capabilities have been built up successfully, or when the support of the central digital unit is no longer needed – for example, when an initiative has been tested successfully and is about to be scaled – the central digital unit pulls out and the core business units take over.[30]

Digital as the new normal (E)

This last archetype is the ultimate target state. "Digital as the new normal" embodies a business where the digital maturity is very high (see Figure 3.9). In this case, "digital" does not feel unnatural anymore. It's something that all employees have accepted and internalized. Thus, employees have fully embedded digital work practices in their daily routine and have developed enough expertise for the central digital (support) unit to become obsolete.[31] However, organizations might choose to keep a scaled-down version of the central digital unit in order to set best practices, coordinate activities, and manage links to external partners.[32] In this ideal stage, companies no longer need standalone digital business units for disruptive 2nd S-curve initiatives, either. This is because the legacy culture and processes that hurt new ideas in the past no longer exist. Digital innovation and continuous renewal are then part of day-to-day operations, so that even entirely new business models can be developed within the environment of the "new core." A well-known example of this is Google, where some employees are able to use up to 20% of their time to work on new, potentially disruptive, ideas within their normal work environment.[33] Incumbents that have arrived at this stage have business units that fully embrace digital work practices and tools and are fully equipped with digital capabilities, that is, all digital capabilities are fully decentralized. This is also

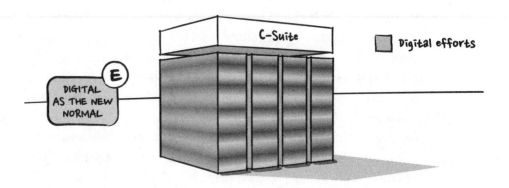

Figure 3.9 Digital as the new normal (E)

when roles such as Chief Digital Officer (CDO) are no longer needed, because the mission is complete.

Under the bottom line, incumbents can move to a more decentralized approach, when digital maturity is higher and business units have the digital expertise in place to drive digital activities themselves. The centralized digital activities can then be reduced to support functions (that is, the digital support center, where business units are driving the activities and the central teams are merely supporting).[34]

Here's how BASF went from less-coordinated efforts to the right organizational setup.

BASF
······

When BASF, the largest chemical producer in the world, started its digital transformation journey, it soon became apparent that "digital" couldn't be neglected and treated as a side project. But how can such a large organization, operating in dozens of countries around the globe and with multiple business units, find the right organizational setup?

In 2015, the CEO wanted to understand what all the hype surrounding topics such as Industry 4.0 really meant for the organization. This triggered a new project with the aim to explore the implications of digitalization[35] on BASF. Due to the importance of the topic, the project was staffed by high-ranking executives who had important operational roles and knew the business well. The seniority of the team members was a signal to the organization. "This setup was important for BASF. The multidisciplinary setup was key to really have an impact," explains Samy Jandali, Vice President Digital Business Empowerment. The CEO deliberately defined a broad scope of analysis, that is, the scope was not limited to digitalization in the core but covered adjacent topics and topics outside the core business as well.

After a nine-month period, the project team came up with a concrete list of active use cases and initiatives (lighthouses) that were pursued to test and learn. These initial initiatives helped BASF get a better feeling for certain topics (for example, predictive maintenance) and allowed them to define a new digital vision for the organization. Over time, the project increased in importance and relevance. Digitalization at BASF moved from being a project to becoming a division. The newly formed Global Digitalization Services division is run by a CDO who reports directly to the Deputy Chairman of the Board of Directors.

How closely the initiatives of this digital division are linked to the core business depends on the similarity to the core, Jandali tells us. If the initiatives are close to the core (for example, when they support the efficiency of the 1st S-curve), the project team consists of people from both S-curves and the initiatives are located within the core, while the digital division is merely supporting. On the other hand, if the initiative is further away from the core (for example, if it's a totally new business model), the potential conflicts with the mothership are too strong. In this case, initiatives are developed centrally within the digital division, or spun off into a separate entity.[36]

Rüdiger Mannherz, Vice President Finance & IT, and Michael Hepp, Vice President Digital Transformation, from the metalwork company Walter would agree. Their organizational setup followed a similar recipe to get the transformation up and running.

WALTER

One of the world's leading cutting tool manufacturers, Walter offers a wide range of specialized machining solutions for milling, turning, drilling, and threading applications. At the beginning of its digital transformation journey, Walter started off with an initiative that was supposed to explore the fuzzy topic of digitization. At this time, a small team was given the task to understand the different facets of the topic as well as possible implications for Walter.

After a few months of work, the findings of the initiative made it clear to everyone that the topic was far bigger than everyone thought. For that reason, Walter decided to shift gears and set up a dedicated digital business unit, with a dedicated Vice President hired from outside to bring in an external perspective.

At first, the main goal of this newly established digital business unit was the exploration of opportunities to introduce new (digital) products and services beyond the core business, as customers were increasingly demanding support beyond the core product (for example, manufacturing support services). Only later in the transformation process did the focus of the digital transformation shift from new products and services to the digitization of core processes. Important in this respect, however, was that this latter part of the transformation could not be delegated to a standalone digital business unit. Mannherz and Hepp explain, "The digitization of the core cannot be done from the outside. You can't have a digital VP telling the other core units 'please digitize this and that,' and even let the core units pay for it. This needs to work with cooperation between the digital unit and the core units."

At this stage, the dedicated digital unit can act as sparring partner to the core, offering digital expertise and advice, but responsibility and decision-making power need to rest with the respective core business units, too. (Comparing this setup with the archetypes introduced earlier, we find that Walter moved from a centralized team to a "standalone digital business unit" archetype, with parallel efforts to establish new (digital) products and services while at the same time supporting the transformation of the remaining core units.)[37]

As you can see, the transition from uncoordinated digital efforts to "digital as the new normal" will not happen overnight. Having a central digital project team can certainly be helpful in reducing confusion around uncoordinated digital endeavors and in starting things off on the right foot. Such a team can also serve as a forum to solve the initial questions we discussed in the **WHY** and **WHAT** chapters (Chapters 1 and 2). After the work of the digital project team has come to an end, it might segue into something like a standalone digital business unit or a digital competence center. Both types are more formal organizational setups to drive the transformation forward.

So far we have barely touched upon the role of a dedicated Chief Digital Officer (CDO). The need for a CDO has been a highly debated question in recent years, including among our interview partners. Is a CDO needed, or not? It depends.

A dedicated CDO role can help drive the digital transformation and push the organization up the maturity curve. Putting a CDO into a top management position, ideally on the board, highlights the importance and relevance of the topic. It thus sends an important signal to the organization and to outside stakeholders. Also, centralizing the responsibility for all digital topics makes it easier to manage the digital strategy and coordinate investments and resources across the organization.[38] However, a digital transformation is a challenge that the entire organization has to face, not just the CDO. Other board members and top executives sometimes think they can outsource the responsibility for the digital agenda to the CDO. As a consequence, CDOs are often overloaded with tasks and end up falling short of expectations. And, because board members are reluctant to relinquish control over their responsibilities, CDOs often end up with insufficient decision-making power and resources.[39] Digital transformations set up like this are doomed to fail, as a former executive of a multinational conglomerate explained.

> If you do not share the responsibility for the transformation with your core business units, the CDO and their digital unit will be rejected like antibodies. We learned we had to get the leadership buy-in first, otherwise nothing happens. So, we decided to have a CDO in the group who aligns and coordinates activities across the organization, but also 'localized' CDOs within each business unit who were responsible for working alongside the Group CDO and applying digital initiatives in their lines of the business. This way, we were able to achieve huge productivity gains across the entire organization.

Former executive manager, multinational conglomerate[40]

An organization that faced similar problems and found a solution is AMAG, the Swiss car importer and dealer.

AMAG
. . . . . .

Who's responsible for driving digital topics within an organization? That's exactly the question that AMAG faced a couple of years ago. Lacking a universal rule, AMAG tried several different digital roles and responsibilities until they found a setup that worked for them. This created several learning opportunities along the way, as Philipp Wetzel, Managing Director AMAG Innovation and Venture Lab, tells us.

Initially, AMAG tried to put the responsibility for its digital transformation in the hands of the Chief Information Officer (CIO). However, they soon realized that digital transformation is not a CIO responsibility. The explanation: IT per se is not innovative. CIOs have to keep down costs for IT infrastructure, unify the architecture, orchestrate the growing complexity of systems, and so on. When AMAG tried to house their digitization efforts within the IT department, they saw initiatives slowed down. New initiatives had to follow a certain legacy architecture or wait for specific release cycles.

Equipped with this novel insight, AMAG tried to put the responsibility within the hands of a dedicated CDO. Guess what? That did not work, either. This time, the reason was not that the CDO lacked an innovative spirit. It was rather the lack of impact he had on the core business units, because they simply did not care. The CDO did not have sufficient resources and power for a significant digital push. With this second attempt, AMAG suffered from something Wetzel calls "the big-company disease." Companies suffer from this whenever they are not well aligned around one (or more) of the following points: who's responsible, who's paying for it, and who's allowed to decide what gets done. As a consequence, the business units weren't willing to accept the costs and do what the CDO wanted them to do.

The realization was that the digital transformation can't succeed if it is not part of core BUs' own goals and strategy, or as Philipp Wetzel puts it, "Digital transformation can't be delegated – it needs to be done by the top management of the core business. It's not enough to have a CDO or digital BU on the side, if the core BUs themselves don't care." Thus, the digital transformation needs to be key priority of the core business, and the business units need to define in advance where they want to be active and allocate sufficient resources to support the transformation.

Based on these experiences, AMAG put the responsibility for the digital transformation back to the core business units and set up one additional digital business unit, called "Innovation and Venture Lab," which is fully separated from the mothership. This new unit is now responsible for all disruptive topics, that is, topics that have a low likelihood of success within the core business. Moreover, the lab acts as an interface unit for all collaborations with external start-ups (including the management and support of these start-ups). From an organizational point of view, AMAG split the responsibility for the digital trans-formation into 1st S-curve initiatives (which were decentralized and reallocated to the core business units), and 2nd S-curve initiatives (which were centralized and concentrated with the new lab for improved coordination and focus).[41]

From our perspective, the need for a CDO role mainly depends on the digital maturity of the organization. It should not be a permanent role. Given that the CDO should help the organization during the transformation period, the role becomes obsolete once the organization calls itself a fully digital organization (where digital is the new normal). Companies that are already digitally mature might not need a CDO. On the other hand, a dedicated CDO, or "transformer in chief,"[42] will be especially important and useful when the organization finds itself in a relatively early stage of its digital transformation, where the overall digital maturity is low. In this case, the strong digital push will be especially fruitful and a more centralized approach, with a CDO or Head of Digital, makes sense. The CDO can then drive the digital strategy and coordinate and align efforts across businesses and functional siloes. Digital topics will be higher up on the organization's agenda, and with the support of the CEO, the organization can get a jumpstart into the digital transformation.[43] It's in these early or middle stages of a digital transformation that a CDO can also be helpful in overseeing and managing digital activities across both S-curves.

Not convinced yet? Let's do a little thought experiment and see what happens when the digital transformation starts with a decentralized approach. In this case, when the digital maturity is low, it would not make much sense to put the responsibility for digital topics into the business lines. This would likely lead to uncoordinated efforts that will not come to fruition, since the business lines do not have the right capabilities (nor the mindset) yet. Starting with a decentralized setting, the business units would need extensive support and guidance so that centralizing digital activities makes more sense.[44] Also, in this scenario, the digital transformation will likely not be high on the agenda of the core business units. It's not that they won't try any digital activities (how could they say "no" if the CEO told them to do so); it's just that they will not approach it seriously. Of course, much of this has to do with goal setting and incentives for business unit heads, too. But if the business units do not have the right digital capabilities, then it's likely that your digital transformation will not end up being a success. Another disadvantage of a decentralized approach is that the digital agenda often lacks top management support and attention, because a high-ranking advocate is missing, and unified standards and practices are missing.

 ESTABLISH CONTACT WITH OTHER DIGITAL TRANSFORMATION BOATS IN THE BAY

It won't come as a surprise that your organization should think strategically, as always, about partnerships and collaborations. In today's hyperconnected digital world, they have become more important than ever before. Many of today's innovations and value propositions have become so complex that almost no organization can deliver them independently. An increasing number of products and services are built based on collaborative efforts of multiple interconnected firms and, as a result, ecosystems and platforms have rapidly increased in importance. Much of this development is fueled by the modular structure of products and services and new technologies that have made it easier to spread the production and distribution of value propositions across multiple actors. The future success of organizations is increasingly dependent on their ability to collaborate with other players in the broader business ecosystem.

That's why it's so important that incumbents undergoing a digital transformation think strategically about their network of ties. They must occupy strategic positions in the broader ecosystems and think about potential new ties. These ties can be manifold and include links to start-ups, company builders, and venture capital organizations and also to universities, thought leaders, tech hubs, players from other industries, and even industry competitors. For some topics that are hard to figure out singlehandedly, an alliance with other players in the industry might make sense. That may be one of the reasons Mercedes Benz decided to join forces with BMW to create an even bigger mobility services platform, encompassing taxi ride hailing, parking, car sharing, charging, and multimodal services.[45]

Govecs, market leader in the production of e-scooters, uses partnerships to broaden its value proposition. It partners with hardware and software providers that deliver solutions for integrated connectivity, data sharing, and so forth. Due to its position as a middleman, Govecs can grab a share of the additional value that's delivered to clients. B2B customers themselves are happy, too, as Thomas Grübel, CEO of Govecs, tells us. Because it would cost clients much more to build, integrate, and test their own solutions, they are willing to pay Govecs for the integration of physical hardware and software components.[46]

Another firm that has learned to leverage the wisdom of the crowd is a chemical and consumer goods company we interviewed. The company set up a broad innovation ecosystem and is about to initiate a broader collaboration platform with industry partners.

CHEMICAL AND CONSUMER GOODS COMPANY

Why should you try to solve all problems internally, when there are smart people around the corner who have the same problem, and/or who have a smart idea at hand that can save you a lot of time and money? That's what the former

CDO thought when he drafted the new collaboration strategy for a dedicated digital unit.

The new collaboration strategy is a good example of what an old incumbent can do to foster a vivid innovation ecosystem within and across company borders. To support and guide its internal digital ventures, the firm established a mentoring program with over 100 mentors from all over the globe. The goal was very simple: to help the company's digital ventures succeed. As for any new venture, the experience of leading venture capital managers, board members of Fortune 100 companies, and knowledgeable (tech) entrepreneurs is of enormous value to the company's internal entrepreneurs. The firm further leverages this network of mentors through regular events, such as "pitch nights," where employees can pitch their ideas and receive feedback from industry experts. The broad network is also a great opportunity to bring in an external impetus to the organization.

In addition to this mentorship program, the firm plans to build a broad collaboration network with industry partners. Operating in an ecosystem environment requires organizations to keep other players in mind when they make investments. That's something many firms neglect when they make uncoordinated, siloed investments, although some technologies, such as blockchain, only work once multiple players align their efforts and set a common standard. In today's environment, "There's often no competitive advantage in what technology you choose. The competitive advantage comes after, when you get everyone to participate," the former CDO argues. For this reason, the firm puts a focus on co-investment in industrial technology – to foster the co-development of new technologies and standards and bring more organizations to the same agenda while reducing uncertainty and sunk costs of all participating firms.[47]

While incumbents have learned to get things done alone, the new reality forces them to open up and collaborate more than ever before. It's better to take an active role and shape the ecosystem than to wait on the sidelines, hoping for others to offer you a seat at the table.

MANAGE THE ORGANIZATIONAL TENSION BETWEEN THE 1ST AND 2ND S-CURVE

Just after you convinced your fellow board members or your boss to separate all 2nd S-curve initiatives and keep them protected within a newly set up digital business unit, separation causes new problems. A separate unit that has more flexibility and freedom than any other unit of the core organization will inevitably upset some of the core employees in your organization. This requires effective connecting links between the two S-curves to prevent these problems.

Even more importantly, however, connecting links are crucial to unlock the full potential of a dual business: incumbents need to leverage their assets to push their digital businesses to new heights, superseding start-ups that don't have corporate backing. The 2nd S-curve can benefit from a number of assets, such as the stable infrastructure, market and regulatory expertise, existing customer network and distribution channels, brand reputation, and access to data. The core business, on the other hand, will benefit from the agility, flexibility, and speed the 2nd S-curve brings to the organization.

One firm that established a new unit to shield its 2nd S-curve activities from legacy problems and cooperate more effectively with start-ups is Munich Re, the leading reinsurance company.

MUNICH RE

How do you align the needs of start-ups with those of a DAX-listed company when you collaborate on new innovations? This is a typical challenge most incumbents face when they bring in new ideas and innovations through collaborative endeavors with start-ups.

Since start-ups are used to quick decision-making and rapid detection and correction of flaws, they are often overwhelmed by the inertia of large corporations. Olaf Frank, head of Business Technology, says that Munich Re, like many other legacy organizations, originally did not boast an environment conducive to cooperating effectively with start-ups. "The standard decision-making process of a large firm like ours is so slow that the start-up will go bankrupt before we have made a decision on whether we want to collaborate or not," he states. To counter this problem, Munich Re set up "Digital Partners," a separate unit that manages all collaborations with start-ups. The new unit is an interface to the start-up world, with managers who have the freedom and flexibility to act in the same speed and take similar risks as the start-ups they collaborate with. As the managers of Digital Partners can speak the same language as their counterparts, and because they can take much corporate hassle out of processes, the collaboration becomes more enjoyable for start-ups. The new unit translates and aligns efforts between the corporate and the start-up side to ensure that the full potential of the collaboration can be exploited. For example, Digital Partners ensures that start-ups get access to customers, experts, or other corporate assets that are necessary to test and iterate new ideas. The unit also evaluates where new start-up innovations can best be leveraged within the larger organization.

Even with Digital Partners as an interface unit, there are still frictions between the old and new worlds. "However, this is totally normal because the old world is tailored to processes and stringent structures, whereas the new world is focused on continuous innovation," Frank points out. The best way to solve this is to discuss and decide on boundary conditions early on. Defining clear rules in advance that both sides can agree on helps manage expectations and avoid conflict later on. Collaboration between traditional organizations and start-ups will also require some understanding and mutual consideration. Start-ups need to accept that some things will just take longer, and that they have to comply with corporate rules that they do not always understand. Corporations, on the other hand, need to understand that taking risks is necessary to compete in the digital world, and they need to accept that a flat hierarchy and fast decision-making can be worthwhile, even if it feels unnatural to them.[48]

We find that ties between the two S-curves are especially helpful when it comes to the growth and scaling of new business models. Many traditional firms see limited success with new ventures because they often do not (or cannot) scale these new ideas.[49] That's exactly where incumbents should become better at leveraging their core. The traditional part of organizations knows exactly how to scale and execute innovations – that's how they ended up being a successful organization in the first place. So, it's about time incumbents do not hide their experience and assets from their little brothers and sisters. And you'll be surprised, people (and S-curves alike) get along once they finally start talking to each other.

AESCULAP

"It all started 10–15 years ago, when the firm realized that further substantial innovations were not to be expected from the product R&D department. We were already market leader in surgical products back then and had a product that was fully optimized. To think beyond the product, we needed to break free and create a new culture and mindset," Bernd Reck and Sören Lauinger told us.

That's how Aesculap came to the conclusion that they needed to build up a separate innovation unit (now called "Werk_39"), that is located at a distance from Aesculap's core business. However, it was also clear that a fancy lab in Berlin, where many other German incumbents locate their new digital businesses, would not work for Aesculap. They decided to keep Werk_39 in the same region because this area was well-known for being a cluster for Medtech products. Also, Reck and Lauinger knew that a strong link to the core was necessary for the lab to succeed, something that was easier to achieve when the lab was not geographically remote.

The lab's links back to the core are manifold. Its scope of innovation is set by the strategic focus of the core. There is a division of labor between the traditional business units, which still focus on core products, and the lab, which focuses on the (digital) extension of core offerings. A further link is established through assets that the mothership provides: established market access, quality standards and controls, stable processes the lab can rely on, established distribution channels with strong customer relationships, trust of customers, and

so on. Links are also built on an employee-level: members of the digital operations team of the core business (a centralized digital team) as well as functional
experts from the core business units work together with employees from the
lab to co-develop new ideas. This makes the handover to the core, and the
integration of ideas within the mothership, much easier later on. The mixed
team with employees from "both worlds" is seen as critical for success because
"Only the combination of mothership and internal start-up unleashes the full
potential. We need the connection to the core to get more power and scale
ideas," Lauinger argues. However, the ties are not restricted to the operational
level only. Lauinger, who is Vice President for Intrapreneurship & Co-creation
at Aesculap, is also the head of the digital lab. This dual role allows him to act
as advocate within the mothership, which is helpful to reduce potential conflicts and to promote an effective collaboration. He also ensures that the lab gets
sufficient support from other executives of the core organization and that digital
topics rank high on the corporate agenda.[50]

Integration isn't easy and there's not a one-size-fits-all solution when it
comes to the appropriate type and the required number of ties between the two
S-curves. The list of integration mechanisms is long and includes many softer
aspects related to leadership, people, and culture (for example, mixed staffing,
shared vision, integrated senior teams), which are discussed in other chapters.

From an organizational point of view, the most effective ties are those at the
top management level (we will explore this topic in more detail in the **Leadership** chapter, Chapter 6). Research exploring successful examples of parallel
business models has shown that an active and credible integrator,[51] and a shared
general manager[52] are effective mechanisms to integrate separated businesses.
Florian Bankoley, Vice President Corporate IT at Bosch, would call these managers "border walkers." They need to be able to function as translators and bridge
builders between both S-curves, he explains. In order to perform this task, they
need to feel comfortable with both worlds, the traditional core environment as
well as the new, digital environment. The key challenge for them will be to handle
the diverging requirements and leadership styles on both S-curves.[53]

Research has shown that the most successful firms appointed an insider from the parent organization as CEO of the new business, which facilitated cooperation and the exploitation of synergies.[54] Another feature of successful firms was that they encouraged cooperation between the old and the new business through shared incentive and rewards systems.[55] Strong management ties help incumbents keep control over the strategy of the new (digital) business and to align digital activities across the organization. Multiple firms we interviewed followed this approach. For example, German bank pbb appointed an experienced executive from within the company as CEO of their new platform business.[56] Similarly, chemicals company BASF appointed a leading executive of the core business to lead their new business model activities.[57]

By appointing an internal manager to lead the new unit, incumbents can thus kill several birds with one stone. One, putting the responsibility of the new venture in the hands of a longstanding executive from the core reduces frictions and prejudices of the core. Two, an internal executive knows the core business well, which will come in handy whenever the incumbent tries to unlock synergies. Such management ties also play an important role when it comes to the overall governance of the transformation. We will reinforce this again in the **Processes** chapter (Chapter 5).

GET MOVING TO AVOID THE DINOSAUR FATE

You will be best equipped to design your organizational setup in the most conducive way if you consider these pointers:

- Define how you pursue digital innovation activities:
  — For your 1st S-curve initiatives, consider digital projects within business units, digital labs as well as links to external start-ups.
  — For your 2nd S-curve initiatives, consider a balanced approach between internal and external venturing.

- Consider how you want to anchor the digital topics in your organization:
  - At an early stage of the digital transformation, establish formal governance and coordination by setting up a central digital unit (competence center) that takes control over the digital agenda (especially for your core business).
  - Once the digital maturity increases, take a hybrid approach where the central digital unit is merely acting as support center.
  - Set up a standalone digital business unit to give your digital activities more freedom (especially relevant for your 2nd S-curve).
  - Once your organization has reached digital maturity, give business units full responsibility for their digital topics.

- Open your organization and establish strategic links beyond organizational boundaries:
  - Think strategically about potential new ties to start-ups, company builders, VCs, universities, thought leaders, tech organizations and tech hubs, players from adjacent industries, and even competitors.
  - Leverage your network to bring in new ideas and evaluate your innovation funnel.

- Build effective organizational links to bridge the gap between the two S-curves:
  - Establish an interface that shields your work with start-ups or other external partners from the red tape of your legacy business.
  - Appoint internal top executives for leading positions of your new (digital) business model to establish strong management ties and keep control over the strategic direction of the new business.
  - Consider shared incentive systems and rewards to foster collaboration and mutual support.

GET INSPIRED (BY ELECTRICITY)

ALPIQ
. . . . . .

When leading Swiss electricity producer Alpiq embarked on its digital transformation, they started with a team of three people. This team was given the task to find out what the word "digital" meant for the organization. After Alpiq had defined their need to act, it became clear that a dedicated unit was needed to get the transformation off the ground.

Alpiq founded a new business unit called "Digital Technologies and Innovation." All digital initiatives that existed at that point were spread across the organization. In a first step, they were moved into the new digital unit (the "digital competence center" archetype). From then on, the digital unit had the overarching responsibility for all digital efforts within the core business. This gave Alpiq more oversight over its digital activities and control over previously uncoordinated digital investments of the individual business units.

But Alpiq did not stop there. The original analysis identified that the organization had to prepare itself quickly, before it got disrupted by others, and that digitization offered opportunities for Alpiq to disrupt others, too. With the newly founded digital unit, Alpiq was all set to digitally transform its core. However, Alpiq knew that to address truly disruptive ideas and business models, it would have to create another unit that was further separated from its core business. For this reason, Alpiq established the "Oyster Lab," a second standalone digital business unit focusing on new disruptive ideas (the "standalone digital business unit" archetype).

When we compare the internal Digital Technologies and Innovation unit and the external Oyster Lab, we observe a number of distinguishing factors. First, the two are quite different in terms of innovation scope and strategic direction. The internal digital unit focuses on topics of "tomorrow," covering all digital innovations close to the core business. The external digital unit, on the other hand, focuses on "the day after tomorrow" and thus deals with all digital topics unrelated to the core business. Second, the distinct strategic foci of the two require different degrees of separation from the mothership. Compared to the standalone Oyster Lab, the internal digital unit is only partially separated from the core; it is still within the mothership, although on a different floor and with more freedom than the traditional business units. The external unit itself was fully separated from the Alpiq infrastructure right from the beginning and the people working there were "allowed to do whatever they want to do," as Markus Brokhof, former head of Digital & Commerce at Alpiq, explains. This brings us to the next important difference: the internal digital unit, being attached to and responsible for the digital transformation of the core business, relies on core processes and structures. The Oyster Lab, as an external unit, has a much flatter hierarchy and only needs to follow a minimum of governance requirements. This separation and the degree of freedom that the external unit enjoys is critical for its success. "The legacy and governance of the mothership would not be a good environment for the Lab. To give you an example, our core would not allow them to buy MacBooks and work on systems that are not compliant with our core IT. So, you end up with conflict after conflict, which would chase away all the digital talent, which is already hard to come by," says Brokhof.

Employees' innovation activities are, however, limited by the boundaries Alpiq set within its digital strategy. Additionally, the external unit has to regularly report to the Group CDO, who monitors the progress and reviews how the lab works toward milestones that were defined upfront.

The link between the two S-curves is established through reporting mechanisms, the CDO oversight and control, and regular management meetings between managers of the core business, the digital unit, and the digital lab.

As Alpiq illustrates, the overarching digital strategy should be translated into an organizational structure that supports it. The degree of separation and the governance mechanisms should be determined in line with the strategy as well.[58]

KEY TAKEAWAYS:

- **Choose an organizational setup that supports your digital strategy, not vice versa** – If you want to be consistent, the overarching digital strategy should be carried over to the organizational structure.

- **The two S-curves play a different game, so give them different rule books** – Your standalone digital business unit, whose main responsibility is to find and scale disruptive business models, will require a flatter hierarchy and less stringent governance rules.

- **Don't forget about the ties** – Although freedom is vital for the 2nd S-curve, consider management ties and control mechanisms (for example, through a CDO who oversees both S-curves).

chapter 4

TECHNOLOGY: HOW TO USE TECHNOLOGY AS A DRIVER FOR THE TRANSFORMATION

The digital era has given birth to a new range of technologies, many of which are increasingly relevant for incumbents. Traditional firms need to keep up with the speed of new technology trends, evaluate their impact, and find ways to develop know-how quickly. In this chapter, we discuss some important trends as well as common pitfalls and success factors related to the implementation of new technologies. We talk about the new role that IT plays as part of a digital transformation and how incumbents can best approach challenges related to the use of new technologies (see Figure 4.1).

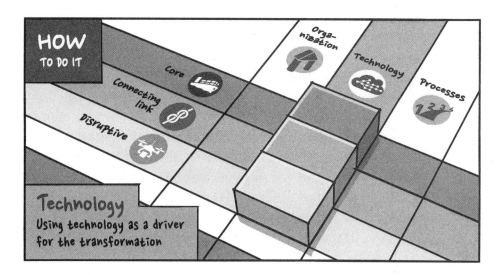

Figure 4.1 Key visual with focus on How/Technology

REALIZE THE TECHNOLOGY CHALLENGES YOUR COMPANY MUST TACKLE

Using a simple but smart combination of new technologies and business model innovation, numerous digital players successfully demonstrate that it's possible to enter mature markets and rapidly gain market share from incumbents. To avoid disruption by tech players – both large and small – incumbents need to address a series of pain points.

First, only when you are aware of new trends and able to build up related competencies quickly, can you fight off attackers. But how can you get up to speed with new technologies quickly? Does it suffice to hire a few experts on the topic, or do you need educate your whole staff and even your management board on the way new technologies work?

Second, the combination of new technology and business model innovation has often been the path to success, but it's easier said than done. How can incumbents identify the right use cases and ideas that build the basis for the 2nd S-curve? Related to this is the question, how are new technologies best used to support the digitization of the core? Are there any enabling technologies that need to be in place first, and how do they differ between the two S-curves?

Third, the increasing importance of technology begs the question of how this affects the traditional role of the IT and R&D departments. While the IT department used to be but a support unit and responsible for keeping IT-related processes up and running, it now becomes a driver for digital activities. What does it take to turn your IT into an integral part of your entire digital transformation? How does the digital transformation affect the technology-related know-how that's required in the IT, R&D, and other departments?

Fourth, an issue that many incumbents face is the struggle with outdated IT architectures and processes. What's the right approach to deal with legacy? Is a fundamental shift necessary, or can small changes to modernize the IT suffice as well? Is there one best way to move from a stubborn monolithic system architecture to more flexible cloud-based, service-led architectures? If you are the one in charge, ask yourself, what are the biggest challenges and obstacles along the way?

Finally, if you have solved the questions above, what do the new development processes need to look like in order to meet customer expectations and deliver shorter cycle-times? Surely such a large migration is time-consuming and costly, isn't it? And how can the transition phase be arranged so that legacy problems do not slow down the transformation?

LOOK BEYOND THE HYPES AND UNDERSTAND WHAT TECH REALLY MEANS

You might think technology has always been around, so it should not be something new for incumbents. You are partially right. Many of the longstanding traditional firms we interviewed experienced the third industrial revolution when new computer and communication technologies radically changed production and work practices. What is new today and what makes the digital revolution so interesting and dangerous at the same time is that it affects so many facets simultaneously. Digital technologies and tools offer an unprecedented opportunity to improve core processes. At the same time, they build the basis for many disruptive innovations. New technologies are therefore a key factor for the success of a new breed of competitors. For example, Netflix, the video-streaming platform, leveraged new technology by moving the majority of its systems to the cloud because this offered them more scale and better functionalities; FlixBus, the European long-distance bus operator, relies on proprietary route optimization and pricing algorithms to give it a competitive edge over its rivals.[2]

We can learn two important things from these examples. One, massive investments into technology infrastructure are no longer an entry barrier, since many of today's hardware and software solutions can easily be rented from third-party providers at low prices. Two, the smart use of new technologies can give new entrants an opportunity to enter established markets, if it helps them to differentiate their value proposition on key dimensions (for example, pricing). Hence, incumbents that don't want to be easy prey need to be on the lookout for relevant technology trends.

Let's look at some technologies that can support your digital transformation (see Figure 4.2). After that, we discuss how you should think about use cases for your S-curves, and how you should go about the development of technology-related knowledge.

Figure 4.2 Technology buzzwords

Key technology trends in the digital era

We have to start with a little warning here – if you were hoping for a complete list of relevant technologies, we will disappoint you. Industries differ, and so do the relevant technologies. According to the McKinsey Global Institute, the research arm of McKinsey, the five technologies with the highest potential for economic disruption in 2025 are mobile internet, automation of knowledge work, internet of things, cloud technology, and advanced robotics.[3] Unsurprisingly, this top-five list does not reflect fully the impressions we got from our interview partners. Quite naturally, the players from B2B industries we interviewed often mentioned IoT or robotics as important trends. On the other hand, we heard from B2C firms that applications based on mobile computing and internet connectivity become increasingly important for them. But no matter in which industry you find yourself, you will likely come across these technology trends in some way. Besides these broader trends, we found that topics related to artificial intelligence (AI), machine learning (ML), and big data are "hot topics" in almost any organization we talked to, irrespective of the industry. So, let's look little bit closer at each topic.

Mobile internet

Mobile computing devices are becoming increasingly inexpensive while computing power and internet connectivity increase. Technology advancements in components such as wireless technologies, computing and storage devices, advanced display technologies, and improved user interfaces enable a plethora of applications related to service delivery and worker productivity and create additional consumer surplus.[4] Even in the luxury industries, where personal interaction and offline-channels remain highly important, the mobile internet offers new opportunities related to customer interaction and communication, such as online customer tracking, self-service tools, and similar use cases, Edouard Meylan, CEO of the Swiss luxury watchmaker H. Moser & Cie., pointed out.[5] A concrete example of an application in the beverage industry is AB InBev's app called "iStadium," which the multinational drink and brewing company is currently scaling internationally. Starting from the customer's point of view, the firm realized that bars in stadiums are often overcrowded during the half-time break, leading to long wait times and a bad consumer experience. As a result, many fans would not order at all, because they fear they could miss part of the game. By using the new app, fans can order beer on their mobile devices and get them delivered directly to their seats. This also has advantages for AB InBev: apart from increased sales, the firm gathers additional insights allowing it to target consumers more precisely at the right moment on their consumer journey.[6] The fifth and latest generation of mobile internet connectivity, 5G, is expected to lift the mobile internet to completely new heights. Although 5G is only in its infancy, it's already clear it will allow for a range of new use cases. The technology will allow connection of devices and services across industries much faster, more efficiently, and at much lower costs than ever before.[7] Connected autonomous vehicles, smart cities, interconnected devices, virtual reality, you name it—technology trends we know today will be accelerated by the use of 5G technology in the future.[8]

Automation of knowledge work

Progress in the development of artificial intelligence (AI), machine learning, user interfaces, and big-data technologies makes it possible to automate tasks that were previously performed by humans. Advancements in this area massively change the way knowledge-related tasks are performed.[9] The availability of complex analytical tools allows us to perform ever more sophisticated analysis and offers unprecedent possibilities to create new insights and draw conclusions about operations and customers alike. The managing director of a multinational bank we spoke with told us they use AI to support their anti–money laundering activities. Based on AI, the bank can filter through large amounts of data and identify suspicious cases more easily than before.[10]

The Internet of Things

The Internet of Things (IoT) systems build on embedded sensors in machines and other physical objects that collect and submit data as part of a connected world. Enabled by advanced, low-cost sensors and wireless and near-field communication devices, IoT systems allow the collection of data and create new insights, opening up new possibilities related to machine and operations monitoring, decision-making, and process optimization.[11] A good example to illustrate this is Schindler, the Swiss producer of escalators and elevators. Schindler equips its machines with intelligent edge devices and sensors that enable performance tracking and monitoring of equipment 24/7. Based on this, Schindler can engage in so-called adaptive maintenance while optimizing service activities: for example, service technicians now know in advance what parts they need to replace and bring to the client site.[12]

Cloud and edge computing

Enabled by cloud management software, data center hardware, high-speed networks, and advancements in software as a service (SaaS), cloud technologies make it possible to deliver IT-related services online.[13] The cloud has become an integral part of the digital transformation strategy of all companies – large and small. An increasing number of organizations have already moved a substantial part of their IT functions to the cloud. The arguments for the cloud are compelling, given its cost, flexibility, and capability advantages. Cloud technology facilitates incumbents, move toward a standardized IT environment with open and flexible application programming interface (API) models. This can free up IT capacities previously used to perform basic infrastructure-related tasks and give incumbents immediate access to the latest technologies and tools.[14] While many organizations have relied completely on external cloud providers, it has become increasingly popular to follow a hybrid approach, using internal and external cloud solutions in parallel. By doing this, companies tap into the advantage of each approach while reducing the risk levels (for example, concerns over security when using external public cloud providers).

While the importance of cloud technology has been well known for some time now, edge computing has also become an increasingly important topic for organizations over the past few years. Incumbents need to find the right balance and focus between these technologies. Edge computing moves data storage and computation away from a central location closer to the edge, that is, the device where the data was gathered initially. Doing this decreases the amount of data that needs to be stored centrally or in the cloud, and reduces latency when the data needs to be transferred (we are talking about huge amounts of data and potentially very long distances) as well as related costs in bandwidth, which can be substantial.[15] Important in this context, however, is the question of ownership and control of the data and algorithms. These and similar questions will become increasingly relevant for organizations as interconnected devices, products, and services gain importance in the future.

Advanced robotics

Advancements in the area of AI, computer vision, robotic dexterity, sensor technology, and related areas have led to massive improvements of industrial robots. While they were traditionally used for physically difficult or dangerous tasks, they are now able to perform complex and meticulous tasks alongside workers, with whom they can interact and communicate. Today, advanced robotics are used across a broad range of fields, such as industrial manufacturing and robotic surgery.[16] Siemens, for example, uses advanced robotics solutions to optimize workflows and perform increasingly difficult machining tasks, such as trimming, de-burring, grinding, and polishing, quickly and efficiently.[17]

Data analytics and AI

No matter whether we are talking about simple data analytics, machine learning, or artificial intelligence technologies, they are all fueled with data, which has become crucial for all kinds of organizations, irrespective of size and industry. First and foremost, it helps managers to make better decisions, by creating new insights into the company's operations and its customers. As a consequence, companies of all shapes and forms are revamping their data infrastructure and are investing heavily into data analytics capabilities. You have probably heard of the saying "data is the new gold" – Riccardo Giacometti, general manager of the Atlantis Hotel in Zurich, couldn't agree more. "The more you can base your decision on data, the smaller the risk that you make an error," he says. He also trusts in the power of data to convince stakeholders of critical decisions: "If you can prove it with data, if you can show the correlation, you can show that the investment and the decision you took actually pays back."[18]

But the impact of data goes much further: data is so valuable today because it powers many of the broader technology trends. The value of data is further increased by the important role it plays in driving machine learning and AI solutions, which wouldn't be possible without massive amounts of data.[19] And the possibilities for AI capabilities are so broad and diverse that we could fill an entire book with it. Possible use cases range from the automated knowledge work described above (for example, language processing, image recognition) to the automation of administrative tasks, thereby freeing up resources that can be applied elsewhere.

The digital era does not have only positive aspects. One of the negatives of the increasing connectivity is the risk of cyberattacks. If a company is affected, it can easily cost millions of dollars and destroy reputations and brand trust within seconds. The costs for the latter might even be higher and affect the business's future long after the immediate damage has been repaired. Although cybersecurity is not a new technology and did not make it into the list of the top five technology trends (measured by economic impact), it becomes increasingly relevant. In fact, cybersecurity is a top priority for many of our interview partners. "Cybersecurity has become much more important for us. It's one of the technologies you either have to master yourself or buy externally," explains Christian Schulz, head of Operations at Schindler.[20] Incumbents need to look ahead, strengthen their hiring efforts, and potentially complement their internal capabilities with reliable external partners that bring in top-notch expertise.

It's also important incumbents establish links beyond the boundaries of the organization that allow for an external perspective. Links to universities, start-ups, accelerators, and VCs can prove valuable. Start-ups deserve special attention in this respect. Many large incumbents have established a rich network of start-up connections because it is often start-ups that experiment with innovative technologies before their potential is broadly discovered. Such links are therefore an easy and cost-effective access point to new technology trends. Second, it can be worthwhile establishing a central team that engages in trend scouting and monitors technological trends in their own as well as in other industries. While some sectors are at the forefront of identifying and using new technologies (for example, advanced industries), other sectors take more time and observe new technology trends before they become relevant for them (for example, equipment manufacturers). ING, a Dutch multinational bank, is a great example. The bank constantly scouts the market for fintechs to identify promising technologies and innovations. Because innovation is part of the bank's strategy, ING decides if it wants to invest in or partner with fintechs or build innovations themselves.[21] In addition to external links and trend scouting, it can also prove worthwhile to attend large tech conferences, such as the Consumer Electronics Show (CES) or the Mobile World Congress (MWC). Although much smaller in scale, the many trade exhibitions and fairs for household appliances can be another fertile ground where managers can discover new technologies and trends. Such conferences and fairs also help build new relationships that might provide value or insights in the future. Regardless of the chosen approach, it's important that firms look ahead and act proactively. If incumbents wait until the new technology trend shows its full impact on the economy, it will likely be too late to capture the benefits and to respond to the implications.[22]

Identifying relevant use cases

When it comes to the identification of new use cases, some firms think they face the typical chicken-or-egg problem, when in fact they don't. What is important to understand is that the technologies themselves are of no value. It's when technologies are used to deliver a better customer experience or when they are used to create new insights that help make processes more efficient that real value is created. Although technologies are important drivers for the digital transformation and the way value is delivered to customers, they are not more than that, Patrick Koller, Chief Executive Officer of Faurecia, the French automotive supplier, tells us. Firms should still focus on their core competencies and assets that create value for customers. The technologies themselves are merely a way to translate or deliver that value. "Firms should not pursue digitization for the sake of digitization. Technologies themselves are enablers, and some of them will become commodities soon," he explains. Firms should think holistically to understand where and how new value is created. It is crucial that this thinking also covers activities that happen before or after the firm's own activities (that is, upstream and downstream activities of partners).[23]

Another best practice example is FlixBus, the long-distance bus operator. The fundamental value proposition underlying their offering is not that different from that of any incumbent: at its core, it's a bus that brings customers from A to B. What makes FlixBus so special, however, is that they combine a smart business model innovation (they use a platform model) with the intelligent use of new technologies. The platform, with its optimized digital customer journey, is a great new way to deliver the underlying asset (a bus trip) to customers; at the same time, proprietary pricing and routing algorithm creates new value for customers—optimized routing and better tariffs. As we can learn from these cases, technology is never an end it itself; it is only a driver to deliver a strategy.

But how does the use of new technology differ between the S-curves, and how can organizations identify use cases in the first place? There are some general points that we would like to highlight when it comes to the application of new technologies.

As far as the 1st S-curve is concerned, strategic initiatives to digitize the core often start with a little twist in the traditional business model in combination with new technology. The digitization of the supply chain should be a top priority for your organization. Technology vendors and service providers offer fast and easy access to powerful and user-friendly tools that help to comprehensively transform supply chain operations. By combining new digital technology solutions with supply chain improvements, incumbents can achieve significant performance gains.[24] The potential of digitized supply chains increases further, once organizations connect with suppliers, partners, and customers and ecosystems emerge. Possible use cases from digitized supply chains can range from machine learning– supported decision making for supply chain managers, over automated real-time data collection and processing, to full transparency in warehousing and transport through trace-and-track systems.[25]

Moving to the customer side, there is state-of-the-art digital marketing. It is more than a digital sales channel and targeted social media ads. Instead, it can help to improve sales productivity, increase customer satisfaction, and unlock new growth areas. By leveraging data and insights, organizations can improve their product development, introduce new and better products and services, new communication channels, or radically redesign entire customer journeys.[26] Many of these use cases are only possible by virtue of data availability.

As far as the 2nd S-curve is concerned, things are different. The key to success is a smart but simple combination of business model innovation and new technology. No matter which successful digital business we look at (Airbnb, Uber, Flixbus, you name it), the key ingredient to their disruptive potential is very likely neither the new technology nor the business model alone, but a combination of the two. Hence, incumbents should systematically explore opportunities to leverage new technologies and consider how they can transition from conventional hardware products to software products and services. New technologies can be applied to and used within the current business, an adjacent business model, or an entirely new business model.

Many of the opportunities for the 2nd S-curve have to do with the build-up of platforms or the participation therein. We find that the active shaping of (IoT) platforms is especially critical for suppliers of legacy equipment. If these suppliers don't find a way to play an active role in the emerging ecosystem and platform game, they risk becoming a "white-label back office"[27] that's merely supplying components or products to the platform without direct customer access and control over the relationships.

An IoT platform can generally be grouped into three layers (see Figure 4.3):

1. The application layer is where the customer-facing applications and services sit. This is the layer where incumbents' additional offering is located.

2. The platform layer is where incumbents' business capabilities are located. This is the heart and brain of the platform that connects the other two layers. The bottom of this layer is the shared infrastructure and support systems.

3. The third layer is the hardware layer. This is where the smart, IoT-enabled things and devices sit, which collect and send data to the platform layer.[28]

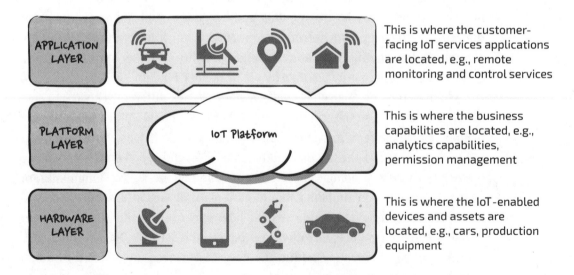

Figure 4.3 Application, platform, and hardware layers in an IoT platform

Successful platforms, such as those of Siemens, Bosch, or Cisco Kinetic, connect millions of sensors, devices, and machines with customers using the broad range of services and applications provided through the platform. The modular platform architecture allows these firms to leverage their domain expertise in the hardware layer, easily connect with (new) customers, suppliers, and other partners, and build an entire ecosystem around their core products.

Development of technology-related knowledge

The breadth and variety of new technologies in recent years is impressive. Many incumbents have neither the know-how nor the resources to work on the development of competencies in multiple areas without the help of others. The IT department, which used to be the focal point for technology-related know-how, can no longer realistically cover all new technologies, explains Thomas Pirlein, CIO of Müller Group, the food corporation. IT departments are occupied with existing technologies and do not have the bandwidth to evaluate the potential of new technologies and build up competencies in these areas.[29] Bernd Reck, head of Innovation at Aesculap, the German producer of surgery products, agrees that IT departments are not well suited because they tend to be chronically underfunded and are usually busy enough with keeping IT operations up and running.[30] Even if IT departments had the resources to focus on new technologies, given their dusty appeal, they could probably not attract the top talent before undergoing a transformation themselves. To source adequate talent for the IT department, incumbents should establish external ties (universities, start-ups, coding schools) through partnerships or even acquisitions.[31] (The **People** chapter will delve into this further, Chapter 7.) An interesting approach was implemented by pbb, the German real estate financing bank. For any new, promising technology, the bank seeks external help to run pilot projects. If pilots prove successful, and the bank invests in the new technology, they put together teams with employees from all units likely to use the new technology. They also assign dedicated resources from the IT department who serve as long-term owners of the technology. When internal competencies are built up, external support is reduced, and the internal owner takes over the lead.[32]

IT talent sourcing and internal knowledge development will not always be enough. Incumbents often do not have a realistic chance of catching up with technology leaders, as the case of Schindler illustrates. Due to increasing connectivity of devices and products, cybersecurity has become a priority for the global elevator manufacturer. The firm realized that developing top-notch cybersecurity expertise at short notice wasn't within its core competency. Therefore, the company decided to access expertise externally via strategic alliances, allowing it to save time and obtain best-in-class protection. Moreover, Schindler has partnered with tech companies to access the required expertise in the area of analytics and the management of edge devices.[33]

Acquisitions are another viable strategy to quickly gain expertise, an approach employed by multinational conglomerate Siemens. While they invest in the build-up of basic software development competencies, they also acquire smaller companies to broaden their expertise. Siemens has expanded from a pure machine manufacturer to a software engineering firm, building the basis for Siemens' new digitally enabled business models, such as its IoT industry platform or pay-per-use models.[34]

One more thing to note: traditional R&D or IT departments should no longer be the focal point for technology-related capabilities as they used to be in the past. Digital know-how should not reside within a single unit or department. Organizations can still establish knowledge hubs within certain departments, but it should not be siloed from other units. All units, especially those that are closely connected to the customer or market, should build up at least a basic understanding of skills important for the digital transformation.

IT DOES NOT EQUAL TECH

The established role of IT departments must change completely. Every digital transformation invariably involves an IT transformation and incumbents face a number of pain points with their legacy IT. A former executive at the Swiss department store Jelmoli stresses that very point: "The head of IT has a completely new role now. Back in the day, the business went to IT and said they needed three new interfaces. And IT just delivered. But today IT needs to be involved in every decision. They assume a completely new role, and that's a huge change."[35]

Establishing a new role for IT

The organizations of many executives we spoke with have moved away from being pure manufacturing companies toward becoming software companies (to a certain degree). As a result, it's quite difficult to think about any digital activity on the 1st or the 2nd S-curve that does not have a direct or indirect effect on the IT department. By definition, digital activities undertaken have at least some software or hardware component to it. Such a transition needs to be supported by the IT department, where many digital capabilities are located and where applications are steered from. Thus, the IT department has a much more prominent role and becomes the key enabler for and driver of the transformation. The IT department must move from a support function to an active facilitator that offers technical solutions and support.[36] An interesting example is WACKER, the German chemical company, that made the IT department an integral part of its digital transformation journey.

WACKER
. . . .

The management of WACKER was well aware of the importance of IT for the digitalization[37] of their business. Realizing a separation of the CDO and CIO roles would not work, they appointed a team of three to lead the digital transformation: Axel Schmidt, at the time CDO of Frontend, who covered the business side; Dirk Ramhorst, CIO/CDO, responsible for IT and the technological foundations; and Jörg Krey, CDO of Operations, covering all topics related to production and processes. Each considered himself a CDO of his area.

Close collaboration with IT was a matter of principle. "There are many CDOs who are separated from IT but I think that's not a promising model. We establish IT as an enabler for the transformation," Ramhorst says. WACKER is a textbook example: parallel to the digitalization of the core business, the organization performs a fundamental overhaul of its IT functions to support the development of new digital initiatives. For the transformation to be successful, the IT department lays out the right foundations for the organization. This includes the development of a functional and forward-looking IT infrastructure and digital collaboration and employee development models for the entire organization. IT literally builds the foundation through digital capabilities and infrastructure investments across business and operations functions. The IT department invested in hiring data scientists and data engineers when they realized the business was going to need more of these profiles. Business units that need a data expert approach the IT department to access their expertise.

The collaboration between IT, business, and operations guarantees that each CDO knows the requirements and opportunities in other areas of the organization. Ramhorst is convinced that he "would not have the same perspective on the core units if it weren't for this close collaboration model."[38]

Incorporating IT avoids "us versus them" tendencies between the traditional business units and the IT department. WACKER formed a strong team that ensures IT develops the right digital capabilities and infrastructure needed for the transformation and that the organization is enabled to deliver digital innovations to those who use them (employees and customers alike).

Integrating old and new IT

The second IT-related challenge concerns the issues that come with legacy systems and processes. In contrast to digital natives that can build fully agile IT from scratch, incumbents cannot – the recurring theme of the digital transformer's dilemma. For incumbents, IT systems and processes are often as old as the business itself. IT systems were expanded and new applications attached left and right as new product lines, new features, acquisitions, and partners occurred. This results in a complexity based on heterogeneous processes, differing software solutions, and complicated linkages between the constituent parts. Further, the development and operation of software applications are often strictly separated. That means in practice, the ladies and gentlemen of the development team program a terrific new application and, once completed, throw it over the fence to the operations team to provide the infrastructure for it. Operations is then responsible for the software deployment and maintenance.

The main problem is that IT departments use traditional waterfall-like development approaches. Teams do not really collaborate with each other and interactions are at a bare minimum. Once developers hand over an application, their request is handled as a ticket, ending up at the bottom of a pile of other ticket requests, an approach that leads to delays, misunderstandings, and sub-optimal results. Developers are often not aware of important infrastructure requirements so that work packages are passed back and forth. Or even worse, the operations team employs a new application that does not meet the established infrastructure requirements, which can result in unstable software and poor customer experience. The production of new software releases – from development to go-live – can take several months (see Figure 4.4).

Such lengthy and error-prone processes do not correspond to high customer expectations to receive top digital products and services (ideally personally

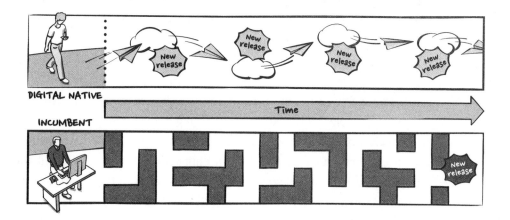

Figure 4.4 Incumbent versus digital native

tailored) in the blink of an eye. Agile software development, on the other hand, is characterized by adaptive planning, rapid testing, and continuous improvements, with regular updates and releases. This development approach is more flexible and faster than the waterfall-like software approach. For these obvious reasons, most incumbents have realized they must move away from their stubborn monolithic architecture and employ a cloud-based, service-led architecture that supports the rapid development, testing, and deployment of software. However, the migration of old systems to new systems is incredibly cumbersome and needs to be well-planned. The costs for such transformations can be massive and can take three to five years – or upwards of that. Most incumbents do not have that much time – fast and flexible IT solutions are needed much sooner.

The solution is commonly known as two-speed IT architecture and it allows incumbents to use new agile development techniques for their digital activities, and at the same time keep their traditional approaches for critical core business functions.[39]

A two-speed IT architecture allows companies to be agile and fast where it really matters, and slow and stable where necessary. IT is split into two parts, which can evolve at different speeds. On the fast lane, there are all customer-facing (front-end) applications developed based on agile principles. The slower lane is reserved for the legacy back-end systems, which keep running at a slower speed, with longer release cycles.[40] Often, these old systems can't be readily replaced as they still play an important role for the operations of the core business. Enterprise resource planning (ERP), customer relationship management (CRM), standard cost model (SCM), and programs related to administration and logistics are run in the back-end; each needs to be 100% reliable, stable, and cost-effective. Because the two IT worlds need to be connected, an integration platform or middleware is installed.[41] It acts as a technical bridge between the two IT systems and allows them to cooperate with each other, passing data between the two (see Figure 4.5).

Such a bimodal approach is a compromise between the old and the new IT world. It allows firms to take advantage of a fast front-end (where customer-facing applications reside and speed is essential) while relying on their stable core systems in the back-end. One advantage of this approach is that it can reduce the risk of a big bang when all systems are migrated at once.[42] A gradual shift will be easier to digest for the organization and mitigates risks if something goes awry because

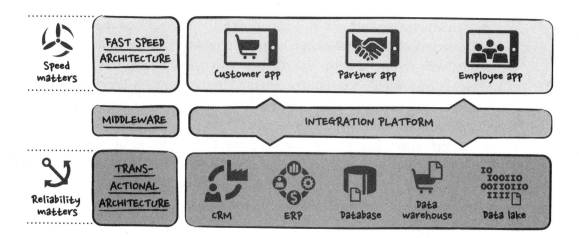

Figure 4.5 IT architecture

core functions can still rely on traditional systems. Bernard Leong, former head of Post Office Network & Digital Services at SingPost, Singapore's public postal service, trusts in this approach. The digital transformation of SingPost was a two-speed process. Their front-end relied on rapid development of new apps and a new website while the transformation of the back-end was much slower. The shift from old to new systems was gradual. "The back-end transition has to be a well-planned process that should happen step by step," Leong maintains.[43]

However, a two-speed architecture is not the holy grail. It is a good compromise and intermediary solution, but it should never be the end state.[44] It keeps the old-vs-new-world dichotomy – at least to a certain extent. This complicates attracting and retaining talent for the traditional part of IT, where talent is urgently needed to transform it.[45] It can easily create friction in the organization when one part of IT is fast and nimble while the other continues to move slowly.[46] Also, when digital initiatives are linked with core functions or systems (1st S-curve initiatives linked to the core platform), the firm runs the risk that these digital initiatives are being held back by the legacy IT of the core if bound to traditional testing and release cycles.[47] As such, the full benefits of a two-speed IT cannot be realized and the approach will fail to meet expectations. By holding onto their legacy back-end, the front-end slows down one way or another. The underlying reason that incumbents' customer journeys are not as user-friendly as those of start-ups is often simply the result of their legacy IT, Fabian Stenger, Vice President Central and Eastern Europe at FlixMoblity, the mobility provider, concurs. Each link to the legacy back-end constitutes a certain boundary for the front-end. The sum of these legacy-related boundary conditions and rules lead to front-end processes that are not ideal. This results in a customer journey that feels complicated and clumsy to users.[48] Konstantin Speidel, Vice President for Digital Transformation at Allianz Global Investors, argues in a similar vein. He says that digital initiatives are often slowed down when there's a link to core systems. When new applications are handed over to the core IT, they often lose speed and traction.[49]

This does not mean incumbents should start their IT transformation with the back-end.

> ❚❚ We know companies that did it the other way around. They say, 'we have to fix our back-end and then we move on to the front-end.' - but I think that's the wrong approach because it takes way too long. You need years to fix the back-end and then the ship has sailed. ❚❚

Gisbert Rühl, CEO of Klöckner & Co, the steel distributor.[50]

Thomas Gutzwiller, expert for platform building and corporate transformations, agrees. He stresses that companies will likely be dead by the time they have cleaned up their legacy. "I can't say I will start by cleaning my back-end because this will take me a solid four years, and the market will have moved on by then," Gutzwiller tells us.[51] Incumbents should start with the front-end and direct their investments where they have the biggest impact. The rapid development of front-end applications is more pressing to meet customer expectations and support digital initiatives. However, they will still have to migrate their back-end systems to new technologies over time. Having said this, incumbents will have to live with a two-speed architecture for a while, at least during the transition period.

MANAGE THE TECHNOLOGICAL TENSION BETWEEN THE 1ST AND 2ND S-CURVE

There exists a technology gap between the 1st and 2nd S-curves before new capabilities and practices take effect across the entire organization. The 2nd S-curve will spearhead the technological transformation while your 1st S-curve will only slowly gain new capabilities and adapt its IT setup until eventually the whole organization moves at the same speed. Incumbents must find ways to bridge potential technology competency gaps and diverging IT development approaches.

From hardware to software and back

The connection between the front-end and the back-end is a critical pain point that incumbents need to address as the transition to a fully agile single-speed model takes time. Therefore, incumbents need to establish new mechanisms to manage dependencies and support the two-speed architecture.

In terms of processes, the development and operations teams should work in a flexible and collaborative fashion. Mixed teams with employees from both departments bring the two sides closer together. The teams should identify dependencies, increase the visibility, and collaboratively manage expectations, timelines, and progress. This increases the joint accountability for the development, testing, deployment, and maintenance of applications.[52]

In terms of technology, instead of manually configuring custom-made infrastructure solutions for every new application, automated systems and self-service tools allow developers to define the infrastructure themselves, independently from the operations team. The operations team can define clear rules and guidelines for developers so that they can manage operational tasks themselves. The integration of applications should be based on fine-grained services with a clear validation logic, instead of integration via large services that are overly complex.[53]

Incumbents can also use automated tools and cloud-based solutions that are available from platform providers that support such a transition.[54] These levers can bring down the time for the deployment of new applications from a couple of months to several minutes. Jenius, the first digital bank of Indonesia, is a case in point – read their case at the end of this chapter.

Reflecting on how incumbents can best solve IT-related challenges and manage the transition period, we suggest switching to a two-speed architecture in the early stages of the digital transformation. This will allow companies to quickly realize the benefits of agile development for customer-facing applications. They should, however, still extend agile work practices to the core back-end to avoid a new bottleneck there. Only when the IT is "all-agile" is it possible to fully leverage the potential across all IT functions.

An interesting example in this respect is Bosch, the multinational technology and engineering company from Germany. Bosch is well aware of the difficulties that come with different release cycles and the integration of hardware and software components. For its eBike business, Bosch had to align its IT environments and integrate its software development cycles with the development and production cycles of hardware components.

BOSCH eBike SYSTEMS

Bosch is well known as an automotive supplier for the big OEMs of this world. As part of their mobility business, the company ventured into the development and production of eBike systems. eBikes provide a radically different customer experience than automotive supplies. For this reason, Bosch established an organizationally independent entity to develop its eBike solutions.

An eBike inherently covers both traditional hardware with embedded software and new digital software solutions. The hardware side relates to the physical experience of cycling while the software side relates to the digital experience attached to it (various lifestyle, navigation, and fitness apps). The challenge was to reflect this balance and to integrate purely physical hardware (for example, bike display), embedded software components (used to run the overall operation of the physical device), and software features (user applications). The development of various hardware and software-embedded elements followed a plan-driven process with release cycles of three to six months. The development of digital elements was more adaptive and had release cycles of one to two weeks. The two processes evolved at drastically different speeds.

To make sure the two melded together, Bosch established an interface team with people from both sides. The team mediated between the two development teams. It was in charge of all programming interfaces (APIs) between the embedded hardware and the software side and made sure all components were on time, on budget, and met all required specifications. The team developed a feature roadmap, which includes all details about upcoming hardware and software releases. On the basis of this, the interface team managed the integration of software features with embedded software and hardware components. Aligning requirements between hardware and software components and syncing the different release cycles was crucial to ensure that the features can function properly.

"To make this setup work effectively, you need to have a team in the middle of both worlds," argues Claus Fleischer, CEO of Bosch eBike Systems. The team members must be able to empathize with and understand both IT worlds. If done correctly, the approach allows the use of waterfall processes for the development of hardware and embedded software components while at the same time using an agile process setup for the development of new software features.[55]

Technology-related capabilities as foundation for both S-curves

As far as the costs for technology development are concerned, incumbents face a difficult discussion. How to split funding between the S-curves is a key question concerning more than just technology-related investments. We will discuss funding from a general point of view in the **Processes** chapter (Chapter 5), but here we want to preempt some technology-related aspects. Incumbents will need to invest in some general enabling technologies, such as analytical skills, software development skills, and so on, in the early days of its digital transformation. These capabilities will be beneficial for both initiatives to digitize the core business and initiatives to establish a new (digital) business. It makes sense to fund these capabilities from a central budget. The transformation will not get off the ground if it is up to a newly set up digital unit, or individual business units, to pay for such upfront investments.

We have seen many examples where organizations located new digital resources in a central unit (for example, digital competence center), and initiatives on both S-curves got easy access when they needed it. As we have outlined in the **Organization** chapter (Chapter 3), this approach is especially fruitful when it is necessary that knowledge is held in some kind of hub to foster the generation of new knowledge, or when the resources can't be fully utilized (for example, when owned by the 1st S-curve). Such a central digital unit can also serve as the driving force to bring technological competencies into the core business, often with the help of external expertise. Remember Deutsche Pfandbriefbank (pbb)? Their central digital unit serves as an interface to the outside world and brings in technology experts. Together with employees from the core, the central digital unit runs pilot projects that help evaluate the potential of new technologies and train employees in the core business.[56]

No matter where the technology-related capabilities are located, it's important that they do not remain isolated. Incumbents need to establish programs that gradually educate employees of both S-curves and across all departments. Developing an understanding of new technologies will be crucial for core employees to understand the benefits and will facilitate mutual discussions and the exchange of ideas. To accelerate this process, incumbents can implement a variety of approaches, ranging from external hiring to internal tech-academies (learn more about this in the **People** chapter, Chapter 7). Partnerships and links to externals should not be designated for one S-curve only. Instead the incumbents should let both S-curves benefit from the external impetus brought to the organization. Regular networking events, together with external guest speakers and start-ups, are one example of an easy but powerful approach to facilitate discussions, internally as well as with externals. Many of the trends and technologies that we have discussed are relevant for both S-curves. For example, capabilities related to data analytics can unfold tremendous advantages to improve core processes but are of course also highly relevant for the new (digital) business. When incumbents set up some form of competence groups or clusters, they should ideally be staffed with external experts and internal advocates from both S-curves. The most powerful approach is one where the two worlds cooperate and mutually support each other. Such moves, however, require foresight and support from the top-management.

Tech-savvy managers as bridge builders

While managers don't have to become tech experts, they need to acquire a basic "technology skill-set" and an understanding of the impact that technologies have on their industry as well as on their own organization. Acquiring such skills is in their best interest. Research shows that today's leaders define technical knowledge as the number-one priority for their future career development and that an understanding of technology for their industry and roles will be key for their future success.[57]

Generally speaking, technical skills encompass the know-how and capabilities required to perform specialized technical tasks. The requirements for such specialized skills depend on the actual role and the duties. Lower-level managers need such technical skills to supervise and review the work of their employees who perform highly specialized technical tasks. This becomes less important the higher up we move on the corporate ladder. Nevertheless, even managers at higher levels need to have a certain set of technical skills.

First, managers need to assess the potential impact of technologies for their organization and industry. Only then can they engage in meaningful discussion with technology experts (to discuss more concrete use cases) and only then can they prioritize and deploy technology-related projects where they make most sense.

Second, managers need to coordinate technology-related tasks within units and across the organization. When managers have no clue what they are talking about, the whole effort is likely to end in chaos and with suboptimal results. The coordination aspect becomes especially relevant when we talk about the connection between both S-curves as managers play a crucial role in this regard. Managers who don't understand a thing about the technologies being used in the newly set up digital unit are unlikely to identify all synergy potentials (if they identify any at all).

Hence, managers from all levels should develop a sound understanding for the relevant technologies, the most recent industry and technology trends, and the use of analytics as decision-making support. Leaders equipped with such a toolkit can engage in more meaningful discussions with technical experts, and ultimately make better decisions (using the power of data). When managers understand the true value and potential of new technologies, the organization is more likely to move to a demand-driven use of new technology, instead of having the IT function push new solutions into business units.[58]

GET MOVING TO AVOID THE DINOSAUR FATE

Make sure to keep the following tech-related best practices in mind:

- Watch out for relevant technology trends and evaluate their impact:
  - Implement a central focus group that looks out for new technology trends.
  - Establish effective links beyond the organization to get insights about new technologies and best practices early.
  - Identify and invest into enabling technologies, especially those that are relevant for both S-curves (for example, data analytics).

- Follow a problem-driven approach when it comes to the identification of use cases and strategic initiatives:
  - Make the digitization of your supply chain a top-priority for your 1st S-curve.
  - Analyze the entire customer journey, encompassing all value-creating activities (even those of competitors) to identify potential strategic initiatives.

- Examine how a combination of new technology and business model innovation can unlock new value pools.
- Consider your role in emerging ecosystems – think about linkages between hardware and software components.
- Prioritize your technology use cases based on impact and in line with your overall strategy and ambition.

● Establish an effective approach to technological competence development:
- Follow a balanced approach and access know-how from a variety of sources.
- Make sure that basic technological know-how does not reside within siloes – make it accessible and educate people from both S-curves.

● Consider how your IT department can prepare for the new role:
- Build strong links between IT, business functions, and operations, to position IT as an important partner and integral part of the digital transformation.
- Provide sufficient capacity and equip the IT department with the required resources to act as a driver for digitization efforts.

● Find ways to integrate legacy and new IT:
- At the beginning, establish a two-speed architecture to unlock the benefits of an agile front-end.
- Make sure you gradually transform your legacy IT and extend agile principles to the back-end.

● Develop a tech-savvy management team:
- Set up formal learning programs to educate managers at all levels.
- Make sure that your managers have an understanding of the impact of new technologies.
- Ensure that leaders in your organization can communicate the use and importance of new technologies effectively.

GET INSPIRED (BY INDONESIA)

BTPN
......

As the Indonesian bank BTPN, which is part of the Japanese banking conglomerate SMBC, embarked on its journey to establish the country's first digital bank, named Jenius, it set itself a high bar in terms of technology requirements. Digital is a core part of the product and value proposition and not just a channel. Delivering the new digital offering required the bank to build a unique set of new capabilities across many dimensions. It had to hire digital talent to bring in new technical capabilities such as user-centric design thinking and modern architecture design capabilities. This required substantial recruitment and training efforts. The bank also had to invest heavily into its IT infrastructure to deliver a flexible and easy-to-change front-end as well as stable and always-available back-end systems. This IT transition was a crucial part because the bank's new IT approach had to allow multiple benefits to meet the internal requirements and rising customer expectations. Jenius used cross-platform frameworks to have a single codebase that works across various platforms (that is, Chrome, Android, iOS) without much manual customization effort. Then, the bank automated as much of its infrastructure as possible, allowing for automatic provisioning, configuration, and management of infrastructure components. Finally, Jenius made use of source-control and packaging tools, which allowed developers and other teams to reuse and build on finished modules. By doing this, the bank was able to cut its development cycle in half.

On top of this, the bank massively reduced its deployment cycle. While the old process included many manual tasks and handovers, the new setup was fully automated, including quality gates and agile testing (user-acceptance testing). The time for deployment went from several weeks to a couple of minutes. The whole IT architecture is now fully microservices-based, similar to that which any modern tech start-up would pursue, while only select systems are still shared with the core bank and integrated via standardized APIs.

Component-based integration layers allow modular access to data, reduce overall complexity, and increase flexibility. This dramatically faster production cycle and the flexible IT architecture enables the bank to release updates more frequently, allowing them to react swiftly to customer feedback and new requirements.

Such a huge transformation rested on an effective development approach. It was done in an agile development setup with multifunctional teams (squads) following a strict agile methodology. The teams held daily check-ins and regular sprint planning and review meetings. Squad leads met regularly to discuss upcoming deliverables to be detailed and complemented in the next sprint, to align the handover of finished products, or to discuss and resolve issues.[59]

KEY TAKEAWAYS:

- **Meeting customer expectations will often require an IT overhaul** – Investing in state-of-the-art IT sets you apart from traditional competitors and allows you to compete with digital natives.

- **Automate infrastructure-related tasks** – This allows the deployment of new applications within minutes, involving minimal (to zero) manual effort.

- **Ramp up your technology team** – Beware that tech teams need to grow if you want to be a tech leader; prepare a comprehensive IT talent recruiting and training program.

chapter 5
PROCESSES: HOW TO GET STUFF DONE

W e split the discussion about processes needed to run a digital transformation into two parts. We first detail how to execute strategic initiatives and what a stage gate development process looks like. In the second part, we explain how the entire transformation should be executed, including governance- and policy-related topics. We outline reasons for why a lighthouse approach is so important, talk about the governance bodies it takes to support the transformation, and how you can solve conflicts related to budget allocation and funding (see Figure 5.1).

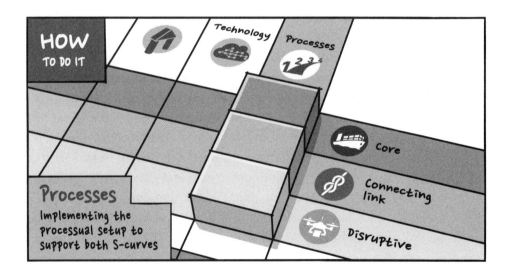

Figure 5.1 Key visual with focus on How/Processes

REALIZE THE PROCESS CHALLENGES YOUR COMPANY MUST TACKLE

Many of the problems related to the procedural setup of a digital transformation have to do with the fact that legacy organizations are run differently than start-ups. More often than not, incumbents rely on waterfall development approaches, resulting in flawless end-products. Start-ups, however, use an approach that's much faster and tailored to the needs of customers. In addition to that, running a digital transformation is not like any other change project, which has profound implications for the way it needs to be set up and governed, as well as the challenges and obstacles along the way. All of this triggers a series of questions.

First, if your organization wants to compete against agile start-ups, it has to adapt and copy some of their characteristics. You can't win a new war with old methods. Does this mean that established development practices need to be thrown overboard completely? To what extent can you stick to your "waterfall approach" that has worked so well for your 1st S-curve? What exactly are the merits of rapid prototyping and iterative testing, anyway?

Second, developing a new business model is not something firms get right the first time they try. How do you implement a pipeline of strategic initiatives and adapt a VC-like approach for the evaluation of new business ideas? Is there a way to improve the success rate, or rule out bad ideas early on?

Third, new business models fail if they do not scale successfully. What is needed to sufficiently support corporate start-ups in growth and scale-up? If you started your digital initiatives in a safe nucleus outside the core, when and how do you integrate a digital initiative into the core business? How can you make sure that the initiative continues to exist and grow once it leaves the lab?

Fourth, developing new things requires resources. How do you decide on the right allocation of resources? Is there a best way to think about budget rules and guidelines, including the split between the 1st and the 2nd S-curve? In addition, governance and politics implications cannot be ignored. What new decision-making bodies are needed to oversee kick-offs and progress? Are the governance rules the same as the ones used in the past, or are new rules needed that are tailored to the freedom and flexibility of digital initiatives, especially those on the 2nd S-curve?

GET YOUR HANDS DIRTY LAUNCHING YOUR DIGITAL TRANSFORMATION

Instead of using an old-fashioned waterfall method (where activities are organized in a linear, sequential design) for the development and launch of new ideas, incumbents should adopt much faster and more efficient methodologies based on design thinking, lean start-up, and agility. While these are common buzzwords, it's important to understand their difference and how they can be combined to launch new products, services, or entire business models.

Design thinking

Consider design thinking as a well-structured, customer-centered, iterative process. It consists of five phases (emphasize, define, ideate, protype, and test) that force organizations to empathize with their customers and focus on customer pain points and needs. The method supports organizations in the idea generation, prototyping, and testing of solutions and is especially useful for problems that are ill-defined or unknown. Design thinking is therefore ideal for organizations at the beginning of the development process.[1]

The lean start-up method

The lean start-up process is another iterative methodology intended to support the fast and efficient launch of new products and businesses. It goes back to a combination of agile software development with the customer development method of Steve Blank. Customer development describes a process in which customer discovery and customer validation mutually stimulate each other. This idea was developed further in Eric Ries's infamous book, *The Lean Startup*, which took the methodology worldwide. The heart of this process is a continuous feedback cycle called "build-measure-learn." It guides organizations during the realization ("build"), data collection and feedback ("measure"), and evaluation ("learn") phases.[2]

The goal is to shorten the development cycles, reduce the amount of time and resources required for the successful launch of new products or business ideas, and achieve this more efficiently and faster. It is an orderly approach to continuously test and realize new ideas. Organizations end up spending less money and time, and create a better product or business that actually earns money (creating real value for the organization).[3]

The first step in the "build-measure-learn" cycle is to understand the problem that needs to be solved and to develop (or "build") a first minimum viable product (MVP) version. This MVP is then used as a basis for the learning process, which requires a solid understanding of customer pain points and needs. Once the organization knows what is most important and what it wants to measure, it can build an MVP. This should help founders (entrepreneurs and intrapreneurs alike) to build a first product version that truly focuses on the customer needs, instead of gold-plating the very first version of the product.

Once built, the MVP is fine-tuned by moving to the measurement and learning phase. The goal is to systematically run experiments and validate elements of the product idea or business model. By applying the lean start-up approach, organizations can radically shorten the development process and reduce the risk of new product or business development substantially.[4]

Agile development

While the lean start-up approach focuses on the optimization of the production process, agility focuses on the optimization of the development process.[5] Agile has have several procedural advantages over the cumbersome waterfall development method; they instill a new way of working and can serve as an enabler for a whole new structure of work. We will now describe what such processes look like in practice and what to watch out for as you go about over-writing your traditional methods with agile processes. Agility as a basis for new ways of working and an agile organization as a new structure of work will be addressed in the **Culture** chapter (Chapter 8).

The basic principles of agility are simple. Organizations empower small, cross-functional, self-managing teams to take ownership over a specific problem or opportunity.[6] Teams normally consist of a product or initiative owner whose responsibility it is to ensure that the team reaches its targets. The team continuously breaks up the larger problem into smaller sub-tasks (modules) and prioritizes tasks based on estimated impact, importance, and so forth. Team members then work in sprints (short cycles of one to three weeks) on intermediate versions of the solution. The whole process is fully transparent to all members and stakeholders, and problems are solved through collaboration among the relevant stakeholders. The approach removes impediments and increases cross-functional collaboration.[7] Continuous, real-time testing with real customers detects flaws early on and lets the team focus on the most important product features. The integration of design and development is where the key benefit of agile processes plays out. Instead of fine-tuning every detail of a product based on a long list of product requirements, teams focus purely on customer requirements and quickly react to changing needs.

The best way to look at the interaction of design thinking, lean start-up, and agile processes is to see them as complementary tools. During the early idea generation and prototyping phase, incumbents can benefit from design thinking, as it helps organizations to really understand and focus on the true customer pain points. Once the organization moves to the realization of the ideas, the full benefits of the lean start-up process play out. The iterative build-measure-learn cycles help incumbents to shorten the development time, decrease the resources and risks involved, and create an end-product that creates and delivers real value. Last but not least, the full advantages of an agile setup will come into effect once the organization moves to iterative and incremental development and refinement of its products and services. The lean start-up method is a valuable supplement and connector between the design thinking and agile approaches.[8] This does not mean these methodologies should be applied in a waterfall-like fashion and that agility only occurs at the end of the process. Nor does it mean that the phases can be performed by different siloed teams. Instead, the methodologies should be used in a complementary fashion within the same cross-functional team.[9]

While agile methodologies are not new to incumbents and have already been applied broadly in many legacy organizations, the lean start-up method has only recently gained in popularity and is now increasingly used by incumbents. The adoption of such iterative prototyping and testing approaches allows for closing the gap between customers' desire ("Oh, yeah, cool product, I might buy that") and customers' commitment to actually buy a product ("Wow, I see the value-add and I am willing to pay for it"), says Dirk Linzmeier, CEO of automotive supplier OSRAM Continental. With modern production techniques (for example, 3D-printing), hardware prototypes can be produced at low costs and without much effort. Companies can easily test if there is an actual demand for their products. Linzmeier is convinced that lean and agile product development processes accelerate the learning curve and radically reduce uncertainty in product development.[10]

We find that incumbents often follow a dual approach. They employ more lean and agile processes for the 2nd S-curve but keep using traditional project management processes for the 1st S-curve. Efforts to digitize the core business will benefit from digital tools and practices but do not have to be managed with an entirely iterative, experimental process. Activities to set up a new, disruptive (digital) business on the 2nd S-curve, however, will benefit from these new methodologies to reduce waste and uncertainty while forcing organizations to emphasize value creation and customer needs.

Another approach is to gradually implement lean and agile practices across the organization. Large organizations often implement an agile set up in one part of their organization (often IT) and when it proves successful, they scale it to the broader organization. One organization that followed exactly this scheme is ING, the Dutch bank. Read the case at the end of this chapter to learn more about their approach.

Let's look at how these methodologies can be employed in practice, and how incumbents can manage a portfolio of initiatives in a well-structured innovation funnel.

Broadly speaking, the development of strategic initiatives can be split into three phases: (1) Ideation, (2) Incubation, and (3) Commercialization (see Figure 5.2).

Ideation phase

It is this initial phase where new ideas for potential use cases or new business ideas are collected. This idea generation process is often organized as

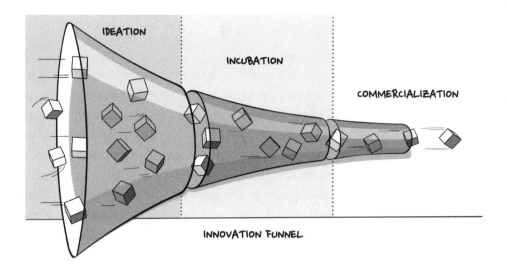

Figure 5.2 Innovation funnel

design-thinking sessions, ideation workshops, or a firm-wide brainstorming exercise. Mibelle, the Swiss producer of health and beauty products, introduced so-called "Rapid Improvement Events," which are held regularly. They are a five-day program in which mixed teams work together to develop ideas and potential solutions for business challenges that are defined by the CEO. At the end of each program, teams present their ideas in a 20-minute pitch and the entire company is invited to watch and comment.[11] In other companies that use similar ideation formats, the ideas may be preselected based on predefined criteria, depending on the number of collected proposals. Quite often, a short-list of ideas is pitched in front of a committee (more on this later) to select the initiatives to enter the next phase. The selection of ideas follows a VC-like approach, in which the future potential of strategic initiatives is assessed. In the early days of the digital transformation, the creation of lighthouse projects is a priority, so the selection criteria might differ depending on the stage of the transformation.

Following the "Business Model Navigator" framework from the **WHAT** chapter (Chapter 2), the ideation phase is part of the initial design stage. That's also where you can find more details about the necessary steps to go from environmental analysis to a complete design of a business model innovation or strategic initiative. The actual realization of an idea really starts in the next phase – its incubation.

INCUBATION PHASE

This is where new ideas are incubated. It's also where the lean and agile approaches come into play. Small teams develop and test products or solution pilots until they're market ready. Ideas are embedded within a lab, accelerator, or incubator environment that acts as safe space where new ideas can be nurtured and refined. Such formats provide digital expertise, supporting infrastructure, financial support, and other valuable functions. The incubation phase is normally split into smaller intermediary phases with regular stage gates where progress is evaluated. The difference between the stage gates is their focus. In earlier stages, the focus is on the development of a viable idea and a first prototype that creates value for customers. In later stages, the focus shifts to the reliability and performance of products and solutions. Topics such as product-market-fit, scalability, and a sustainable business case become more important.

ALPIQ
. . . . . .

The leading energy company from Switzerland established a six-step development process, called "Innovation Framework." In the first step, so-called "spark owners" prepare a one-pager about their idea and they get 15 minutes to pitch it in front of a committee. In a second step, the committee decides which ideas to pursue further. The decision criteria for this first stage gate center around the novelty of the idea and potential synergies with the core business. Ideas that pass this stage are detailed further and then evaluated in the third step, which is also the second stage gate. At this gate, the spark owners get 30 minutes to present plans for the development and validation phase and address any open questions. Ideas that pass this stage gate enter the validation phase, in which a first proof-of-concept is developed (fourth step). The fifth step is another stage gate meeting, where the management discusses the results of the proof-of-concept and the business case for the product. Here, management asks three basic questions: Does the initiative have a positive impact (is the business case positive)? Can all important questions related to the product based on existing knowledge within Alpiq be answered? Did the validation phase answer all the questions we had about the market viability? Initiatives that pass this third stage gate enter the design sprints and agile development phase, where a market-ready product is developed.

When it's not possible to find a positive answer to all three questions, the last step (validation phase) is either iterated, or an external expert is consulted to answer remaining questions.[12]

Commercialization phase

Once the idea has proven its market readiness, it needs to find a home outside the safe environment. This means that market-ready innovations have to be either reintegrated into the core business or spun off into a separate standalone entity or business unit (particularly those close the 2nd S-curve). A reintegration makes most sense for 1st S-curve initiatives that were developed in mutual collaboration with the core, and a natural owner from the core business who will be responsible for the further development of the initiative is identified. A spin-off and the setup of a new entity is often the path forward for initiatives on the 2nd S-curve, business models that have little or no overlap with the traditional business. The growth and scaling of initiatives are often where incumbents tumble. It is in this commercialization phase where the stable processes and structures of incumbents (the 1st S-curve) regain importance. Also, once innovations leave the safe environment, follow-up financing is critical so new innovations and business models can exploit their full potential and pay back the original investment.[13]

If done correctly, a well-structured development approach can help incumbents convert ideas into real prototypes within a few months. While these three phases illustrate a general blueprint from ideation to go-live, firms often develop unique approaches tailored to the organization (as Alpiq did). We have seen multiple successful incumbents, however, that followed the above blueprint and used internal accelerator programs for the early incubation phase, followed by an internal incubator program later in the incubation phase. Their internal accelerators provide guidance to build a first prototype, and offer technology know-how, strategy, and business model development support as well as coaching related to customer development and the lean start-up process in general. Their internal incubator programs, on the other hand, provide lab space, shared services, legal advisory, and additional support related to strategy and business model development. Once the ideas leave their internal incubator programs, they are normally ready to enter the commercialization phase. It is at this point – or even earlier, depending on the situation – where the incumbents decide whether an idea should be reintegrated and pursued within an existing business unit of the core, or if it's better to build a standalone entity or business unit (that is, a separated spin-off). Similarities to the core business, potential synergies, as well as conflicts are among the top decision-making criteria in this respect. Important to notice in this context, however, is that all successful incumbents we interviewed were well aware of the fact that not all their new business model ideas will eventually grow into a fully fledged business (most will actually fail). Therefore, they continually evaluate their internal start-ups and reject or exit them if necessary (see Figure 5.3).

Let's look at some more examples of what this can look like in practice.

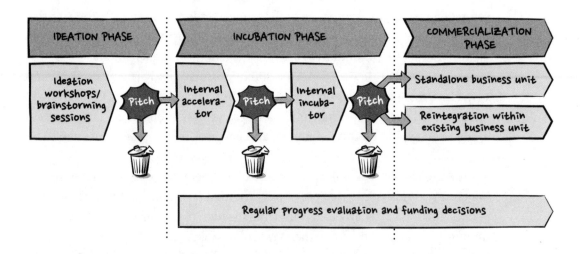

Figure 5.3 Ideation, incubation, and commercialization phases

SWISSCOM
. . . .

Swisscom, Switzerland's leading telecommunications provider, uses a novel three-stage development approach to foster explorative innovation behavior and connect intrapreneurs with externals.

David Hengartner, head of Intrapreneurship, explains the workings of the Swisscom Kickbox concept: "We 'innovate innovation' through a novel three-stage approach to decentralized intrapreneurship in cooperation with external partners and customers. The first stage is the RedBox. Every employee with a good idea can apply for such a RedBox." The box contains 1,000 Swiss Francs seed money, an official authorization by HR to spend 20% of working time on the venture for two months, contacts to innovation experts, and other useful tips, tricks, and tools for the innovation process. "The initial two months are spent refining the idea to a point where it can be pitched to a jury of the Digital Business Unit or to another sponsor within Swisscom, which ultimately decides if they make it to the next round and are given a BlueBox," Hengartner details. If a BlueBox is handed out, that means another 10,000 to 50,000 Swiss Francs capital injection, more experts, coaching, and mentoring to draw from, the possibility to attend workshops to refine the team's ideas, and an extension of the 20% rule for an extra four to six months. During this time, a proof of concept needs to be developed jointly with customers. "The final GoldBox is awarded by a sponsor from the Digital Business Unit if the proof of concept is convincing. The team gets another 100,000 to 500,000 Swiss Francs and can devote 100% of their time to scaling up the business and potentially spinning it off as a standalone entity. Our goal is to hand out a couple of GoldBoxes per year," Hengartner declares proudly. Being awarded the GoldBox also means additional support is provided, for instance, in the form of introductions to business angels or venture capitalists and participation in international acceleration programs.[14]

BÜHLER
. . . .

Ian Roberts, the CTO of diversified tech conglomerate Bühler, initiated the company's Innovation Challenge as an internal competition for employee teams proposing solutions to solving key strategic goals of the company.

"The Innovation Challenge helps our company think in networks, much more so than traditional companies would," Roberts points out. Teams from across the world and from different functions gather to develop ideas addressing Bühler's customers' problems. "Last year, our focus was on digital solutions for energy and waste consumption. In the years prior, we've asked for digital business models supporting the sustainability vision of our company," Roberts recalls. The Innovation Challenge starts in January with a kick-off meeting of the 100 top leaders at Bühler. A video and a website detailing the scope of the Innovation Challenge is then distributed across the organization. The call for submissions is open for six weeks during which time the employees need to submit an initial proposal. "Then we go to all of the regions, spend a day in each, and listen to the best pitches. From that, we pick the ones we believe are most promising," Roberts describes the process. Once the best ideas are picked, they are published online for the whole organization to access and respond, thus advancing the idea, or to join the respective teams. Ultimately, it's the employees who get to vote on the best ideas. The teams with the highest scores are flown to corporate headquarters in Uzwil, where they receive a four-day training to prepare them for their final pitch in front of an executive jury. Roberts is one of the jury members who eventually decides which of the roughly eight pitches they listen to will receive funds and further support.[15]

DIVERSIFIED TECHNOLOGY COMPANY

The company's innovation cycle starts with regular ideation workshops held in the firm's digital unit. The resulting ideas are presented at so-called "stage gate meetings." At the first stage gate, the employees have to pitch their ideas to a committee, explaining their idea, the market environment, and their assessment of the market potential.

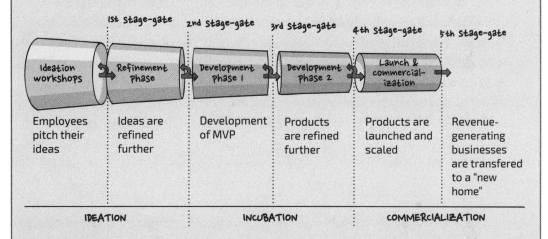

Figure 5.4 Stage-gate approach

Ideas that pass this first gate are then expanded (see Figure 5.4). Product features have to be detailed, the impact has to be estimated more precisely, and first assumptions regarding market focus and positioning are outlined. Ideas that pass the second stage gate enter the development phase (note, this is what we called the incubation phase earlier) in which a first MVP is developed with an actual lighthouse customer. The products that pass this third stage gate enter a further development phase, in which the product-market-fit is optimized and tested. All ideas that pass this second development phase are pushed through the final two stages, where ideas are scaled and developed into full-fledged products.

With every stage gate, the committee decides about further resources that the initiative needs for its next phase. This can include budget, personnel resources, additional time, technical expertise, digital expertise, and so on. At the beginning, the digital unit is more heavily involved as it provides digital resources (for example, UX/UI developers) while the initiative owners from the core spend about 20% of their time working on the initiative. This changes after stage gate three, where they spend at least 80% time on the initiative, otherwise they can't pass the stage gate and the initiative is put on hold.

The company learned a heavy time commitment at the beginning does not work because the employees who contribute ideas are typically already busy in their main roles. In fact, they are normally the ones who are already very engaged in the core business, so they simply can't spend 100% on this new endeavor. Stage gate meetings are broadcasted on the internal YouTube channel, and everyone is encouraged to watch. This transparency also creates visibility of the initiatives across BUs, which helps to create acceptance and detect synergies.[16]

V-ZUG, the Swiss market leader for household appliances, provided details of the rather turbulent journey it experienced until one of its 2nd S-curve initiatives passed the final stage gate and received approval.

V-ZUG

. . . .

When Julian Schubert, managing director at V-ZUG Services, first presented his idea to his CEO, he could not imagine how much sweat and tears were going to go into bringing it to life.

His idea to set up a new digital business model posed a real threat to the core business, as it was a plan to move partially from a B2B to a B2C model. Due to the dependence on key distribution partners, the core was afraid to cannibalize its own sales channels with an uncertain new business model. And rightfully so: Why should an organization that has been market leader for decades risk its core business when it is unclear whether the new idea will ever take off?

For Schubert, it was clear he had to address those concerns or the new business model would never get sufficient support and backing. "The doubters are the best challengers. If you can't answer their questions, then you should consider dropping the idea altogether," he argues. So, instead of seeing the doubters as opponents, he saw their questions as a chance to rule out uncertainties.

The concerns raised were valid points. Addressing them properly – particularly legal concerns – was necessary. Testing with customers, obtaining legal advice, and so forth helped Schubert determine the viability of the idea and gauge demand for it. Every new answer was not just a milestone to convince the board; it also gave the initiative owner more confidence he was on the right path.

Looking back, Schubert is convinced that a well-structured approach, good arguments, and a clear plan were key success factors in persuading others in the organization. Incumbents have something at stake: they are at risk of losing their reputation, trust of customers, established distribution channels, and so on. A lot of what the incumbent has built up over the years (107 years for V-ZUG) can be damaged when the corporate start-up makes poor decisions. To win corporate over, Schubert needed a clear action plan. This, however, is not inherently incompatible with agility. V-ZUG's innovation unit was empowered to explore new ideas, and they also applied rapid prototyping and testing approaches, but only after key assumptions were verified and critical questions answered.[17]

No matter which S-curve is concerned, a well-structured development approach used as a blueprint for idea development and testing will prove worthwhile, especially when employees of the core work on digital initiatives on the side, as innovation expert Harald Brodbeck argues.[18] It promotes the use of a common language and a mutual understanding of how things get done.

 GET YOUR HANDS EVEN DIRTIER RUNNING THE DIGITAL TRANSFORMATION

Now that we have discussed the process to execute individual strategic initiatives, let's zero in on how incumbents can successfully steer the overall digital transformation (the entirety of efforts related to digital transformation), which will include important governance, politics, and funding decisions among other things.

Incumbents should start at the beginning with lighthouse initiatives to initiate the process and gain momentum quickly. Do not underestimate the importance of a good start. The first initiatives will set the tone for everything that follows.

❜❜ when the first idea fails massively, the board will be very skeptical about future initiatives. There's a great responsibility for lighthouse initiatives to open doors instead of closing them. ❜❜

Julian Schubert, Managing Director at V-ZUG Services[19]

❜❜ we knew that the start was critical, that's why we spent some time in the beginning to carefully select not only the most promising use cases, but also the willing ones, whom we knew were supportive for our digitalization efforts. ❜❜

Samy Jandali, Vice President Digital Business Empowerment at BASF[20]

❚❚ We figured out it's important to start with lighthouse projects in each business unit to prove success
and create visibility inside the businesses. **❚❚**

Deborah Sherry, former Chief Commercial Officer of GE
Digital in Europe[21]

If the firm can demonstrate success early on, this creates enthusiasm and excitement, which can spread across the organization. It is an important first step to raise awareness, acceptance, and support. Short-term wins will also be helpful to free up capital and release important key resources from the core.[22] Companies should consider carefully which initiatives to turn into lighthouses. Other aspects to consider include the allotment of financial resources, a highly skilled digital team (often led by a CDO), the right organizational environment, and the right governance model to support it.[23] Let's look more closely at these.

Selection of lighthouses

Selection criteria for which initiatives to turn into lighthouses will be different from the criteria used once the digital transformation is up and running as priorities are completely different. The following story from BASF illustrates this well.

BASF
......

When they embarked on their digital transformation journey, BASF's focus was to generate excitement broadly throughout the organization. Later in the process, the focus changed from reach to impact. However, it was difficult to find the right criteria to select lighthouse initiatives. The executive team in the project discussed long and hard about the most relevant selection criteria. They thought about short-term versus long-term relevance of use cases, including factors such as profit potential, growth prospects, and so on. They considered whether it was better to start with business units that already had a high digital maturity. They even discussed if they should choose business units with low profitability where a successful digital use case could be a strong positive sign.

At the end of the day, these criteria did not bring clarity or direction. "We realized those decision criteria are never completely right or wrong. It's almost a religious discussion," says Samy Jandali, Vice President Digital Business Empowerment. Instead of predefining the "right" impact measure, they agreed on selecting business units and initiatives that had the most supportive and willing leadership in place. An "alliance of the willing" was most central to generating excitement and learnings for the organization.[24]

If you find yourself in the lucky position to have many supportive business unit heads who want to spearhead the digital transformation, you may want to apply a more rigorous selection procedure – like ABB, a Swiss-Swedish technology conglomerate active in such areas as energy, industrial automation, and robotics. ABB defined a number of conditions to be met before an idea even qualified as a lighthouse initiative. The idea has to be new and testable, meaning fielded, with a real customer willing to give feedback. The idea has to be a cross-functional effort and bring together employees from different departments. It has to be one for which it is possible to develop an MVP of a marketable solution within six to nine months. Finally, the idea needs to have a digital technology component to it (for example, AI, AR, Blockchain, or any other technology ABB has an interest in). These selection criteria make sure that lighthouses are not just digital lighthouses but also important first steps toward an agile setting in general.[25]

It is important to manage strategic initiatives as a portfolio and start with the most promising idea to increase the chances for early successes. However, a portfolio approach is not just important in the beginning, but should be maintained throughout the transformation. It is also a useful tool to demonstrate progress to relevant stakeholders (especially the supervisory board).[26]

Governance

Incumbents must establish a digital decision-making board or committee with the authority to decide on the pipeline of strategic initiatives for both S-curves and on how and where opportunities will be pursued. It can decide whether strategic initiatives should be developed fully internally, or with the help of externals.

This board can be the governance body to regularly review and evaluate the overall progress of the transformation – a supervisory board for the digital transformation. It controls the activities of the central digital unit (depending on the setup) to ensure that digital activities are in line with the overall digital strategy. Such a board should also be kept informed about new technology trends, the progress of ongoing initiatives, and the pipeline of future strategic initiatives. Together with the digital unit, this board needs to regularly revisit the strategy and discuss changes in direction or pace, if necessary. In fast-moving industries, both the strategy and the transformation plan should be revisited and adapted on a regular basis. Not only the execution of strategic initiatives but also the planning itself has to become more iterative and agile.[27]

At the beginning of V-ZUG's digital transformation journey, it had no dedicated decision-making body to decide on the pipeline of digital initiatives. All they had was an R&D body, which decided on improvements rather than truly digital innovations. Thus, V-ZUG established a new steering board for its digital activities, which had a completely different area of competence than the R&D body. This board analyzed, prioritized, and managed digital initiatives for the entire firm. Julian Schubert, managing director at V-ZUG Services, remembers the road to establishing this body was rocky.[28] Reshuffling and redefining competencies is never an easy task, but it gets even more complicated when the executive and supervisory boards are affected. The effort and time it takes to establish a new decision-making body in such a large and traditional organization must not be underestimated.

Funding and budget distribution

At the beginning, incumbents are advised to fund lighthouses from a central budget pot supported by all business units, avoiding budget discussions and the courtesy of the core business units. When Osram, the multinational lighting manufacturer, started its digital transformation, individual business units were responsible for the funding of core initiatives. However, this setup did not really work well as funding was subject to long and cumbersome P&L discussions. Therefore, Osram decided to fund strategic initiatives via a levy – each business unit had to contribute a certain lump sum to a central budget every year that was then distributed back to the business unit with the more pressing digital transformation needs and the most relevant digital transformation ideas. Thorsten Müller, former head of Innovation and Research, remembers this approach worked much better as discussion centered around content and the question of the best way for all to drive the transformation rather than business units trying to dodge investing in the transformation. Overall, the new funding policy was well received and the adjustments quickly paid off for the business units.[29]

Once the lighthouses are successfully completed, the organization can move to a more balanced approach, where funding is provided from both a decentralized and a central budget. Differentiating between the location and the purpose of the initiative is helpful to facilitate the discussion. Most organizations have different rules and guidelines depending on whether the initiative is close to the core business, focuses on new business models, or is concerned with an investment into a general digital capability, which can serve as an enabler for both S-curves.

1. **Strategic initiatives close to the core business:** these activities are often very business unit-specific and core business units usually sponsor the initiative and provide the funds and other relevant core resources. To create additional incentives for the digitization of the core, some incumbents provide the service of the central digital unit for free, so that the core only has to pay for its own resources but not the digital capabilities it borrows from the central digital unit.

2. **Strategic initiatives far from the core business:** new (digital) business models are not normally a primary interest of traditional business units. You can try to ask them for funding, but the odds are slim. Fund these initiatives from a central budget. The size of this budget has to be defined by the digital board and should be reflective of the strategy and the priorities of the organization.

3. **General capabilities and technologies:** the organization will also have to invest in some basic digital capabilities, especially at the beginning. The exact nature and size of this investment depends on the gap between the existing digital capabilities and the company's digital target. Most incumbents will have to undertake substantial investments to build up analytics and data capabilities. As these assets can be seen as general enablers helpful for both S-curves, it makes sense to fund them from a central budget.

The general rule is: those who earn the benefits should also bear the costs. When it comes to follow-on investments, the required funding for 1st S-curve initiatives can be estimated in advance in most cases. For example, when a core business unit wants to digitize a customer interface, it can ask the digital unit for its support and request an estimate of the required effort. Initiatives on the 2nd S-curve, on the other hand, are developed in iteration cycles, so the funding process should match the development process. This means funding is only provided in small tranches and contingent on reaching milestones. Organizations have to adapt a VC-like approach with evaluation and funding, where investment decisions are based on criteria that venture capital firms use to evaluate start-ups, such as team composition, market potential, and viability of the business model. Although the build-up of a new (digital) business will require more perseverance and patience than incumbents are used to, the regular stage gate development (and funding) process makes sure that uncertainties are reduced early in the process, and large investments are only granted once market viability is proven.

Digital team support

A common problem is that traditional organizations demand entrepreneurial behavior, but when push comes to shove, they are unwilling to support it. Boards should incentivize and promote entrepreneurial risk (you will hear more about this in the **Leadership**, **People**, and **Culture** chapters, Chapters 6, 7, and 8). Without it your best talent will not take on these risks and will not move into the digital team, or elsewhere altogether.

" When digital topics are talked about as being 'the future of the company,' they should be respected and supported accordingly. Digital teams need sufficient backing and freedom, otherwise all digital activities are no more than 'innovation theater'. **"**

Sören Lauinger, Vice President Intrapreneurship & Co-creation at Aesculap[30]

" If digitization is really the most important strategic topic for the years to come, the board should mobilize the best people the organization has to offer to really emphasize the importance and create strong momentum right at the beginning. Many top talents don't like risky career moves, even less when the backing of the board is missing. To solve this issue, the board needs to be credible, communicate the importance of the topic, mobilize the best talent, and give them their backing. **"**

CDO of a large discount retailer[31]

" Senior leadership buy-in is absolutely critical, otherwise you can't digitally transform the organization. I've had so many people come to me telling me things they want to do and it's breaking your heart because they can't get the budgets and the traction because their senior leadership doesn't get it. **"**

Deborah Sherry, former Chief Commercial Officer of GE Digital in Europe[32]

184

What should the digital team be allowed to do, how much freedom do they need, and why are different governance rules so important? Forcing your digital team to comply with core business processes would be counterproductive and thwart all the speed and innovation power you build up in the first place. To avoid this, incumbents should establish a new rule book that provides more freedom and autonomy along a number of dimensions. First, new financial rules are required. Pressure to deliver short-term returns only leads internal entrepreneurs to make decisions that hurt the long-term success of the corporate venture.[33] Management has to use different KPIs (key performance indicators) and targets than in the traditional business (we will talk more about this in the **WHERE** chapter, Chapter 9).

Second, the compliance and governance process requirements need to be less stringent. Do not require your digital team to comply with all the legacy rules and procedures; otherwise, you should not be surprised if your digital talent flees in panic. This will be especially important in the early phases of the 2nd S-curve, where incumbents should establish "minimum governance requirements" for new ventures.

Third, incumbents need to implement new decision-making structures. To make agility work, management has to delegate responsibilities to the development teams. One organization that chose an interesting approach was BASF. With the introduction of agile processes, BASF decided that no single person or decision-making body in the organization – not even top management – was allowed to evaluate the quality of ideas. Only the market was, meaning feedback from the market determines if an idea is promising or not. Right from the start, everyone was forced to get in touch with the market and validate ideas with real customers.[34]

This doesn't mean no rules, but different rules. Organizations need to find a balance between setting rules and giving freedom to avoid conflicts with the core later on.

Reintegration and scaling

This is another common problem related to digital transformation processes. Once again, we have to differentiate between the two S-curves, since the problem is more severe for the 2nd S-curve. The initiatives on the 1st S-curve will be close to the core so that the number of required adjustments and changes once initiatives have been handed over to the core are low. In fact, 1st S-curve initiatives should be developed in close collaboration and with the strong contribution of employees from the core business. To prevent potential problems later on, it makes sense to start the collaboration as early as possible. An early integration of core staff makes the handover and incorporation of ideas within the mothership much easier. Core employees who are part of the team are more likely to support and promote the idea within the core business, instead of rejecting it. Once the initiative is completed, the core business can start to leverage the lessons and approach new use cases independently, with reduced support from the central digital unit. So, in the long-run, digital capabilities are integrated within the core and employees from the core are enabled to approach new use cases on their own.

When we look at the 2nd S-curve (and 1st S-curve initiatives that are developed independently from the core), things get a little bit messy. Special challenges arise when the incumbents decide to reintegrate digital initiatives into the core (for example, 1st S-curve initiatives that were started in a lab environment or in a separate digital business unit). Similar challenges occur when digital initiatives have reached a stage where the company decides to spin them off into a standalone entity (for example, 2nd S-curve initiatives with little or no overlap with the core business that have reached market maturity). We identified common challenges in our research.

First, when initiatives leave their safe environment (for example, lab or incubator) to find a new home, the team setup often changes. Product ownership is passed from the central digital unit to the core business, or the ownership for certain topics is handed over from central digital experts to employees from the core. Such change in personnel can smash momentum and negatively impact team dynamic. Even when the transition period is well planned (for instance, through a partial overlap between roles), team productivity might experience a dip.

Second, when digital activities are reintegrated into the core, they often receive a subordinate role. Initiatives end up waiting in line with other initiatives, vying for budget and attention. Progress is further slowed down by long decision-making cycles and non-agile processes.

Third, more problems arise when initiatives are attached to the core's legacy. When initiatives are reintegrated, they are often forced to comply with or run on legacy systems. Significant time needs to be invested into technical integration and testing, instead of into growth and scaling. Even worse, teams are suddenly bound to corporate release cycles, instead of daily or weekly updates which they are used to, points out Konstantin Speidel, Vice President for Digital Transformation at Allianz Global Investors, the global asset management firm.[35]

Fourth, scaling new business models requires different capabilities than those start-ups are known for. Scaling requires efficient execution and doing things over and over again, consistently and efficiently. This does not come naturally to start-ups. In this phase, start-ups have to adjust some of their internal processes and start to act more like corporates. Sometimes this will involve the recruitment of more experienced employees and managers. Whenever 2nd S-curve initiatives are about to be scaled, the organization should refer back to and leverage the proven and reliable processes from the 1st S-curve.

Fifth, when business ideas leave the lab environment, it is often assumed they no longer need financial support. Incumbents forget that business-building is a long-term investment, and support should not stop at the point where business models are pushed out of the incubator. When a venture is handed over to the core, the respective business unit should take full responsibility for further costs. At BASF, the incubation phase is funded through a central budget. But once initiatives have proven their potential, they are handed over to the business units of the core, with all costs and benefits.[36] If the venture is spun off into a standalone business unit or into a separate entity, further central funding will be required, unless the organization opens up its venture to outside investors.

The sixth and final challenge is the lack of commitment by incumbents. It happens quite often that business ideas successfully leave an incubator but organizations decide not to invest and scale them any further. When companies fail to manage their ideation phase in accordance with their strategy, or when they fail to set clear boundaries for the incubation phase, they end up with a venture that has indeed proven its market viability but does not fit into the overarching strategy or vision. To avoid this, companies must stick to their strategy during the ideation and incubation phases. Harald Brodbeck, the innovation expert, explains, "Firms tend to set up an accelerator because it's cool to have one. But the ideas that go through it are often stopped afterwards, even if they are successful and have a positive business case. The reason for this is that the ideas are not in line with the strategic direction. Thus, firms should only accept ideas that are based on the strategic focus areas that were identified as important to the firm, creating a clear link between the strategy and innovation activities."[37] Besides a misalignment of strategy and initiative, the lack of commitment may also be rooted in an unawareness of the required investments to scale a business. Firms may have to fight competitors trying to move into a similar space, which can easily result in excessive spending. Incumbents that find themselves in this position can either take a half-hearted approach and invest only a little, go all-in and try to win the race to the top, or they stop and try to sell off the entire business.

One firm that mastered the separation and reintegration of digital activities very successfully is CEWE, the European-wide leading photo service company.

CEWE

When the company started to work on innovations that were at the intersection of digital photography and traditional printing of photo images, the internal opposition was substantial. Although CEWE managed to nurture a culture of entrepreneurship, the internal doubts and fears that existed originally within the core business were not the ideal environment for the digital pioneers.

For this reason, the management decided initially to separate all digital activities and put them into a safe nucleus. This was a standalone entity called "CEWE Digital," located in a separate hanger where the digital pioneers (both internals as well as newly hired external staff) could work and innovate with little interference from the core business. This setup was something that one would call an internal incubator today, CTO and head of R&D Reiner Fageth explains. But CEWE did not stop there. Because there were many promising synergies between the traditional core business and the new innovations that originated in the new digital unit, CEWE didn't forget about the colleagues from the traditional business. Once the digital unit completed new digital innovations, they were reintegrated into the mothership, where they were then combined with core products and services. This process not only allowed CEWE to scale new ideas within the core but also helped to achieve high acceptance rates, as employees from the core could gain a first-hand experience of the benefits that the digital innovations had for the core business.[38]

Suffice it to say, such a transition period is critical but difficult.

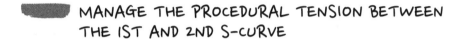

MANAGE THE PROCEDURAL TENSION BETWEEN THE 1ST AND 2ND S-CURVE

Unaligned activities and decision-making processes can cause serious difficulties between the two S-curves, for example, when the corporate start-up makes decisions that make a future reintegration into the core business difficult. But it's not just the potential for negative consequences that makes building bridges so important. Only a strong link and alignment between the two S-curves allows incumbents to unlock the synergy potential and make the best out of both worlds. Let's look at the most useful procedural mechanisms we can recommend.

Integration manager

Incumbents should appoint a well-connected top executive from the mothership to act as integration manager (or gate keeper). Such a manager can represent the mothership and serve as a catalyst for the 2nd S-curve within the core business.[39] This will be especially important when the organization sets up a separate entity not directly managed by a central digital unit. This integration manager has two tasks. One is the management and prevention of conflicts between the two S-curves. That means having an eye on decisions of the new (digital) business and ensuring that a future integration – should it ever happen – is possible without problems. Critical in this respect are, for example, decisions that affect the branding, the data architecture, or the hardware interfaces. Such a review or control function should neither slow down the new venture nor hurt its agility. So, whenever a deviation from the direction of the core is essential, the (digital) business should be allowed to do so. However, many decisions are made without consideration of a future reintegration. An integration manager must have profound knowledge of core business processes in order to assess the impact of decisions being made on the 2nd S-curve. The integration manager is also responsible for the aggregation and orchestration of information: only when the core is informed about important decisions can conflicts be prevented. The integration manager should know which decisions are important enough to coordinate with the core.

The second main task relates to the management of synergies and overlaps: only when there's a procedural link between the two S-curves can the 2nd S-curve build on core assets, and vice versa. The integration manager should inform digital teams about the relevant assets of the core and help them get access. On the other hand, whenever digital teams work on concepts that are relevant (or likely to be relevant in the future) for the entire organization, it makes sense to coordinate them accordingly.

This function is often performed by a central digital unit (or a dedicated CDO), in which case a separate role is not required. If, however, a central function does not exist, incumbents might want to consider introducing such a role to establish a procedural link. The role requires a good understanding of the strategy of the organization, of both the core business and the new (digital) business. To perform well in this role, the manager needs a strong network within the core, especially to the top management of the core and business unit heads. Under the bottom line, an integration manager should act like a business angel – he or she supports the digital unit, raises concerns, and avoids pitfalls.

Florian Bankoley, Vice President Corporate IT at Bosch, calls this manager type "border walkers" because they need to constantly switch back-and-forth between both S-curves. They can then build ties where needed, and avoid or solve potential conflicts more effectively, as they know the pain points and language of the core business much better than leaders who are only familiar with the digital world.[40]

Samy Jandali of BASF makes a similar argument. It's crucial to have business people on board who can convince business unit heads with business arguments.

This allows discussions at eye-level with the business managers. This does not mean that they need specific knowledge about the individual operation, but they need a general understanding of business problems and the needs of business unit heads to address their concerns and build good proposals.[41]

In addition, it's also important that these talents bring sufficient technical knowledge, Deborah Sherry, former Chief Commercial Officer of GE Digital in Europe, points out. "You need to find the digital migrants in the core business who are willing to promote the idea in the core," she explains.[42]

These employees can then become important ambassadors or catalysts for the digital activities, thereby forming an important link between the two S-curves.

Shared assets

As stressed earlier, a key reason why incumbents do not succeed with their new business models is because they fail to leverage the core asset appropriately. Although we have touched upon this point here and there, we have not yet discussed which assets are most useful. Let's look at the main advantages incumbents should try to unlock to strengthen and accelerate their new (digital) business.

- **Market and technological expertise:** many incumbents have built up remarkable market expertise. Start-ups do not have such market experience and can benefit from advice (for example, regulatory requirements, licenses, and so forth). Incumbents have built up technological know-how and skills in specific fields over years or even decades, which can then be leveraged in the new venture. Finally, incumbents often have a sea of data (about markets, customer behavior) that can save the new unit a lot of money and time.[43]

- **Existing customer base:** while normal start-ups have to build a customer base from scratch, corporate start-ups benefit from the existing customer relationships of the parent firm. This allows the 2nd S-curve to scale up quickly.[44] The decision to tap into the parent's customer base will depend on channel conflicts and cross-selling potential (if the new venture is too far from the core business, the existing customer base might be irrelevant).

- **Establish distribution channels:** building up a distribution channel can cost a lot of money and time. Leveraging existing channels makes a lot of sense, especially when the customer base is similar.

- **Brand power:** the importance of an established and trusted brand should not be underestimated, especially in industries where the brand is important for customers' confidence in the product quality.

  Werk_39, Aesculap's digital innovation unit operating in the market for surgery products, benefits greatly from the trust that customers put into the brand of its parent company.[45]

- **Management capabilities:** once the start-up grows into something like an established business, the management skills and expertise of the core become increasingly important as the new business has to prove stability and efficiency, skills that the core business has developed and honed for years. The know-how of core managers in the setup of operations, structures, processes, and the scaling of ideas becomes a valuable asset for start-ups.

Incumbents will only be able to unlock the full potential of their new (digital) business when they translate crucial core assets into a competitive strength of the 2nd S-curve.

GET MOVING TO AVOID THE DINOSAUR FATE

Be sure to consider these action items as you think about the processual setup of your digital transformation:

- Adopt a lean and agile process setup to execute strategic initiatives:
  - Apply the lean start-up approach to turn your ideas into working products, services, or new business models.
  - Have agile teams work on strategic initiatives (see **Culture** chapter, Chapter 8).
  - Set up a structured development approach with various stages that is tailored to your organization.
  - Adapt a VC-like approach for the evaluation of initiatives.

- Establish effective governance mechanisms to manage the transformation at an aggregate level:
  — Run lighthouse initiatives to create enthusiasm and excitement.
  — Establish a digital decision-making board that decides on the pipeline of strategic initiatives, evaluates the progress, and ensures alignment with the strategy.
  — Define clear rules related to the funding of initiatives on the 1st and the 2nd S-curve.
  — Define a new rulebook for the initiatives on the 2nd S-curve; let the customer/the market decide on the viability of new ideas.
  — Develop a plan for the reintegration (especially the 1st S-curve) or spin-off of initiatives (especially the 2nd S-curve).

- Bridge the gap between the 1st and the 2nd S-curve:
  — Establish an integration manager or gatekeeper who avoids conflicts between the two S-curves and makes sure that synergies can be realized.
  — Leverage your core assets to unlock the full potential of your new venture, especially for scaling.

 GET INSPIRED (BY BENELUX)

ING
. . . .

How do you turn a large bank into an organization that embraces an agile way of working? Dutch-based ING successfully made this transition and is now organized around small cross-functional teams.

ING's innovative ideas are often born in so-called "innovation bootcamps." Organized once a year, employees contribute their own ideas. Proposals are evaluated using the PACE methodology, something the bank invented for itself.

Essentially, PACE is an innovation methodology that combines elements of design thinking, lean start-up, and agile scrum. Prior to developing PACE, these modern working techniques were already used to some extent but there was no central comprehensive development approach. With the introduction of PACE, ING established a common innovation standard and language. This has made the whole development process more efficient and collaboration across countries easier, and contributed to the transparency and comparability of initiatives. ING even used agile principles to design PACE in the first place: they designed it, tested it, redesigned it, improved it, and finally rolled it out across the organization. A distinguishing feature of PACE is that it starts with the problem, not with the solution. At the beginning of the process, there is always the customer problem, or pain point. This approach brings two main benefits, as Katharina Herrmann, Global Head of Platforms and Beyond Banking, identifies: First, it ensures that the organization does not jump to solutions too soon. The second advantage is that it makes sure that the organization works on problems that matter to customers.

ING's innovation process is split into three phases. The first phase is the "problem-fit phase," in which teams start with understanding what problems customers struggle with today. From the beginning, employees interview customers to test their hypotheses and collect information for the next phase. The second phase is the "solution-fit phase," where teams work on concrete solutions that are tested with real customers (for example, A/B testing, observation test). The last phase is the "market-fit phase," in which a business case is calculated and the solution is tested and improved in the field. In line with agile principles, each team has a clearly defined goal before it starts into the next phase. The type of goal and the topic that the teams work on depends on their purpose, which is closely connected to the overarching strategy. For example, while there are some teams working to improve the loan conversion rate, others work on the improvement of customer satisfaction.

This hypothesis-driven testing approach gives teams flexibility to adjust their course based on the insights generated. Each experiment can have one of three outcomes: (1) When the hypothesis is proven, the team continues to work on the proposed solution. (2) When it detects a new angle or an alternative, more promising solution, the team can decide to change direction, in which case it makes adjustments. (3) When the team finds out that the hypothesis is fundamentally wrong, and that the proposed solution does not work, the work is stopped. This is not considered a failure but an important learning that allows the team to move on and focus on a new hypothesis. ING's approach, being all about testing and validating assumptions before ideas are built, ensures that innovations are desirable, feasible, and viable.

ING's structured innovation process is also used within the bank's so-called "ING Labs," which are physically located in London, Amsterdam, and Singapore. These labs, which focus on certain predefined value spaces that ING aims to disrupt, allow the bank to collaborate with external partners, explore new areas and business models, and accelerate disruptive innovation globally. The partnerships can include start-ups, scale-ups, researchers, entrepreneurs, and even other corporates. The central idea is always a mutually beneficial partnership that turns ideas into minimal viable products. Once ready to scale into minimum viable companies, the initiatives are either integrated in the core business or can pitch for funding from ING Ventures or other potential investors.

When it comes to the overarching management of innovation initiatives, ING separates between two types of innovations. As far as incremental innovations are concerned, responsibility is put on the shoulders of local teams (so-called squads and tribes), which know customers' pain points well. Disruptive innovations are steered and pushed from a central team and at a global level (through its ING Labs). The coordination between the two S-curves – the incremental innovations close to the existing business, and the disruptive innovations on the 2nd S-curve – is facilitated by several councils and forums. There are management and expert meetings to decide how topics should be tackled and how efforts can be best coordinated across the organization, especially when local and global teams work on similar topics.[46]

KEY TAKEAWAYS:

- **Develop a unified approach** – Having a standard procedure for the innovation process makes communication and collaboration much more efficient.

- **Use different approaches for different types of innovations** – Manage disruptive ideas centrally (for example, through labs) and establish different formats (for example, councils and forums) to align efforts across the organization.

- **Define a purpose and set clear goals** – Agile teams need to have a purpose that drives their activities and a crystal-clear goal; don't be afraid to make adjustments or to stop initiatives based on the testing data gathered.

GET A GRIP ON THOSE "SOFT" FACTORS OF YOUR DIGITAL TRANSFORMATION

"Instituting the right talent and mindset" encompasses three distinct action areas – with an emphasis on their distinctiveness. Our **Leadership** chapter, next, answers the two guiding questions: "What kind of leaders does it take for a digital transformation? And how can these be sourced?" When we inquire about the kinds of leaders it takes, we look for the kinds of leadership styles and attributes that are needed on the 1st and 2nd S-curve. And when we ask about how they can be sourced, we talk about how existing leaders can be morphed into digital leaders and how external leaders can be attracted to join. Our **People** chapter (Chapter 7) answers very similar questions, but related to employees with no managerial responsibilities: "What kind of people does it take for a digital transformation? And how can these be sourced?" Again, we want to know what types of skills are necessary to succeed on either the 1st or 2nd S-curve for regular employees – arguably the vast majority of your total headcount – and how you may go about building your workforce of the future. For both leaders and people, we will talk about how to bridge a gap between those on the 1st and those on the 2nd S-curve. Chapter 8, **Culture**, is also rooted in a distinct definition of culture – the values, beliefs, and behaviors that govern how a company's staff (leaders and employees) interact with each other. This is the glue that ties everybody together. Hence, this part's final chapter asks, "What kind of culture is most conducive for a digital transformation? Specifically, what (change in existing) beliefs and behaviors will you need to strive for?"

If you're still having trouble fathoming how these three things differ, imagine building a house. You have your load-bearing walls made of bricks – these are your leaders. You have your non-load-bearing walls, which are also made of bricks – these are your non-leader employees (what we refer to as "people"). Note that both leaders and people are made of the same DNA (bricks) because they are both ultimately of the same substance. Relatedly, note that "load-bearing" only refers to the figurative weight on leaders' shoulders and is not to be interpreted as people being inferior to leaders but more as their being more numerous than leaders. To make this all stick together (both the leaders and people in their own groups as well as leaders and people across group boundaries), it takes mortar to connect them – that's your culture. Notice that the foundation of your house – your strategy – will have been laid before piling bricks and mortar on top (refer to Chapter 2, the **WHAT** chapter, for details). This foundation is made of concrete, so is even more durable. It literally and figuratively guides the building structures that are yet to be added on top.

chapter 6

LEADERSHIP: WHAT TO LOOK FOR IN LEADERS AND HOW TO FIND THEM

This is your guidebook for the review of the load-bearing walls in your digital transformation house, aka the leaders of your digital transformation. We will talk about what kind of leadership styles and attributes are needed on the 1st and 2nd S-curves, respectively, and why these need to differ. Then we will talk about how to build the leaders it takes to run a digital transformation, including how to evangelize the middle-management layer. We will also give you advice on how to maintain your 1st S-curve leadership in parallel with your 2nd S-curve leadership and how to best manage exchanges between the two (see Figure 6.1).

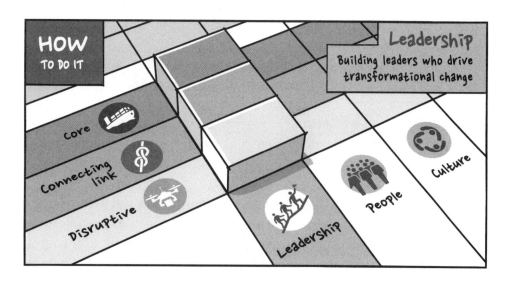

Figure 6.1 Key visual with focus on How/Leadership

REALIZE THE LEADERSHIP CHALLENGES YOUR COMPANY MUST TACKLE

Let us give you a sneak peek into one of the main conclusions – and biggest challenges – of this chapter: it takes different leadership styles to succeed on different S-curves. This begs the question: How do you reconcile two vastly different leadership schools of thought in one company?

Taking a step back, what exactly are the different leadership styles and attributes needed for leaders on the two S-curves? How are the requirements of these exacerbated by the presence of a VUCA (volatile, uncertain, complex, ambiguous) world? From everything you have heard about the 1st S-curve (and everything you know about it from your own experience) you can infer that 1st S-curve leaders typically focus on efficiency and productivity, adhering to the business-as-usual success formula of perfect solutions and no failure and trusting in hierarchies – they (project) manage very effectively. To what extent do they need to change in the context of a digital transformation? Meanwhile 2nd S-curve leaders inspire their teams to give their best and take initiative, trusting in networks rather than hierarchies. A transformational leadership style attracts and retains the best talent, particularly in VUCA times. How can this new leadership style best be introduced to the organization without sidelining 1st S-curve leaders?

How do you source these leaders? How do you build such leaders internally? In which external sources will you find executives who can comfortably and authentically lead on both S-curves and walk their respective S-curve talk? Looking long-term, how can you potentially transition some 1st S-curve leaders into 2nd S-curve leadership positions? Can they at all be morphed into the type of transformational leaders it takes to be successful on the 2nd S-curve?

Once 1st and 2nd S-curve leaders are in place, you need to circle back to your original point of departure – namely the coexistence of two such vastly different sorts of leaders in one company. How do you make space for both of them? How can you ensure a functioning exchange between them? And how can you avoid the negative overtone of such an "old school/uncool" and "new world/hyper-cool" dichotomy in leadership behaviors?

LEADERS MAKE OR BREAK THE DIGITAL TRANSFORMATION DEAL

"Leadership, people, and culture really are the most crucial elements to tackle. They're more important than everything else. The rest is just process."

Ian Roberts, CTO, Bühler[1]

"What matters to us, what I really want to focus on, is instituting the right leadership, people, and culture."

Philipp Leutiger, CDO, LafargeHolcim[2]

"Getting leaders – and employees alike – on board with the digital transformation, motivating them to personally drive it, will make or break the success of your transformation."

Automotive expert, automotive supplier[3]

"The key challenge of a digital transformation is not money, or how you set it up. It's a matter of leadership and culture."

Cristian Citu, Digital Transformation Lead, World Economic Forum[4]

These and similar statements were common among the 100+ interviews we conducted. Finding and cultivating the best leadership is the most decisive decision for the real-life success of a digital transformation.

Why is leadership so important? As companies become more digitally mature, leaders have to evolve alongside their employers. An MIT Sloan Management Review and Deloitte Digital report found that digitally maturing firms are implementing organizational changes necessary to moderate the shift from traditional to digital environments. But much work remains to be done, particularly in leadership development. In excess of 50% of digitally maturing companies reported needing new leaders.[5] Getting and developing these leaders is a top priority for companies because they drive digital transformation success, bringing initiatives across the finish line and inspiring employees to be a part of the journey. Particularly when employees are faced with a VUCA world, they need extra guidance and strong leaders who can act as role models and sweep through the organization to win approval for and rid fear of the digital transformation. Companies often succeed or fail based on their leaders' ability to move the organization forward at times when the path is hazy. The best leaders find ways to provide steady, realistic direction to their teams, and lead with excellence, even in times of volatility, uncertainty, complexity, and ambiguity.[6]

While VUCA is a trendy managerial acronym, there is much truth to the applicability of VUCA in the context of a digital transformation. The digital transformation game is a *volatile* one where unexpected and unstable challenges undermine businesses' ability to strike preemptively. Think about fluctuating demand, short time-to-market, and other examples of industry dynamism (like disruptions from start-ups and tech players revolutionizing entire industries). The digital transformation environment is also inherently *uncertain*, marked by limited abilities to predict the future. Having unexpected competitors emerge as if from nowhere contributes to blurred future prospects of individual companies or industries. *Complexity* denotes the number of factors that need to be taken into account, including interconnections. In a digital transformation, the sheer overwhelming volume of influencing factors makes it impossible to fully analyze the environment and make accurate projections. *Ambiguity* refers to a lack of clarity in information and causal relationships. Incomplete, potentially contradicting information is something any digital transformation practitioner can attest to being present in a digital transformation context.[7]

Seeing how the already challenging phenomenon of digital transformation is further exacerbated by the presence of a VUCA environment, it is all the more necessary to institute leaders who skillfully and authentically steer an organization and its people across rocky roads.

KNOW YOUR LEADERS INSIDE AND OUT

There is no *one* perfect leader. No leadership holy grail. No universal leader-philosopher's stone. Instead, three types of leaders exist, or should exist (see Figure 6.2). They differ significantly in attitudes, skills, background, and profile. Importantly, they each have their raison d'être. None of them enjoys higher value than the others. Despite portrayals deviating from this nonjudgmental evaluation, the three different leadership styles are all needed to the same degree.

Figure 6.2 Leadership types

The traditional 1st S-curve leader

These leaders are the executives of your core business. They often have decades of experience managing that business, or similar kinds of businesses. Their professional environment (and potentially their academic background) socialized them to prioritize efficiency, productivity, and perfect solutions. They are firm believers in hierarchies, a zero-failure-tolerance policy, and escalations where necessary. They tend to manage daily operations rather than lead inspirationally. Their no-failure acceptance makes production lines operate at minimum downtime while employee efficiency is maximized. They are the ones who – given a goal – manage for excellence in achieving that goal along a pre-defined path. They follow and give orders, making sure they and their teams achieve or surpass targets in maximum-focused fashion, in time and within budget. This type of executive most resembles "command-and-control" leaders. Their professional upbringing predisposes them to be classic managers and to employ a more authoritarian-directive leadership style.

While we believe there is a difference between management and leadership, we – like many others[8] – oppose the strict manager-versus-leader dichotomy. In effect, there is only one role that one person has to assume. Which of the two potential foci – management or leadership – this one person emphasizes ultimately is either up to them personally or determined by the job description. Yet, the job description is unlikely to read "We are looking for a clear [insert <manager> or <leader>]." Just as unlikely is for the person in the position to think of themselves as "I am a clear [insert <manager> or <leader>]." Some roles (for instance, a production manager) require more classic management skills, like the ones a traditional 1st S-curve executive would be drawn to.

The digitized 1st S-curve leader

Your go-to "do as you're told" approach for the 1st S-curve won't reap the maximum results once the 1st S-curve undergoes a much-needed digital transformation. A leader in charge of the digitization of your traditional customer journey – 1st S-curve – may have a traditional 1st S-curve background that will need to be adjusted to the requirements of the new task. To modernize the core business and steer it toward a digital one, executives need to focus on leadership and corresponding leadership attributes. Such elements may include shifting toward more other-oriented leadership activities and opening a two-way street between executive and employee. This may take the form of an open dialog, where executives encourage team members to give (and not only receive) feedback. Similarly, digitized 1st S-curve leaders will rely more on networks of people and teams rather than on strict hierarchies, both to source ideas and resolve problems.

Employing these new leadership facets, digitized 1st S-curve leaders may not be transformational leaders just yet. But their transactional leadership style already goes beyond what a traditional 1st S-curve leader envisages in terms of exchanges with their subordinates.

A shift toward more (transformational) leadership is necessary to steer the digitized 1st S-curve business and indispensable for attracting and retaining talent. If you think only the 2nd S-curve needs inspirational leaders to mobilize recent graduates, young professionals, and mid-career job hunters, you are mistaken. For the 1st S-curve to digitize, it takes young blood. They need leaders to look up to rather than managers to simply carry out tasks for.

The 2nd S-curve leader

This type of leadership is a completely different ballgame. Executives no longer command and control, neither do they interact with subordinates in a transactional way. Also, their subordinates are no longer subordinates but team members whom leaders are at eye level with. These executives act as coaches and advisors to their team members. While traditional 1st S-curve leaders focus on leading the business and digitized 1st S-curve leaders add to that a focus on leading others, 2nd S-curve leaders focus on leading themselves so they can be their own team members' strongest supporters.

Transformational leaders are more willing to take risks, to act as intrapreneurs, and to promote intelligent failures. They seek maximum diverse teams, drawing in people from a variety of different backgrounds across expertise, ethnicities, culture, and other demographics. Highly skilled diverse profiles are easily drawn to such transformational leaders. Another upside: a lot of the qualities important for digital transformation leaders have become generally more important as leadership roles have developed, so executives can capitalize on that.

One must not assume the 2nd S-curve type of leadership will be optimal throughout the entire lifecycle of the new digital business. The more the new venture matures and eventually reaches the scaling-up phase, the more important 1st S-curve elements of management and leadership become. Not only will 1st S-curve leaders have to learn the ropes of transformational leadership but 2nd S-curve leaders have to get accustomed to 1st S-curve leadership. Ideally, both types of leaders are able to command both types of leadership styles. To "walk the talk" across two types of businesses is easier said than done. The good news: leadership styles are not innate, and any type of leader can learn other leadership styles – traditional leaders can become digital leaders and vice versa. Under the bottom line this means that executives need to be able to lead authentically across both S-curves, adapting their style to the environment. Leadership teams (for example, the C-level team and the business unit leadership teams) should exhibit requisite diversity in leadership styles, ideally covering all three of them.

Organizational consulting firm Korn Ferry confirms the distinction between inherently digital (2nd S-curve) leaders and those from a traditional background using their company's digital transformation as a steppingstone for their own leadership transformation (digitized 1st S-curve leaders). The two differ in what they do, specifically in what kind of experiences and competencies they bring to the table; they also differ in terms of their personal values and drivers as well as character traits. For instance, 2nd S-curve leaders have a stronger focus on managing themselves than managing others, and they emphasize independence more than their digitized 1st S-curve counterparts. Eventually a hybrid leadership strategy, combining both under the same roof, is necessary for the success of digital transformation.[9] Or, as one of us, Markus (an executive in his previous life before turning author), likes to put it: "In hindsight, I wish I'd had two hats – one blue, one orange. The blue one for the 1st S-curve; the orange one for the 2nd S-curve. I would have worn the respective hat when the situation demanded either 1st or 2nd S-curve thinking. Then my team would have automatically known what the situation was about."

What bears repeating is that leaders will have to adapt to different degrees and intimately familiarize themselves with the transformational leadership style, even if they don't (have to) employ it themselves as much. The 2nd S-curve leader will arguably have to undergo the least changes in her leadership style and can largely continue to rely on most of her previous attributes and attitudes. The digitized 1st S-curve leader will have to undergo more change, adopting a leadership style more closely akin to the 2nd S-curve leader, who will represent the new leadership norm for the future business. Going forward, everybody will need to (be able to) wear multicolored hats. For 1st S-curve leaders to be able to stand their ground in an organization that will increasingly rely on transformational leaders to drive the business forward, they will have to be able to speak that language, relate to their counterparts, and impart some new leadership characteristics for the benefit of their teams and themselves. Even those who continue to practice business as usual for the most part (for example, because they continue to lead a production line) need to fully internalize what this transformational leadership style is about. In the future, no strict distinction can be drawn between these three leadership types. Any one leader will have to understand all others, and vice versa.

The real challenge lies not in the fact that leaders currently have different styles and need to embrace new leadership attributes going forward. The predicament is rather the necessity to switch between styles and to embody all roles to an equally authentic and convincing extent. The key message to leaders is: all three types need to be able to empathize with each other and need to at least learn to understand each other and, to varying degrees, adopt new leadership habits.

GO SHOPPING FOR YOUR PREFERRED LEADERSHIP ATTRIBUTES

Assembling a digital transformation leadership team that brings a number of attributes to the table safeguards the success of your transformation. It also benefits leaders as they will enjoy a general sense of satisfaction by bringing their best selves to work. It also benefits people who are motivated working with inspiring leaders they hope to emulate. The leadership job is not done, though, by simply ticking off these boxes. Digital transformation leaders experience additional pressure because they need to bring the same qualities to the table that they ask of their team members. As you select your leaders, there are attributes specific to digital transformation leadership positions (all three leader types) in addition to their general leadership skills.[10] Also note that our definition of "digital transformation leaders" encompasses all three leader types because they are all equally needed for the success of the transformation.

Speak the language of and lead authentically on both S-curves

Leaders need to be able to lead authentically in the core business and in the new digital business. Their job is to unite the two businesses rather than run them as disconnected silos. They need to build bridges, form connections, and get "buy-in" from employees on both teams.[11] And they need to bust the myth that the 1st S-curve is tired and dated while the 2nd S-curve is hip and cool. A digital transformation leader needs to convey that both are equally important. This needs to be done authentically, seemingly with no effort, so as to avoid second-guessing or appearing to favor one business over the other.

Carola Wahl, former Chief Transformation and Market Management Officer (CTMO) at insurance firm AXA, stresses that leaders need to situationally adapt their leadership style if they are to succeed in a digital transformation environment. AXA is one example of a firm holding onto its traditional core, including well-proven hierarchies, in some areas while working in agile mode in other areas. "If this is the chosen model, if you decide to pursue both in parallel, it takes leaders who bridge the divide between these worlds," Wahl explains.[12]

Another executive who actively manages to bridge that divide is Otto Preiss, Chief Operating Officer of Digital at ABB. ABB Digital is the central digital team at ABB, which is led by the ABB CDO and for which Preiss runs operations and acts as the deputy. He says he is a translator between two worlds. For him and his fellow digital transformation leaders, a key prerequisite is to know both S-curves well. In practice, in addition to knowing how the wind blows in new digital businesses, he has a long standing in the core organization and a good reputation throughout, which established his credibility in the core. That background from the legacy business was crucial so people in the core would perceive him as an ally and as a bridge to the digital business, instead of as a rival. He considers it one of his key responsibilities to link the classic legacy business with the digital S-curve. In fact, he says that digital leadership is about convincing people, presenting projects in the language of the relevant business unit, explaining effects on them, and building connections. While there will invariably remain a chasm between the two S-curve leadership types, creating alignment is key. Day in, day out, that's what he does.[13]

A diversified technology holding follows a similar recipe for success whereby executives need to know the specifics of the old-world problems while also understanding the potential of new world solutions, like customer-centric rapid development. The CDO explains that traditional leaders are equipped with digital know-how so they can navigate both S-curves skillfully, and vice versa. Traditional leaders are sent on field trips and experience tours to Silicon Valley, Tel Aviv, and other innovation and digitization hubs. They experience how digital initiatives work in practice. Witnessing the kind of momentum around digitization creates a sense of urgency to act. Similarly, digital leaders need to bring the requisite understanding for the traditional business with them. The CDO explains, "Only if you have knowledge of old-world problems do you understand why you can't just copy and paste solutions from the new world to a traditional business. That's why bridging this gap with mutual communication is so important."[14]

Act as a sparring partner

Gone are the days of authoritative instructions from executives and passive submission by subordinates. What evolves in a digital transformation setting is a dialog between the two, where the leader can and should challenge their team members while making sure to have their professional development at heart. Regular one-on-one feedback sessions are a key tool in facilitating that dialog. Team members should feel free to bring up the topics that matter to them and draw in their superiors where they see fit. Leaders should act as coaches, giving advice where helpful and needed. But that advice should not come packaged as a to-do list, but as food for thought, leaving the decision if and how to incorporate that feedback to the team member. The leader should provide guidance but no hand-holding. Their purpose is to spur team members to reach their maximum potential. They succeed when they can sit on the sidelines cheering their team members on as each brings their tasks across the finish line. "We need to move away from leaders demonstrating a 'we colonize the world' attitude," Ian Roberts, CTO of Swiss-based hidden champion Bühler, a technology company, explained.[15]

Former AXA Switzerland CTMO Carola Wahl confirms that leaders are increasingly no longer know-how bearers or specialists who pass on information. Instead, they are personnel developers who make it their mission to lead by purpose and to coach their team members in solving ill-defined problems so they can exploit their full potential. She stresses that, "today, we still see many leaders that are good at, and focus on, scaling efficiency. They are the people who have all the answers in any given situation. Instead, we need to change to leaders who have the most inspiring and thought-provoking questions and can admit when they don't have the answers."[16]

Thorsten Lampe even goes so far as to say, "Classic top-down leadership models are outdated. We see leaders as servants who create a safe space for employees to perform at their best." Lampe is the CEO of Asellion, a Dutch-based e-platform for chemicals. Asellion fully spun off from its former holding company, material sciences conglomerate Covestro, where it started out as a corporate venture. Lampe admits they have even experimented with such alternative organizational models as Holacracy, where authority and decision-making are distributed to self-organizing teams, making leaders obsolete.[17]

Whether you go so far as to completely abolish the leadership position or you assume a more sparring partner type role, the importance of feedback in a digital transformation leadership context cannot be overemphasized.

Inspire and empower employees

To act like an entrepreneur. To think like an owner. To take initiative. To decentralize decision making. To radically innovate. To follow a common vision. To dedicate themselves to a shared purpose. To pursue a joint cause.

When leaders are sparring partners to their team members, they provide guidance when and where needed. The rest of the equation only works, though, if they are then willing to relinquish control and motivate team members to venture outside their comfort zones when pursuing digital transformation projects. Leaders need to fully embrace delegating their decision-making authority to their team members. Only through empowerment can they make sure team members reach their full potential (which, as a sparring partner, should be their goal). They must create a safe space for them to experiment and pursue their own hunches, to make decisions without prior approval, and to demonstrate ownership of their digital transformation work packages. In fact, leaders need to turn their teams into mini-entrepreneurial (or intrapreneurial) squads, so their own job moves away from managing the business and more toward managing people. After all, developing a new digital business has much in common with developing any standalone business from scratch, aka founding a start-up. Motivating employees also has a lot do with creating a vision for the digital future and to translate a strategic course of action the team can work on. Leaders must prove their ability to inspire others to gather around a joint vision.[18]

In the same breath, leaders should ask themselves, why do entrepreneurs pursue their ventures so eagerly? There's a whole host of benefits that come with being an entrepreneur. To motivate employees to become mini-entrepreneurs in the context of a digital transformation, leaders need to provide the necessary inspiration – and incentivization. Inspiration can come from the freedom to pursue your own ideas; incentivization often comes from more tangible things, such as equity compensation, bonuses, or prizes. Leaders first need to create an inspirational work environment, where they serve as beacons of motivation, inspiring employees with their own stories of successes and failures. Then comes an equally hard part – creating the hard-wired incentives to attract and retain the best talent. Think: an award for the "digital transformer of the month"; any other public recognition (like an intranet article) for a successful digital transformation project team; bonuses tied to achieving digital transformation KPIs; equity participation in the venture if it spins off; quick career progression, including more responsibility and higher compensation, and so on.

Markus Streckeisen is Chief Transformation Officer and head of Sales at SBB Cargo, a subsidiary of the Swiss federal railways, specializing in rail freight. He is convinced that inspirational leaders who know how to empower their employees is what it takes for a digital transformation. "A key requirement for digital transformation executives is that they know how to excite people, leading them by providing them room to maneuver freely rather than subjecting them to restrictions and rules."[19]

Welcome intelligent failures

One aspect of entrepreneurial (or intrapreneurial) life that founders have (much) first-hand experience of is failure. Empowering employees means creating a safe space for them. A safe space includes the ability to fail without being judged. Any conclusion needs to center around what to do better next time.

In the serial entrepreneurial world, failure is accepted and to some extent even encouraged. If you fail, you get up and you start over again. (Of course, there's some permissible criticism to serial entrepreneurs[20] but that often does not stop them from pursuing their ventures.[21]) In the established corporate world, if you fail, you may have a hard time recovering. John Sculley, Apple's CEO, initially hired and then in 1993 culled Steve Jobs, who had hired him. He also made a number of other bad decisions before Apple eventually forced him out, overturning many of his previous decisions, including hiring Jobs back. Kay Withmore orchestrated the downfall of Eastman Kodak. Former CEO of Sun Microsystems, Jonathan Schwartz, derailed the company to a point where it had to be acquired by Oracle. Were these inherently bad leaders? Probably not. Were they given a second chance after previous failures? Definitely not. On the other hand, was LinkedIn Reid Hoffman's first venture? Was Twitter Evan Williams's first start-up? And was Amazon Jeff Bezos's first business idea? Nope, nope, and nope. If failure was as accepted in the established corporate world as it is in the entrepreneurial realm, you would likely still see Jonathan Schwartz and friends around. The point is: failure in a digital transformation context needs to lose its bad overtone. Only when failure is accepted are employees empowered to pursue their digital transformation projects. "Failure is just a part of the process. If a project dies, it doesn't mean you have personally failed. It just means next time something should be done differently," Martin Watzlawek says. Watzlawek is in charge of strategy and innovation at the Swiss-German polymer business REHAU.[22] He would probably agree with Samuel Beckett's much-known wise saying: Try again. Fail again. Fail better.

Gisbert Rühl, CEO of Klöckner & Co, the German steel distributor, would agree. He posits that leaders and entire organizations need to change how they deal with failure. An open failure culture needs to be promoted, and leaders need to demonstrate where and when a failure is okay. "That's a tough nut to crack, particularly in a business steeped in tradition. To drive your career forward, the number-one mantra has always been to avoid mistakes – not even so much to do things well, but to avoid mistakes. Doing nine things well and making one mistake has traditionally had more repercussions than doing ten things half right."

To make failing the new norm among leaders, Klöckner & Co now orchestrate "Failure Nights," which enjoy great popularity. Even members of the board get up in front of a large audience and admit "I committed a terrible blunder this week, and I'd like to talk to you about it." This has made all the difference for Klöckner & Co leaders.[23]

Onur Erdogan, former general manager at Estée Lauder, chimes in, saying, "You not only have to give people the freedom and the tools to be successful, but you also need to tell them what you're expecting. And if you want people to be bold and take risks, you need to encourage this boldness. You have to celebrate even failures. You have to tell people 'It's great that you failed. Tell me what you learned and now keep going.'"[24]

Be pragmatic

As repeatedly stated, digital transformations usually do not fail for a lack of ideas or a lack of strategy but for a lack of implementation capabilities. These include the execution skills leaders need to bring to the table, including their pragmatism when making decisions as well as clarity when communicating them.

"It's one thing to inspire people; it's a completely different thing to drive them to act and to finish what has been started," Markus Streckeisen, CTO and head of Sales at the Swiss rail freight operator SBB Cargo, says.[25] Martin Watzlawek of REHAU adds that it takes leaders who are prepared to make the right decisions quickly, who don't hesitate and waste time. It's not necessary to turn every decision into a committee discussion; instead capable leaders need to evaluate situations and determine what is to be done next.[26] Similarly, Otto Preiss, of ABB Digital, agrees that it's necessary for digital leaders to know not just what to do, but how to do it, and to be pragmatic in pursuing the right things.[27]

This does not mean leaders make all decisions blindly. They should remain true to the principle of empowering their team members, but when needed give purposeful input and not shy away from making swift decisions.

Trust in the power of networks

Networks, in this context, has two meanings. One, leaders need to be willing to let go of hierarchies to solve problems. Escalating issues as the go-to problem-solving approach no longer reaps the aspired results.

Raphael Dölker, co-head of the Digital Office at EnBW, a large German utilities company, says there are still areas of the business where traditional hierarchical leadership is best suited (1st S-curve operations). "These include our power plant operations and our grid operations. This is standard business for us, with classic processes where a hierarchical organization is best suited. But in an environment where it's unclear what everybody should be doing the next day, it takes a different leadership model where responsibility is more distributed across a network of people. For our new ventures or in product development, it takes that trust in the network."[28]

The second meaning of *network* encompasses external partnerships and the wider ecosystem a company finds itself part of. Inward orientation is a thing of the past or, if it isn't, it's a dangerous pitfall. What is needed is the openness for an impetus to come from the outside world.

"The best digital ideas, the most interesting and promising digital transformation initiatives often do not emerge from within the organization, but from the ecosystem around. We need leaders who have not spent their entire adult lives working at the same company and drawing on 30 years of uninterrupted experience doing similar things. To drive innovation and digital transformation, it takes leaders who have experience in other companies, industries, and countries. Leaders who know the world is larger than a single company. Leaders who bring in a network and draw inspiration from their network to solve problems differently," Martin Watzlawek of REHAU explains.[29]

Demonstrate emotional intelligence

That EQ (emotional intelligence) trumps IQ is something we have long known to be true in many situations. It also proves to be true in a digital transformation leadership context. To be a leader whom team members want to emulate, empathy and being able to slip into someone else's shoes for a while are key. A certain degree of inward-orientation is also necessary. Digital transformation leaders need to be beacons of self-reflection, able to look at past and future from a bird's-view perspective. Falk Bothe, director of the Digital Transformation Office at Volkswagen, says digital transformation leaders need to be human temperature sensors, assessing what is being said between the lines even more than what is written on paper.[30]

Digital transformation is an intricate topic. Often it is met with distrust and suspicion, many people assuming their jobs are at stake. Sensing this, understanding people's motivations, and elegantly addressing their concerns with reason and sensitivity is a necessity for digital transformation leaders. Ridding them of fear that comes with hearing the words "digital transformation" or "digitization" alone is important to avoid antagonizing what should become strategic allies. This very point was stressed by many of our interview partners, all of whom agreed that leaders must demonstrate approachability and be happy talking to shop-floor employees and addressing their concerns.

Show adaptability

To exemplify that emotional intelligence outdoes IQ, that networks trump hierarchies, and that all the other previously mentioned dimensions are adopted as new norms, leaders themselves need to demonstrate willingness to change. They need to adopt these new standards, thus they should be happy venturing outside their comfort zones. Only if they do this can they ensure their teams' success and their own leadership progression in a digital transformation environment. That openness to change and willingness to adapt along with it is crucial.

Adaptability also means keeping up with the latest digital developments and showing a genuine interest in acquiring the necessary skills and functional expertise. While digital transformation leaders are not necessarily required to be expert C++ coders, they should have an interest in engaging in new topics and learning about them. Andreas Sturm, former President of the Board of Directors at Bank Cler, and his colleague Matthias Häne, former head of Strategy and Digital Transformation, are two proponents of this school of thought. In early

2018, Bank Cler launched Zak, Switzerland's first mobile bank. When assembling their leadership team, Sturm and Häne made sure to evaluate for willingness to learn. "Some aspects of hard knowledge, specific to the relevant leadership position, are simply a prerequisite. But there are many people who would be able to contribute these hard skills. What sets a good digital transformation leader apart from others is their willingness to adapt to new leadership realities – be it openness to take risks, to share failures, to depart from hierarchic structures, to introduce a more cooperative rather than a command-and-control leadership style, to lead interdisciplinary teams in an agile fashion. Even if they don't already bring a lot of experience in this realm, leaders at least need to be able to credibly demonstrate that adaptability."[31] Or as Kurt Straub, a senior executive at luxury hotel chain Hyatt International, puts it, "We need tech-embracing leaders. Ideally, they are already tech-savvy. But if not, they need to be able to say: okay, so this is a tool or a way of working I'm not used to but I'm happy to learn about it."[32]

Lead by example and walk the talk

All of the above characteristics are worth nothing if not demonstrated in real life. Digital transformation leaders (of all three leader types) need to show that what they ask of their team members (see the **People** chapter, Chapter 7) are standards that they hold themselves. For instance, when they encourage intelligent failures, this means that not only must their employees be okay to fail, but so must they. Ideally, they would even share their failures so as to make failing the new normal, like Gisbert Rühl in his Failure Nights. When leaders ask team members to be willing to learn, they themselves have to demonstrate the requisite openness to embrace change. Leaders must lead by example and walk that talk.

TX Group is the largest private media conglomerate in Switzerland. Chairman Pietro Supino makes no bones about holding his leadership team to the same standards as new hires when it comes to openness to change and willingness to learn. He expects that leaders act as authentic role models, and he only promotes those who do. One story astutely highlights this. When the board had to plan the succession for a top executive position, the best qualified internal candidate was invited to partake in a three-and-a-half-month coding course at Columbia University in New York City to beef up his digital knowledge. He genuinely welcomed this opportunity, took the course excitedly, and was promoted. Supino is convinced that this is the kind of attitude, adaptability, and authenticity it takes for leaders in a digital transformation environment to succeed.[33]

As you consider the elements of our attribute list, think about how these will apply to the three different types of leaders – your traditional 1st S-curve leader, your digitized 1st S-curve leader, and your 2nd S-curve leader. Digital transformation leaders need to be able to lead the business, others, and themselves (see Figure 6.3). The above attributes cover exactly these points: leading the business refers to making pragmatic decisions, trusting in networks, and welcoming intelligent failures to reach better outcomes, among other things; leading others covers being a sparring partner to your team, being able to speak the language of both S-curves, encouraging feedback, as well as inspiring, empowering, and incentivizing employees to put their best foot forward at work; and leading yourself refers to being self-reflective, emotionally intelligent leaders who demonstrate adaptability, lead by example, and walk the talk.

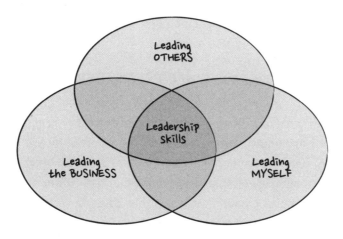

Figure 6.3 Leading the business, leading others, leading myself

Of course, becoming such a transformational leader must be a voluntary commitment if it is to succeed – though a little nudging and inspiration may help.

(Leaders themselves can also use a little inspiration.) What Falk Bothe of Volkswagen does is to offer a creative mix of learning formats, "For one, we have developed a simulation where participants can experience a digital transformation. Specifically, they are led through the development of the automotive industry from the early days of manufacturing and production lines to its current status." In addition to this business simulation game to draw leaders and employees alike into the world of digital transformation, Bothe introduced more maverick formats. "I recently hosted a series of seminars to which I invited a number of extravagant profiles. One day, we had a brain researcher visit us to give a talk about why our brains are wired the way they are and what we can do to change our habits and inclinations. Then we had a magician and a hypnotist over who demonstrated that the only barriers we have are mental barriers and that the mind determines reality. We also had a violinist visit us who had a very different approach to strategy development." Such events are meant to calmly nudge people to leave their comfort zones. But, importantly, participation is optional. These formats are only useful to leaders who are intrinsically motivated to engage. While it's crucial to offer these events and to make them accessible to everyone, leaders at least have to contribute their own motivation to partake. "Or else there's no point in them participating to begin with," Bothe concludes.[34]

GO SHOPPING FOR YOUR PREFERRED LEADERS

Now that you know what to look for, the question is, where do you get those leaders from? The options are binary: internal sourcing or external hiring. You will see these – and more – options reemerge in the **People** chapter (Chapter 7). But staffing digital transformation leadership positions is a markedly different undertaking than staffing digital transformation team member roles for at least two reasons. One, your leaders are your load-bearing walls, so having each of them "tick all the boxes" is of utmost importance for the stablity of the whole digital transformation construct. (This is also the reason why some of the options for filling positions are only applicable to team members and not leaders.) And two, the composition of your digital transformation leadership team – the percentage split of internal versus external leaders – will be different from the composition of your workforce.

As far as leaders are concerned, the mix will be skewed toward internal sourcing over external hiring for three primary reasons. The first is practical in nature – scarcity. Compared with the number of digital transformation leaders needed, the existing market is quite limited. Demand way exceeds supply. This makes it an uneven playing field, to the detriment of employers who are often faced with a limited selection. Slim pickings, in other words. The second reason is also practical in nature – speed of availability. Typically, internal leaders are more quickly available than new hires whose previous contracts may have included exclusivity clauses, in which case they are unable to work for a competitor for a while, often half a year or more. Even if there is no exclusivity clause, there is usually a notice period and the added time factor associated with (potentially) relocating. The third reason is moral in nature – responsibility vis-à-vis your existing leaders. You are not going to turn your existing leaders adrift without having given them a chance to transform themselves into digital transformation leaders. Many have served the organization for many years so it's only fair the organization gives them a shot at proving themselves.

Let's now examine internal sourcing and external hiring to see how you best go about them (see Figure 6.4).

Figure 6.4 Sources for digital transformation leaders

Building leaders internally

Turning existing leaders into digital transformation leaders is no minor feat. Your upper echelons are not the real challenge here. Having a capable CDO or a supportive CEO is the least of your worries. The real gauntlet is evangelizing your middle managers to jump on board with the digital transformation.

❝Buy-in from the c-suite is a necessary precondition. But it's not sufficient.❞

Uli Huener, Chief Innovation Officer, EnBW[35]

❝The greatest resistance for a hierarchical organization like ours comes from middle management. In order to break this resistance, you have to find ambassadors within the organization. They are middle managers who have enough capacity and find an interest in supporting the transformation. I think that the role of the ambassadors, who will reach out to the top management and become the voices of the transformation, is essential.❞

Jean-Charles Deconninck, President of the Board of Directors, Generix Group[36]

The CDO of the large discount retailer points out, "Leaders on middle and lower management ranks will experience the most marked change in the course of a digital transformation. The board or top management will not have to switch over to agile ways of working, or maybe only to a very limited extent. But the ones whose daily worklife will change fundamentally and who must adapt to such new realities are mid- and lower-level managers. It is vital to properly onboard these leaders and to prepare them for a new way of leading."[37]

Setting up leadership campuses to train middle managers, often over two or more years, is one way of imparting knowledge. At Bosch this meant training all executives, including board members, as well as senior and middle management over three years in how to be a transformational leader in a VUCA world. External experts moderated many of these workshops, which were designed to be interactive to engage leaders and get everyone to contribute. Participants were also invited to engage in self-reflection after these workshops. Eventually, formal feedback processes were adapted to reflect the focus on transformational leadership, with executives getting 360-degree feedback.[38]

That knowledge alone does not suffice is something that Mercedes Benz also realizes. "To make sure our leaders are best prepared for the digital transformation journey ahead, we trust in experiential learning," explain Mercedes-Benz Bank Chairman of the Management Board Benedikt Schell and CTO Tom Schneider. "Sitting in SCRUM meetings, shadowing a team when they work on a Kanban board, getting to know UX/UI designers are, in our opinion, crucial for future digital transformation leaders."[39]

Automotive supplier ElringKlinger trusts in yet another tool – reverse shadowing. This allows leaders to shadow younger, more digitally astute colleagues in how they go about employing digital solutions. This is an optional offer for leaders; the ones who really want to "become more digital" take advantage.[40]

The lesson is that traditional executive education will not do the trick anymore. Luckily there is a host of providers vying for Chief Learning Officers' corporate training budgets. They include business schools with open programs, business schools with customized programs, strategic consultancies, human resources consultancies, corporate universities, and remote personalized learning platforms. MOOCs (massive open online courses) and training providers such as Udacity and Coursera may ring a bell. Such digital solutions make it easy to deliver training value efficiently. As a result, the Personal Learning Cloud (PLC) is on the rise.[41] When determining how to train your digital transformation leaders, consider incorporating platforms that provide interactive content online, paired with the aforementioned on-the-job learning, be it in the form of reverse shadowing or similar.

Recruiting leaders externally

For the leaders you intend to recruit externally, it's a seller's market. This means you will battle for the best talent on the market. Demand is huge for several leader profiles: one, executives with a proven track record in digitally transforming legacy companies; two, executives coming from a digital pure-player background; and three, entrepreneurs. The last are particularly evasive and hard to get a hold of because they don't often look for a new position to begin with (almost never openly and seldom proactively). That makes them all the more sought after. For all three categories, bring your poaching A-game.

The competition for these three types of leaders is tough, and the pool is even shrinking because, as Korn Ferry explains, there is a growing temptation for managers with ten or more years of experience in the digital field to move into plural careers early on – that is, assuming several nonexecutive board positions, responding to the clamor made by board of independent directors with digital experience.[42]

If you do manage to snag leadership talent, you will need to put together a highly compelling offer package. This may include such perks as equity participation, like restricted stock units and stock options; a signing bonus; a relocation bonus or executive housing support, plus potentially a child-care package; other performance-based bonuses and incentive plans; potentially ("Silicon Valley–feel") perks, such as free food, gym access, and the like; and several softer factors related to job design, such as flexible work schedules (both time- and location-wise) and a reasonable amount of vacation days (particularly relevant in non-European countries where a default of 20, 25, or more vacation days a year is usually unheard of). The extent to which this is necessary, of course, depends on the leadership level you are hiring for.[43] But across all leadership levels one thing will remain true: you get what you pay for.

MANAGE THE LEADERSHIP TENSION BETWEEN THE 1ST AND 2ND S-CURVE

Once you have sourced your 2nd S-curve leaders, you need to ensure a functioning link with your 1st S-curve leaders because your very goal is to avoid silos and to create buy-in for the transformation from everyone in the firm. Working hand in hand is the key to success. The very definition of a digital transformation is digitizing the core while establishing a new digital business – and that can only be achieved if leaders on both sides are acting in concert and pulling together.

The following three examples illustrate that bridging the gap between leaders is a function of the organizational setup for the transformation. Each example outlines different instruments and approaches to bridge the gap between 1st and 2nd S-curve leaders.

ABB
· · · · ·

The Swiss-Swedish enterprise pursues efforts on both the 1st and 2nd S-curve. Its 1st S-curve portfolio includes any non-digital and digitally enabled products (for example, machinery like robots or drives for motors – it is a hardware product but at its core needs software to function). The 2nd S-curve portfolio spans a variety of software solutions, which include asset management, predictive maintenance, and lifetime extension solutions.

While such new digital business models qualify as 2nd S-curve efforts, their undertaking rests with the relevant business unit, arguably a 1st S-curve unit. The central digital team, however, supports the business unit, and does the same for all other digital endeavors. One example of support and momentum creation is the digital lighthouse projects, initiated by the relevant business unit, which also staffs that project while the funding is shared among the central digital unit and the business. The business units themselves state what they can best use the central digital unit for (for example, how to think about digital business models, how to go about strategic customer engagement, and so forth). Eventually a scaling-versus-no-scaling decision is made. If the decision is pro-scaling, the central team typically leaves, and the business unit takes over and runs the remainder of the project with regular project management and governance.

The exchange between 1st and 2nd S-curve is seamlessly orchestrated thanks to the organizational design of business units pursuing a venture in tandem with the digital team. But it is also thanks to a close leadership exchange.

Before launching lighthouse projects, every business unit had to set up a digital strategy. This happened in close alignment with the central team. Various levers of continuous communication are in place, among them so-called monthly inter-lock meetings, where the central digital leadership teams meet the business unit heads and key members of their management team to discuss progress and give feedback. This continuous exchange helps both – business unit heads can get feedback and brainstorm jointly on how to overcome barriers while the central digital team keeps an overview of how the business units are progressing, even and especially outside the lighthouse projects they have visibility over.[44]

Having BU heads develop their BU's digital strategy jointly with the CDO is a strong lever for ensuring transparency during the planning stage. Similarly, progress check-ins help sustain that level of transparency during implementation stages. If your organization is receptive toward a setup model similar to ABB's, consider formalizing leadership exchanges through joint strategy formulation and regular progress updates.

EnBW
......

The digital transformation setup of this German utilities company features a clear distinction between 1st and 2nd S-curves, led by two individuals who are in constant exchange with each other but who run quite separate efforts.

Uli Huener is EnBW's Chief Innovation Officer, in charge of disruptive new (digital) business models. These models are developed not as part of the core organization but in a relatively autonomous space, physically separated (in an "innovation campus") and processually detached from the parent company. Many eventually spin off completely as separate start-ups. Meanwhile Raphael Dölker is co-head of the Digital Office, which is the umbrella term for EnBW's efforts to sensitize the core and its traditional business units for how they may benefit from and can integrate digitization in their business model. The Digital Office is not a central unit but serves as a digital accelerator for the core, similar to ABB's central digital team.

Huener and Dölker facilitate frequent exchanges with one another, and they do more and more events together (like hosting joint hackathons). Originally, their exchange was more event-driven, but gradually it is becoming more formalized. While formalizing their discussions is a positive development, they want to consciously avoid introducing bureaucracy that would hamper the immediacy of the exchange.[45]

Though similar to ABB in function, the leadership exchange approach taken by EnBW is different. They cooperate across the S-curves by hosting joint events. Covestro uses yet another approach, due to its differing digital transformation setup.

COVESTRO

Material sciences company Covestro made a conscious decision against establishing a separate digital unit, either for the 1st or for the 2nd S-curve, for fear it would be hard to integrate and scale results and to keep them connected. Instead, the digitization of the traditional business happens directly in the core organization and new business models – at least during their incubation period – are developed in the corporate area, under Hermann Bach, head of Innovation Management & Commercial Services. Once the corporate venture is ready to be spun off and if the business model necessitates a separation from the core, it is separated from Covestro. An example case is Asellion, an e-commerce platform for the chemical industry. The idea for the business initiated in 2016 within Covestro and it is now a standalone subsidiary based in the Netherlands.

Thorsten Lampe heads Asellion and talks about how it manages the interaction with the parent Covestro and how he orchestrates a leadership exchange: "Once we spun off from Covestro, we were met with sentiments revolving around 'those guys no longer belong to us – they do their own thing, they even have their own name.' Then it didn't even matter anymore that we developed the name with Covestro trademark experts and that Covestro has a 100% stake in us. As soon as we were out, we felt a 'not invented here' backlash from the core – including leaders in the core – despite the fact that we were indeed invented there. What helped us overcome this was a lot of communication with leaders in the core organization. The communication didn't happen as a push whereby we provided transparency on what we do. Instead, we reached out in a maximum friendly, pleasant way to understand their pain points and how we can help them, how we can deliver value to them. Our platform actually does deliver a lot of value so convincing them with content was one way to build the trust needed to establish an ongoing dialog. In addition, we also made sure to institutionalize the exchange, where possible – for example, by setting up Slack channels to be able to easily converse with relevant decision makers on the Covestro side."

What helped Asellion leaders strengthen the connection to the core was an empathic, proactive dialog, clearing away any reservations vis-à-vis e-commerce and outlining the concrete value-add for the core business from the newly spun off digital business.[46]

If your organizational setup is such that the digital venture is already fully separated and standalone, the not-invented-here syndrome can kick in. To overcome the divide, empathy and patience are key. Discussions between 2nd S-curve leaders and their 1st S-curve counterparts may be necessary. It may be particularly helpful not to formalize these exchanges but to let them mature over time, with no pressure. The goal needs to be to de-alienate the 1st S-curve, which can be done outlining the value-adding aspects of the 2nd S-curve to the 1st S-curve, as Lampe did.

GET MOVING TO AVOID THE DINOSAUR FATE

When you think about assembling your digital transformation leadership team, make sure to keep these best practices in mind:

- Source your digital transformation leaders mostly internally:
  - Make sure to provide ample training and (reverse) mentoring opportunities to your internally sourced leaders, potentially as part of institutionalized leadership campuses.
  - For the leaders whom you do want to source externally, make sure to put together a compelling compensation package for them, potentially including incentive plans, equity participation, signing bonuses, relocation bonuses, and similar.

- When sourcing digital transformation leaders, regardless of where from, test for their ability to lead the business, lead others, and lead themselves, including some key leadership attributes:
  - Have them demonstrate that they can lead authentically across both S-curves (for example, have them explain in their own words why both matter for the continued success of the company).
  - Have them explain how they plan to lead their teams; make sure to test for the kind of leadership style they would employ (directive/boss-like versus empowering/coach-like) by giving them hypothetical scenarios they need to resolve.
  - Have them lay out in detail how they plan to inspire, empower, and incentivize their teams to act like entrepreneurs.
  - Have them exemplify situations where they themselves have demonstrated openness to admitting failures and willingness to adapt and learn, and ask them how they would create a risk-free environment for their team members where this is possible.

- Orchestrate a regular exchange between 1st and 2nd S-curve digital leaders so as to ensure maximum transparency over what the respective other is doing, keeping in mind that the exact setup of this will depend on your organizational setup :
  — Irrespective of your organizational setup, ensure a collaborative, non-judgmental environment in the leadership exchange (avoid a 1st-versus-2nd-S-curve mentality and focus instead on cross-fertilization).

 GET INSPIRED (BY CAR TIRES)

MICHELIN
. . . .

You may know the tires. You may know the restaurant guide. You most likely know the chubby, friendly looking Michelin Man. You may not yet know Eric Chaniot – the Chief Digital Officer of infamous French tire manufacturer Michelin.

When tasked with assembling his digital transformation team, it was of utmost importance for Chaniot to keep his digital squad as nimble and lean as possible. He leads the team as CDO. There is one layer of his direct reports – the digital transformation leaders. Beyond that there's only their direct reports – the digital transformation team members. This ensures minimum red tape and maximum agility.

"Sixty or seventy percent of my direct reports were recruited from within Michelin. There are some exceptions, of course – like our Chief Digital Architect came from Salesforce, our Chief Data Officer from GE. But the majority have a long Michelin background. My direct reports held very senior positions before joining my team – just under executive level," Chaniot explains. He trusts that their great network and excellent reputation within Michelin makes them bridge builders, ensuring buy-in from the core business for what the digital transformation team does. "These are very good leaders but, to be fair, they needed to adopt a new leadership style, given the kind of mode we operate in. It's almost like they are now working in a new era. To get to that point, they got trained and were mentored. But most importantly, I always kept an open dialog between them and myself – I think this also helped the cause a lot. I bring the fresh external perspective and the expertise and experience in digital business building while they bring the knowledge about Michelin and a great network. We complement each other very well."

Overall, however, a solid 60 or 70% of his entire team, particularly driven by the layer below his direct reports, were recruited from external sources. These are digital natives who bring the functional knowledge and the experience with new ways of working. "Also, they don't see – or choose to ignore – the complexities of a large organization, which is exactly the kind of mindset needed for our digital transformation," he says.

This means Chaniot's team is comprised of influential, well-connected executives from the holding company, experienced practitioners hired from outside the holding, and specialists who bring the requisite functional knowledge. Freedom to source that talent as he saw fit was important for him to be able to assemble the best team possible.

Chaniot makes sure to point out the role of the setup. "Sometimes you can hire or build all the right leaders and you are still doomed to fail because the setup didn't empower you and your team enough. Then it turns out it's not a question of how smart you are or how apt you are as a digital transformation leader. It's just a question of the setup. That's why I love reporting directly to the global CEO. No one ever tells me 'that's impossible.'"[47]

KEY TAKEAWAYS:

- **Focus on internal recruiting for your leadership positions** – These proven executives' reputation and network might just work wonders; add to the mix experienced practitioners, specialists, and potentially past entrepreneurs.

- **Keep your leadership team close together** – Avoid excessive hierarchies and ensure an open dialog between the different types of digital transformation leaders across the two S-curves (especially when they are sourced internally).

- **Setup is key** – Make sure digital transformation leaders have as direct access to the CEO as possible.

chapter 7

PEOPLE: WHAT TO LOOK FOR IN TALENT AND HOW TO DEVELOP THE WORKFORCE OF THE FUTURE

This chapter refers to the non-load-bearing walls of your digital transformation house. It does not mean they are not a crucial asset; people are most certainly a success factor for a digital transformation. It just means that the leadership load rests with the leaders from the previous chapter. In this chapter, we talk about what types of digital transformation team members there are, and the attributes they should bring to the table. We include a section on how talent can be sourced or built. Finally, we detail how 1st and 2nd S-curve team members can stay closely connected to ensure maximum alignment between the two S-curves (see Figure 7.1).

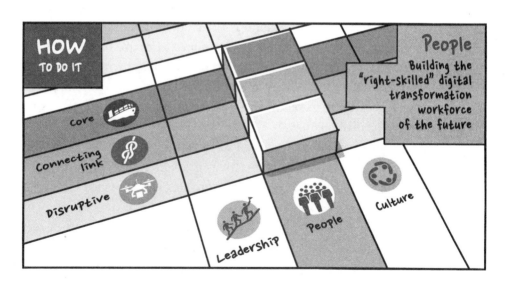

Figure 7.1 Key visual with focus on How/People

REALIZE THE PEOPLE CHALLENGES YOUR COMPANY MUST TACKLE

The bulk of any digital transformation team will be practitioners in non-leadership roles. You are faced with no small task when it comes to assembling your digital transformation team. Several series of questions should be top of mind.

One, what types of people does it take on the 1st versus the 2nd S-curve? Different attributes matter depending on a 1st or 2nd S-curve initiative. How can you avoid a dichotomy of two types, particularly a long-lasting dichotomy of winners versus losers? The "winners" being those apt for a digital transformation (the digitization of the 1st S-curve and/or the build-up of the 2nd S-curve); the "losers" being those that have only traditional 1st S-curve competencies.

Two, what is the perfect mix of externally versus internally sourced talent, if there is any at all? What kind of internal training programs best prepare current workers for the digital transformation future? How can you transform people who do not have the requisite competencies for a digital transformation? How can employees on the 1st S-curve even be motivated toward digital transformation initiatives, where new rules of the game apply?

Three, for external talent, how are they identified and hired (potentially poached) or contracted? What new approaches are necessary to seek out and attract talent? When the 2nd S-curve eventually turns into a 1st S-curve, how can you make sure this new talent is not lost but keeps pursuing a new business that has exited the exciting beginning stages and is on the verge of turning into an established business?

Four, once talent has been attracted, how are they retained? For externally and internally sourced talent, providing long-term career options with development potential is key. To transport this message to employees, showcasing attractive career options on both S-curves is necessary.

Finally, for the two S-curves and their respective talent to remain closely linked and not turn into silos, a proper exchange must be facilitated. How can this be arranged such that people from both sides have mutual trust in and respect for each other?

PEOPLE, TOO, MAKE OR BREAK THE DIGITAL TRANSFORMATION DEAL

The critical element to a digital transformation is the human element. The leader of the flock is only one part of the equation – the flock itself is a whole other story. Even if the leader has done everything right, this does not guarantee success. A leader also must pick the right people for the transformation. Without these willing and able employees, companies will struggle to benefit from the latest technological advances and new methodological approaches.

Companies have started vying for the best talent. A severe shortfall of skilled digital talent is expected worldwide.[1] The question then is, how can this be avoided, and what do companies need to do specifically to prevent this from happening?

A large part of the answer (but, to be fair, also of the root cause) surely lies in skills. Lacking requisite skills ranks among the top barriers to digital transformations; the most functional expertise gaps reside in artificial intelligence, blockchain, IoT, and big data analytics. Only 15% of companies say they have enough staff with the needed skills for their digital transformation today.[2]

The OECD agrees. Their "Skills for a Digital World" report highlights that to seize the opportunities that digital technologies and digitization bring with them, skills to make meaningful use of these technologies first need to be developed.[3] Useful technology exists to respond to many of our most pressing business needs, and it takes qualified people to operate such technologies before their value can be translated into real-life business value. The OECD sees three particular areas of skills as paramount to taking that step: specialist digital skills (for example, skills to develop and program new applications); generic digital skills (for example, skills to use new technologies for professional purposes); and complementary digital skills (for example, skills to perform new tasks associated with new technologies). These digital skills along with higher-order thinking competencies, social, emotional, and select other skills are necessary to drive real value for employees, companies, and eventually sovereign states from digital technologies. This conclusion is also in line with findings of a McKinsey Global Institute study. It highlights that by 2030 the demand for technological skills will experience the most significant uptick, followed by social and emotional skills and higher cognitive skills. The conclusion is a call-for-action to companies, which need to change themselves and their workforce to accommodate these expected changes, as well as to other stakeholders, which can also play a role in preparing the workforce of the future.[4]

KNOW YOUR TALENT INSIDE AND OUT

Just as with leaders, there are also three types of digital transformation talent (see Figure 7.2). They are equally needed, and a winner–loser dichotomy should be avoided at all cost. It is a myth that it only takes cool, paleo-bar-eating hipsters to digitally transform a business. It also takes your more grounded and experienced colleagues to keep the shop running as others engage in the digital business–building side of things.

Figure 7.2 People types

Your traditional 1st S-curve talent

These are the colleagues doing the heavy 1st S-curve lifting. Their task is to squeeze the last ounce of efficiency out of the core business, milking its productivity. They do so in consultation with their managers – or, more realistically put, they do so as an outcome of their managers providing targets and directions. The main criterion for their career advancement is a strong record in doing exactly that – reaching or surpassing targets set by their superiors, which are almost exclusively tied to core business performance.

Despite them owning the traditional 1st S-curve, their work realities will not remain untouched. They must keep upgrading their skills to ensure they maintain the best-in-class skills in the core business. And their ways of working, including how they collaborate with others, will also be affected (see the **Culture** chapter, Chapter 8).

Your digitized 1st S-curve talent

These are the colleagues who either will undergo a transition from being traditional 1st S-curve talent to becoming digitized 1st S-curve talent or will be hired or contracted from external sources to aid in the digitization of the 1st S-curve. The latter will most definitely bring new perspectives to the organization – or at least the unit they operate in – and the former will need to adjust quickly to fundamental changes in the types of skills they need to put to use in their daily work, which in and of itself will change drastically.

Motivating traditional 1st S-curve employees to use their company's digital transformation as an opportunity for their own development and as a stepping–stone for their career advancement is easier said than done. Mercedes-Benz Bank executives Benedikt Schell and Tom Schneider realized they needed to show the benefits and opportunities of digitization and a clear vision of moving forward, rather than deliberating the "what-ifs" and fears of digitization. In a similar vein of thought, both Daimler and Mercedes-Benz Bank had undergone several transformations in the past and came out stronger than before every time. So why should they not be able to master the digital transformation this time around? Employees also needed to realize that change is omnipresent in society and an economy. Asking "What's in it for me?" helps realize how digital transformation contributes to employee development and how each can benefit from interesting new responsibilities.[5]

One benefit is through training, upskilling people in new technologies and preparing them for a world of automation. To be eligible to partake in trainings, employees should be able to reference strong performance in their core jobs. The most marked changes will not be felt by customer service representatives but by the IT and R&D departments, whose roles will shift fundamentally from being peripheral to being vitally central in nature.

Your 2nd S-curve talent

For this category, learning new skills and competencies is key, as a good portion of people will be sourced internally. Being open to and eventually succeeding in applying the needed new skills, plus thriving in a demanding digital business–building environment that differs from what they are used to, is a lot to ask of these employees. It involves high risk but major payoffs, including much visibility by senior management and the associated shot at accelerated career progression.

A significant share of new people will need to join from outside the firm to drive the change, throwing new personalities and characters into the mix. Such talent must be presented with attractive career opportunities along the full spectrum of 2nd S-curve efforts and an environment they can be sure to thrive in.

While these job profiles may sound "fancier" than 1st S-curve positions, "there is no difference in value attached to 2nd S-curve talent as compared with 1st S-curve talent," says Claus Fleischer, CEO of Bosch eBike Systems. Founded in 2009 as a standalone entity embedded in the Bosch Group, the large automotive supplier with over 400,000 employees, Bosch eBike Systems is a leading manufacturer of eBike systems in the bicycle industry. Fleischer is convinced that "the realities of people on these two S-curves differ enormously. There is a different time-to-market. Customers are served differently. Of course, technologies are different, but it's so much more than that – business model, marketing, sales. These differences predispose different kinds of people to best address them. Understanding among both groups needs to be created for the respective other. The embedded world needs the digital world as much as the digital world needs the embedded world. Any organization needs 1st S-curve teams as much as it needs 2nd S-curve teams."[6]

While the three talent groups differ significantly, some aspects matter to all of them. Career development is one. With the increasing pace of change facing organizations, their employees, too, need to develop themselves further – and not only laterally (learning new skills) but horizontally (assuming more responsibilities). Particularly, the talent affected by digital transformation the most will want to (and need to) advance, even in a networked (agile) organization. Just because hierarchies are loose in 2nd S-curve businesses does not mean that people do not want to progress. For many, future opportunities are a reason to join a given employer. That's why companies have to be über-clear in emphasizing career progression, identifying specific options, paths, and support provided.

While upward progression is top-of-mind for many people – especially Gen Y and Gen Z – lateral movements, including switching from a 1st S-curve to a 2nd S-curve role, are also of interest. Showcasing that a firm can be a long-term home and that internal opportunities for learning new skills in new roles abound is a must for firms. Both for upward progression and for lateral moves, real-life testimonials from the organization best help to illustrate the validity of company claims.

This is very much in line with overall employee expectations, especially those of the younger generations. The ability to plan a long-term professional future, support in learning new skills, and flexibility in work schemes (for example, through remote working and freelance work) are key, if employers want to appeal to younger generations.[7] All are requirements in a digital transformation workplace.

While this is what people want, what attributes and attitudes, skills, and competencies do digital transformation talent need to bring to the table?

 GO SHOPPING FOR YOUR PREFERRED PEOPLE ATTRIBUTES

People and leaders need to walk hand in hand if they are to effectively address their organization's digital transformation. For the people of a digital transformation to be successful (and to even fit into the team), they need to accept the realities their leaders create for them (see the **Leadership** chapter, Chapter 6).

A sizeable share will happily do so because they have spent the majority of their professional lives in similar settings. (This is especially true of externally sourced 2nd S-curve talent.) But it's important to remember that those less familiar with the realities of a digital transformation need to accept these new realities just as much. (This is a hint at the internally sourced, formerly (traditional) 1st S-curve talent.) The ideal digital transformation team member is a hybrid of the two – the experience of a core business veteran paired with the attitude and skills of a digital business builder. The more of that type of employee you have, the luckier you should count yourself. Ultimately, all digital transformation team members have to get excited about the environment, including the realities of everyday work, their leaders create for them.

Because (desirable) 1st S-curve experience cannot be manufactured magically, let's consider the characteristics digital transformer talent can develop and demonstrate more readily.

Have courage

To accept the challenges posed by leaders. To stand up for your ideas when challenged. To dare to fail.

This makes intuitive sense if you accept the initial premise that staff have to respect the realities their leaders create. Leaders as sparring partners who empower their team members and support intelligent failures only works if employees are willing to take on difficult tasks assigned to them; if they are able to withstand when their leaders challenge their ideas; and if they are ready to fail without seeing it as a personal failure but using it as a springboard for learning.

Martin Watzlawek of polymer producer REHAU describes this trait as the "rebellious gene." "I need people who dare to think and do things differently," he exclaims. He wants a sound mix of people seeing things through but being willing to let go of them quickly if failure looms around the corner, not being married to the idea but realizing when to cut off money supply. The people for REHAU's innovation unit "Unlimited X" were often sourced externally. "We consciously made an effort to look for people who have worked in start-up environments before. We were also open to people from completely different industries. You can be daring in any industry, so if you've demonstrated this elsewhere, you can demonstrate this here, too." To make sure Unlimited X has the internal approval it deserves, especially when a good chunk of the team was recruited externally, the leader of the unit was recruited from within REHAU.[8]

The courage to venture into uncharted territory also matters to Carola Wahl, former CTMO of insurer AXA. "A transformation in and of itself is new, has never been there before. So, you need people who embrace the inherent uncertainty and make the right decisions even when they don't exactly know how things will develop. They need to be courageous enough to own the vagueness of the situation. And when they fail, they get up again."[9]

Be a self-starter

Take initiative. Drive your own ideas. See things through from conception to implementation. Step outside your comfort zone, learn new rules of the game, and adjust to ever-changing circumstances. Work independently, with minimal supervision.

We spoke with a former executive at a Nordic bank who said that this very requirement is a double-edged sword. "These kinds of people are exactly whom we need, but they are the furthest removed from our traditional DNA. We need hands-on self-starters who aren't afraid to make decisions on the spot," he mentioned. "One example was our in-house IT colleagues. These developers used to be told exactly what the aspired output was. They were given detailed instructions and the requirements were crystal clear. But in this new setting, they were expected to play an active part in finding the solution. However, they were not at all used to themselves chasing after what features were supposed to look like in the end," the former bank executive explains. In the end, some people intrinsically own their problems and are okay with being held accountable for them while others have a harder time adjusting. "It was a learning process for all involved. But no doubt, if we could have staffed exclusively those intrinsically motivated self-starters, that would have been roses, roses all the way."[10]

NOVARTIWS
. . . .

Novartis likes to refer to the self-starter, independent work attitude needed for digital transformation talent as "unbossed," a term adopted by their CEO, Vas Narasimhan. A supersized, eponymous neon sign flashes as we step into the Novartis headquarters in Basel, Switzerland. "We need naturally curious learners who have the courage to act like entrepreneurs," CDO Bertrand Bodson says as we overlook the River Rhine from one of the meeting rooms. "I give my team members the freedom to be self-starters, to employ the ways of working that they deem most suitable, to follow their instincts and lead the change themselves. There are, of course, some rules. And the burden of the digital transformation does not rest solely on one team member – the whole organization is responsible for bringing this to fruition. But I did hire my team precisely because I want to empower them to take initiative themselves."

Novartis, like many other pharma players, is astutely familiar with extensive drug development cycles that are anything but agile. "It still takes on average 12 years and US$2.5 billion to bring a drug to market, with a return on capital employed that has decreased from 10% to less than 3%. This is worrying. It means the usual way of doing things won't do the trick anymore. Instead we need to be intrinsically innovative," Bodson explains, hinting at the kind of people it takes in such an environment.[11]

In 2018, Novartis sold its 36.5% stake in its consumer health joint venture with GlaxoSmithKline to focus on expanding their footprint in transformational medicine and on becoming a digitally powered pharma leader.[12] This move was further underpinned in October 2019 by announcing it was going to start a multiyear alliance with Microsoft to transform how medicines are discovered, developed, and brought to market, leveraging data and AI in the newly founded Novartis AI Innovation Lab.[13] "Digital transformation is a crucial topic for us. For many of our drugs, adherence [the extent to which patients comply with the prescribed medication intake; authors' note] is 50%, excluding chronic diseases and cancer. Technology surely has the capacity to change things for the better. While we know this, it still takes people who actually make the change happen and bring the customer experience to a new level," Bodson points out. "We need solution-driven entrepreneurs, only we call them 'unbossed.' We empower them and give them a mandate. We are trying to get the whole organization to be more 'unbossed.'"[14]

Put the customer first

Customers are paramount to the digital strategy and the digital business model. They need to be at the forefront of conceptual thinking and employees' thinking. Putting their interests first is indispensable in a digital transformation context. Ultimately, you digitally transform to better satisfy (or anticipate) your customers' needs, or the whole transformation is in vain.

Carola Wahl, formerly of AXA Switzerland, swears by a customer-first attitude. "A commitment to achieving high NPS [Net Promoter Score – a metric to gauge the willingness of a firm's customers to recommend them; authors' note] is so important. We introduced this customer-centric dimension as part of our digital transformation, so this was virgin land for us. Getting people on board who had already internalized this mindset was key. We didn't shy away from looking for such people in other industries unrelated to insurance."[15]

BTPN
......

Digital bank Jenius could not agree more that people from nonfinancial industries sometimes bring more of the customer-orientation mindset needed for a digital transformation than industry insiders. Jenius is a 100% daughter of BTPN of Indonesia and the first digital bank in the country. BTPN's history lies in the pension business but their intention in the early 2010s was to extend into retail banking.

When it came to assembling the digital transformation team, senior leadership employed an industry-agnostic approach. For the leadership team, it mattered that they had some financial services experience. But for the digital transformation staff, that requirement was waived. In fact, about 70% of Jenius's headcount did not have a meaningful financial services background before joining. Instead, senior leadership made a conscious effort to recruit people from industries where customer experience was traditionally paramount, like the hospitality and retail sectors, whose primary goal is to provide a great customer experience when vacationing or shopping.

For a digital bank, customer experience equals in-app user experience. When customers are asked "What is Jenius?," they say, "The app." This means a lot of thinking needs to go into designing the best, most convenient customer journey possible. It's easiest to employ this customer centricity to everything you do when you already have a background in industries where this is common practice – or at least more widespread practice than in banking. In most countries, when you walk into a bank branch, your experience will be decidedly less pleasant than when you walk into a hotel or your favorite clothing store. Jenius wanted to meet that same standard. So, they said, if they want the best customer experience, they will need to hire from the most customer-centric sectors.[16]

The CCO of a luxury jewelry retailer we spoke with mentioned some other examples of a customer-first mindset: "Nike and Porsche, among other prestige brands, have really mastered customer centricity by involving customers early on in their product development. We need exactly this attitude and the corresponding people who bring a relentless focus on customers to the table."[17]

Bring the relevant (functional) skill set

Finally, besides soft factors revolving around a positive can-do attitude, an entrepreneurial mind, resilience to bounce back from failure, willingness to take risks, and a customer-first mindset, there is no way around contributing a set of hard skills (as in, functional expertise).

"While softer factors may be harder to influence and in the end are better determinants of how happy both the employee and the team will be, people are eventually also hired for the functional expertise they contribute. Actually, I should say, for the functional expertise that the digital transformation project needs them to contribute at that point in time," elaborates Mirco Mäder, former manager of mobility venture Kollibri. "If I had to choose between two equally qualified candidates, I would pick the one whose mindset fits better. But the qualification first needs to come from their specialized know-how."[18]

Across our interviews, we heard many different things about what specialized know-how is needed. Agile development, machine learning, AI, UX/UI design, design thinking, to name a few. Ultimately, it depends on the specifics of the digital transformation. Some of the studies discussed earlier have done some fine-grained analysis on exactly which skills will be in more demand, and most of this is perfectly in line with what we heard in our conversations. Basic and advanced digital skills, including programming skills across a variety of languages, are sought after today and will continue to experience a drastic increase in demand. Other technological skills that will experience stark increases are (big) data analysis as well as technological design skills (including engineering skills). In an environment where large datasets can be analyzed with ease, requisite brainpower is needed to make sense of this data, necessitating critical (and creative!) thinking, problem-solving, and decision-making skills, as well as analytic skills needed to process and interpret complex information. There is evidence for the increasingly important role of these hard and soft skills.[19]

GO SHOPPING FOR YOUR DIGITAL TRANSFORMATION WORKFORCE

Just as leaders are sourced internally and externally, so, too, are team member talent, but the spectrum of options becomes larger. We present another 2 × 2 matrix in Figure 7.3 that summarizes the four options of building your digital transformation workforce.

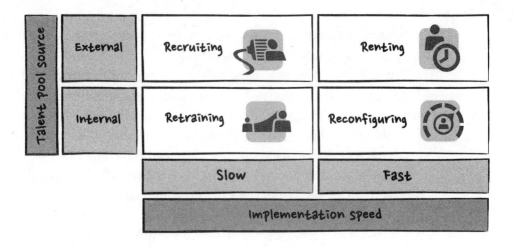

Figure 7.3 Sourcing digital transformation talent

Given that the volume of digital transformation staff needed is large, building your digital transformation workforce comes with a set of distinct challenges, like, how can you upskill headcount in the 4-, 5-, or (yes!) 6-digit area. Let's proceed one by one.

Retraining

Retraining refers to the practice of training current employees to develop their existing skills such that they can use these new or more advanced skills in a digital transformation context, where their previous role may have changed (see Figure 7.4). Such trainings can revolve around congeneric skills, those that are a natural extension of a person's existing job profile. An example would be helping traditional offline marketers acquire online marketing skills to run digital marketing campaigns. Expanding the skills portfolio of an offline marketer to include digital marketing skills is not a very far-fetched idea. However, skills taught as part of retraining programs can also be quite different from the ones people are used to for their jobs. Teaching an offline marketer how to code in Python to sit alongside website developers as they jointly digitize customer journeys is a less intuitive line of upskilling. No matter the type of skill conveyed, retraining is one of the foremost levers in building your digital transformation workforce.

Figure 7.4 Retraining

Currently, companies are more inclined toward skill-based staffing than the overall credentials of a candidate. This means if you bring the right soft and hard skills to the table, you are more likely to be put on a project than if you bring good references, big employer brands, or good grades. It is in this light that the crucial role of upgrading skills of existing employees should be seen.

Large-scale retraining programs are a considerable investment in employees – in both monetary terms for the employer and symbolic value for the employee. Many companies we spoke with have sent employees through retraining programs, realizing their value to employees and themselves.

NESTLÉ
·······

Vevey, Switzerland–based Nestlé is known for brands such as Nespresso, Kit Kat, Vittel, and many others, and has in excess of 300,000 employees worldwide. Imagine the effect a digital transformation has given this order of magnitude.

245

That in fact is Sebastien Szczepaniak's job. A former director at Amazon and Procter & Gamble, Szczepaniak is now Vice President of eBusiness at Nestlé. His job is to think through how the transformation of Nestlé's core can inform new business models. Of course, the repercussions of these strategic decisions manifest in changed job descriptions and ways of working, so Nestlé provides on-the-job trainings across "15 key competencies to win in digital." On-the-job training reflects new skills that cannot be taught in a single day and that bosses are no longer able to carry out in their support jobs. "When your boss can't help you out and a one-day training doesn't suffice, you need a more holistic approach," Szczepaniak argues. What they do is a market-based skills assessment. For each individual brand, they assess the maturity of the market and the sophistication of existing skills. For instance, people in the US division of pet food brand Purina have a higher digital maturity than the same brand in Argentina. Skill and training requirements will thus differ. Typically, every market defines and then homes in on five to seven of the 15 key competencies that their teams need upskilling in.

Relatedly, Nestlé has launched the Digital Academy – a platform that provides learning opportunities to over 60,000 employees. Staff learn basic digital skills and acquire expert knowledge or training in special-expertise areas, earning a certification at the end.

"And then there is also the Digital Acceleration Team, DAT for short," Szczepaniak continues. The DAT is an eight-month training program for Nestlé employees worldwide, 20 people each time. They meet in Vevey to learn digital transformation skills and then put them directly to use. Digital transformation at Nestlé is more than e-commerce and social media. It encompasses such topics as IoT, as Nestlé has a vested interest in understanding how IoT will affect the kitchen of the future and how they can best fit into that picture. Having acquired the requisite skills, the DAT members think through exactly such challenges.

While on-the-job training and the Digital Academy platform are meant to reach a large number of Nestlé employees, the DAT is geared toward a more exclusive group. At Nestlé, at least two roads lead to Rome.[20]

KLÖCKNER & CO
. . . .

When you think of steel, you don't necessarily think of a particularly digital-savvy workforce. Well, think again. Gisbert Rühl, CEO of Klöckner & Co, recognized early on that digitization would have a bearing on his entire staff, not only the executives leading the digital transformation. He instituted a program to educate all employees in digital-related topics.

Klöckner & Co's Digital Academy is based on the belief that digitization will affect all employees, including those who have spent their entire adult lives focusing on the traditional core of the business. Rühl considers it Klöckner & Co's responsibility to prepare staff for the digitization of the business and the changing requirements of their work environment and jobs. The call-to-action was clear ("upskill yourselves now") and the offer was enticing: unlimited, free retraining programs to be taken during work hours. In line with fast prototyping, the Digital Academy started out as an MVP but has meanwhile expanded to include a variety of learning paths, including certifications verifying employees' commitment to taking a full set of courses and passing an exam at the end.[21]

DEUTSCHE BAHN
. . . .

Germany's Deutsche Bahn is another unexpected candidate contending for the title of "digital skill builder." They have introduced a number of training formats to reskill both employees and leaders.

They first assess employees' current level of skill sophistication. The "Digital Self-Check" determines where an employee excels and where there's room for improvement. It doesn't stop there – the test is a platform that internal job offerings and corresponding skills profiles are fed into. Based on employees' input and performance in the test, they are presented with a list of recommended internal positions for which they would be suitable.

One learning opportunity on offer is the Intrapreneurship Program, aimed at Deutsche Bahn employees who have the intention to become entrepreneurs. Instead of losing them to the start-up world, they are trained in business model planning, market assessment, product design, and other entrepreneurially relevant areas. They can then pursue their ideas internally instead of having to leave the organization.

Another program is the "Digital Trainee Program." As an attempt to attract digital talent for the 1st S-curve, it is aimed at recent graduates who work on digitization projects in the core business to drive digitization and introduce a digital spirit into a traditional business from within. This brings with it learnings for the core organization, stemming from recent graduates' fresh ideas. And it provides learning for the recent graduates, who build up their credibility in the core business.

Finally, the "Digital Base Camp" is aimed at managers and employees alike (though only managers are required to attend). The program establishes connections to digital companies so participants can see for themselves what AI, design sprints, and other digital ways of working really look like. Says CDO Stefan Stroh, "Management and employees experience first-hand how agile methods, digital tools, and so forth work in a real-life setting. Not in a classic training room format but in a real lab. It's important they experience this in practice and not just in theory."[22]

As you consider instituting such large-scale retraining programs, how do you estimate how many people will be affected and what kind of training capacity you need to provide? A comprehensive strategic workforce planning exercise is the best instrument, management consulting firm BCG suggests. Core digital profiles need to be identified and the relevant skill set for each of them needs to be laid out. Then companies need to analyze their current and expected digital talent base, estimating the manpower and competencies needed for their digital transformation initiatives to yield a model forecasting skills demand, supply, and any gaps for each profile. Depending on where staffing gaps are the most pronounced, the need for action is the strongest and most pressing – action needs to be taken fast to have a shot at safeguarding digital transformation success.[23]

Recruiting

By recruiting (see Figure 7.5) we mean hiring employees long-term from external sources, including the open job market and competitors. Companies also can engage in acqui-hiring, the practice of acquiring companies in an effort to take over their talent. Recruiting is certainly one of the key levers to build your digital transformation workforce as it – like retraining – lends itself well to being applied to a large number of talents that need sourcing.

Recruiting

Figure 7.5 Recruiting

Hiring long-term employees from external sources is a big effort. It takes time and investments to get it just right. The timing factor comes from the fact that there are often months between advertising a position and someone actually starting the job. This is due to extensive time needed to advertise the position broadly, screen initial candidates, conduct interviews (potentially multiple times), determine contractual details, and negotiate a start date. In addition, there is often a month-notice period, putting off start dates by a significant stretch of time.

The investment factor comes from the costs associated with administering the entire process – posting ads in job forums, lodging for applicants, not to mention the internal costs of having HR colleagues handle all this. If you need to hire hundreds or thousands of people, you need to stock up on HR specialists also. This also points out one of the major challenges associated with hiring: there just may not be enough supply to fill your demand. If pressed to find talent, you may lower your sights, potentially leaving you dissatisfied with the performance of your new hires.

But if you get it right, rewards loom. Hiring new people sends positive signals to outsiders and potential candidates alike, underlining serious growth plans. Long-term hires bring a fresh perspective into the company, potentially reviving its corporate culture – much needed in a digital transformation setting.

Getting it right is not a walk in the park. You have to be creative to source the talent you really want. Incentivize existing employees for help finding suitable new talent. For instance, try roping in your existing employees for finding suitable new talent. This can be done by incentivizing employee referrals. When an employee recommends someone for a vacant position, you are more likely to end up with someone suitable because the employee will only refer people they see potential in, as they will only be rewarded if the referral is successfully hired. Plus, the candidate may be more naturally excited about the job, having been sold on it by their contact. If you as the employer want to assume a more active role in seeking out talent – particularly developer talent – explore source code repositories on sites that host community discussions among programmers. Consider making training resources available on your website to help candidates increase their skill levels in the skills you want them to bring. For instance, if you are looking for cybersecurity experts, offer cybersecurity training resources on your website, drawing knowledgeable practitioners to you, increasing your chances of being able to sneak in and secure them as talent. Plus, they will already bring a lot of the skills you need when hired.[24]

When looking to recruit digital transformation talent, make use of the vast array of digital tools available to aid in the process. Consider online gamified assessment systems, machine learning algorithms that improve with use, new data analytics to identify the best channels for hiring and the types of candidates to target. Automated CV screening can help avoid the cost of hiring executive search firms, prevent bad hiring decisions by turning a gut feeling into an analytical process, save time, and rule out unconscious biases in recruiting, thus fostering diversity.[25] While these technologies can optimize hiring processes in general, they are equally applicable for digital transformation talent.

Let's look at an example of how digital transformation talent can be recruited.

EISSMANN

Eissmann is headquartered in the quaint village of Bad Urach, Germany. Driving into a quiet valley tucked away in the Swabian Alps, you would not guess that this spa town's most prominent business is an automotive supplier whose executives are devoted to addressing how digital transformation affects some 5,000 employees worldwide.

Former CFO Norman Willich and director of IT and Business Services Alexander Maute describes their talent strategy: "Many of our employees have been working here for a good 10, 20, sometimes 30 years. What they expect – and what they excel at – is fundamentally different from what we need to deliver to a younger generation. But we depend on the younger generation and their fresh ideas for survival, just as we have an obligation to our tenured employees. So, we really need a mix of established employees and new, externally sourced talent. We'd be doomed if we didn't bring in people from the outside."

What they trust in to source this talent are partnerships with universities. "Several of our employees teach at various universities in the area," Maute says. This affords Eissmann to enter into cooperation with educational institutions to get access to young professionals and apprentices. They often recruit directly off campus.[26]

An inspiring example of large-scale recruiting awaits at the end of this chapter, so stay tuned.

As you recruit digital talent, you will be faced with competition between the two S-curves that are both vying for talent. Separated digital units or entities that focus on 2nd S-curve initiatives will likely find it easier to attract new digital talent. If the core business has a hard time attracting any talent, using the 2nd S-curve as a recruiting channel might be a viable option. Once the candidates are on the hook, it's easier to channel them to the core business. Imagine a situation where applicants are not an entirely good fit for the 2nd S-curve but may be for the core business. Rejecting such applicants would be negligent when the core is struggling to find talent. Of course, if the core business can't attract any talent at all, it makes sense to leverage talent across both S-curves. The disclaimer here, however, is that this should only happen on a non-permanent basis, for example, in the form of short-term job transfer or mutual projects.

Given that recruiting is one of your two biggest levers in building your digital transformation workforce (retraining is the other), you need to estimate the number of new recruits necessary. Make sure that your strategic workforce planning quantifies both retraining and recruiting demand. The next two categories, renting and reconfiguring, should of course also be included, though it's worth noting they will amount to smaller numbers.

Renting

Renting (see Figure 7.6) is Recruiting's little brother. In fact, it's his shorter-term brother. Mostly, it entails contracting workers for a confined amount of time or for an agreed-upon scope of work with a certain desired output. In other words, it means bringing in new blood for a limited time. If the terms "gig economy," "freelance work," or "contract work" pop in your head, you've hit the bull's-eye.

The advantages include the pace with which this can be done and the flexibility in deployment. Often, employment agencies, job centers, or staffing agencies can source candidates quickly, circumventing effortful and time-consuming hiring processes. Integration into the company is often easy, especially when work is project-based. While even entire functions can be outsourced, one must

Renting

Figure 7.6 Renting

not walk into the trap of assuming renting is equivalent to recruiting or retraining. Some staff can be contracted but it is a minority.

Several reasons make renting a supplementary option in building the workforce of the future. Long-term viability of a largely rented workforce is questionable. If companies intend to cover short-term needs, quickly available contractors and freelancers are a useful resource. For companies looking at a longer time horizon, wanting to build a lasting solution, insourcing may make sense. Employee motivation may also dwindle if a large-scale shift to a contractor-led strategy is undertaken – consider the morale of the few remaining full-time employees. Companies may also see their reputation wane. A contractor-led strategy gives negative signals to the job market and potential new recruits, who may perceive such companies unworthy of consideration. Knowledge retention will also suffer. After all, how well can institutional knowledge be built or retained in an organization if the majority of its workers are employed by another entity? In the same vein, a lack of succession planning is a similarly concerning side effect. How well can future leaders be groomed when the majority of employees get their paychecks from other external entities or, if they get their paychecks from the company itself, are only guaranteed that for a handful of months? Company culture may also be impacted. It stands to reason that a largely external workforce with limited affiliation and loyalty to the company may have a detrimental effect on corporate culture.

This is not to say that renting isn't a viable option. On the contrary, with platforms that connect businesses with skilled talent (such as Upwork or

Freelancer.com) becoming more and more efficient in matching and thus increasingly sought after, contract work is a growing phenomenon. Up to 30% of the working-age population in the United States and the European Union already engage in some form of contract work – with a large share of these workers preferring contract work over traditional jobs – and the gig economy is expected to grow much further in the coming years.[27] However, to set up your digital transformation talent, you cannot rely on contracting alone, although you should certainly use this option as an additional lever in building your workforce of the future – like the following companies have.

FOOD PRODUCT CORPORATION

The CDO of a globally leading food product corporation suggests thinking strategically about what, who, and which capabilities to internalize versus what to externalize or outsource. "When there is a chance that capabilities will become obsolete fast, it makes sense to externalize these, using contractors. For example, predictive modeling to foresee business outcomes – that is a topic where we activated a community of agencies, especially data science agencies, to help us out," she says. "But there are other functions where the internalization of skills is crucial. That is especially true for areas that are core to the business. For instance, demand forecasting, procurement, or supply chain management are so central to us that we would not rely on external talent to run these departments."

The CDO suggests formulating a roadmap detailing what skills need internalizing versus those that can be externalized. But in the end, a reality check is needed. "Ultimately, we need to be source-agnostic. Eventually we decide opportunistically about where to get talent from," she explains. " Some roles grow into new job profiles; others are recruited or contracted externally, when needed. The preference is to source people internally but often there aren't enough capable people, or sometimes not even enough willing to undergo retraining. That's when they look to external hiring and using contractors, freelancers or other specialized agencies. Necessity, after all, is the mother of invention."[28]

EnBW
· · ▪ ▪ · · ·

German utilities company EnBW banks on sourcing students directly off campus – not only to recruit them but also to rent them. To do so, they make a little detour, using the wisdom of the young crowd in an innovative way: hackathons.

"Especially when demand is high and supply is scarce, you need to think of innovative ways to attract qualified talent who have a variety of career options," explains Raphael Dölker, who co-heads EnBW's 1st S-curve digitization efforts. "There is a real shortage of data scientists, UX specialists, and developers who have Blockchain expertise. While we made an effort to find Blockchain experts even within our company-internal community and while we recruited several UX specialists off the job market, we did turn to cooperations with external partners to find other able developers that we collaborate with for contract work. Specifically, we got involved in a series of hackathons hosted by KIT [an elite technical university] in cooperation with Microsoft. We were quick enough to also pose some challenges and to stay in touch with the winners after the competition. That team ended up founding their own company but they do work for us as freelancers."[29]

BÜHLER
· · · · · · · ▪ · ·

"Of course, we use contractors and agencies. They bring in experience and they can add value from day one," explains Ian Roberts, CTO of Swiss-based diversified tech company Bühler. He also points to an important accounting aspect, "This is variable cost," alluding to the fact that internal employees are part of fixed costs.

But one needs to be wary. Roberts warns that contracting can only work if there is a sound strategy in place detailing which functions, which positions, and which capabilities are key to retain in-house and which ones are peripheral enough to warrant outsourcing. "It's a case of strategically ensuring access to relevant skills for the company," Roberts proclaims.[30]

Reconfiguring

This is probably the least intuitive option for most companies. Reconfiguring (see Figure 7.7) refers to several ways of reallocating workers around the company, including moving workers between S-curves.

Figure 7.7 Reconfiguring

First, it can refer to the disassembly and recombination of tasks to yield reframed job profiles.[31] Think about it this way: every job has a job description, a set of responsibilities that come with the role, and a list of qualifications and other requirements needed to fulfil the position. Imagine all the constituent parts of the various jobs were to be taken apart and recombined in new ways that make sense for the digital age. At an insurance company, the responsibility to build an app for reporting a claim instead of by phone may no longer sit with the IT department, but may be redistributed among a set of teams that did not used to be involved in developer work. Perhaps the marketing department because they know the customers best, the customer service department because they know the claims handling process best, the finance department because they know the workings of the pay-out process best, and others. Given such fundamentally new responsibilities, everyday tasks of people change dramatically, often leading to new – reconfigured – job descriptions altogether. This also means that historically purely 1st S-curve jobs may gain 2nd S-curve components along the way.

Second, reconfiguring can refer to the (geographic) re-placement (not to be confused with *replacement*) of workers to areas – or functions – with higher demand for their profiles.[32] If a US-headquartered organization has built up a digital transformation unit to conceive new digital business ideas that work well for the US market, why stop there? Their European subsidiary, though faced with different customers and preferences, is in just as much need for business model digitization as the US mothership. Expanding the transformation unit may best be begun by sending some of the US pioneers overseas, where they are now more needed.

Third, reconfiguring can also mean redesigning work processes such that workers, as part of their same job, carry out additional tasks that are part of a new business model, which increases employees' responsibilities beyond their usual 1st S-curve work to encompass 2nd S-curve elements.[33] It is common in Germany and beyond that gas stations double as parcel service shops. This is customer-friendly because of generous opening hours. It also increases employee utilization which, at gas stations, is often manageable. The use cases of reconfiguring in the sense of redesigned and extended work processes in the context of digital transformation are manifold.

None of these variations entail adding new talent to the firm, making reconfiguring somewhat a counterpart to retraining in that it relies on an internal talent pool as a source. In practice, reconfiguration is often paired with retraining to make sure employees transition smoothly into their reallocated positions.

One pioneer of reconfiguring jobs is IBM – the IT giant founded in 1911 and known for its innovation track record and the US business entity with the single most patents on record. They introduced their own term for job reconfiguration: "new-collar jobs." This means tasks are reallocated among workers of different skill levels, creating a whole new class of jobs. These new roles are in growing tech fields, such as cybersecurity, cloud computing, and digital design. Instead of preserving such jobs for university-trained engineers, new-collar jobs are in reach for people who do not have a traditional degree but whose skill set can be honed by undergoing IBM-provided trainings. This goes to show how reconfiguration can empower a class of workers previously neglected while freeing up time for university-trained workers. It also illustrates that reconfiguring is most effective when executed in tandem with retraining.[34]

Striking a balance between these four options to build your digital transformation workforce is necessary. Ultimately, the exact mix depends on what you have available in your company, how willingly your workers embrace trainings or reconfigured jobs, and how scarce the supply on the external market is (be it for short-term or long-term solutions). The mix may also be influenced by geography. A survey among private sector organizations with more than US$100 million annual revenue found geographic disparities for resolving skill gaps. European companies lean more toward using retraining or a mix of retraining and recruiting to resolve skills gaps, compared with US companies, which are much keener on recruiting new people.[35] As a rule of thumb, the people mix will lean more strongly toward external hiring than your leaders mix. You most likely will realize that it does take quite some new blood to get the digital transformation machine up and running.

Reducing

Now that you have heard about the four matrix fields, you will wonder what the deal is with another obvious option related to workforce development in the context of digital transformation: reducing work(ers) (see Figure 7.8).

This is deliberately not included in our matrix because, compared with retraining, recruiting, renting, and reconfiguring, reducing focuses on ways of cutting back on workforce. We do not deny the fact that as you add to the pie, you may have to consider taking away from the pie as well. But none of our interviewees stressed that removing work or workers was a preferred, or even the most relevant option. However, none negated that reducing the number of workers or the amount of work no longer needed post-transformation may have to be considered, if all else fails. Many of our interview partners underlined their obligation toward workers but did point out that some lines of work are

Figure 7.8 Reducing

particularly susceptible to this option (such as production, which is subject to largely increased automation and process digitization). But, panic is uncalled for. Removing employees does not necessarily mean firing them. It can mean letting regular attrition occur and not refilling positions. The same can be done for retirement, where the former roles of retirees are no longer filled with new talent. It can also mean reducing work hours for jobs that are no longer as needed – for example, moving full-time to part-time positions.[36] This spares companies having to let go valued employees but it does allow downsizing, when needed.

MANAGE THE PEOPLE TENSION BETWEEN THE 1ST AND 2ND S-CURVE

There's no one-size-fits-all strategy for bridging the gap between 1st and 2nd S-curve people. Just like with leaders, it depends on your organizational set-up and, not least, the people themselves (for example, their level of skepticism versus openness). However, there certainly are several examples of what can work and has worked in some companies. Take this as inspiration of how you might go about bridging – or better yet, narrowing – that gap.

By bridging the gap between 1st and 2nd S-curve, digital transformation teams (2nd S-curve) act as internal service units that selectively and temporarily provide the needed skill profiles to traditional business units (1st S-curve) that would otherwise have a hard time swiftly sourcing the needed experts. This design inherently leads to talent exchange. This implies that the 2nd S-curve people need to be found and attracted to the digital transformation unit first, but, once hired, they represent a knowledge pool that many more traditional business units can draw on. This interwoven digital transformation design where BUs get support from a central digital unit is a great way for exchange between 1st and 2nd S-curve talent.

You met several proponents of this type of model in earlier chapters, including ABB, where many digital transformation initiatives that impact ABB's customer offerings start as lighthouse projects, initiated by a business unit and supported by the central digital team. The central team's consulting and client success teams are comprised of experts in various digital-relevant fields, such as those bringing expertise in business model digitization, digital customer engagement, diverse technologies (like AR/VR), and ways of working (like agile development). These 2nd S-curve experts support many transformation efforts, such as developing an IoT platform, a digital ecosystem, a business model, or a go-to-market innovation. They might be staffed on lighthouse projects for a limited time – usually until they reach the scale-up phase. Then they are moved to the next project where their expertise is needed, thus rotating around 1st S-curve units and meeting a variety of 1st S-curve talent, initiating exchanges and mutual learning. "When people from both S-curves come together and join forces to solve problems for customers and work on a real customer project together, this is when legacy and digital people start to understand each other," Otto Preiss says. What he has seen happen in his teams is that speeches and logical reasons for digital transformation never fully get through to people. Instead what they need is first-hand experience with the digital transformation team and with customers, such that the legacy business as much as the digital team can see live where their value-add originates from and how this can be applied to the benefit of the business units. "As long as you work in the theoretical-conceptual realm, the worldviews seem to differ so vastly that they are nearly impossible to reconcile. Different IT requirements, different assumptions – heck, even different terminology. People often talk past each other. But when colleagues from the traditional business units see the new value propositions – for instance, in how we do co-design with customers, how we incorporate customer perspectives into product design – that makes them realize that we can jointly bring something valuable to the table," Preiss elaborates. "In action," not "in promise," is the key to realizing value of the respective other S-curve.[37]

In the last chapter you also met German utilities provider EnBW and their Digital Office, which supports the digitization of the 1st S-curve. This team follows a similar approach, whereby they act as coaches to internal digital transformation initiatives and thus also function as bridges between legacy business and the digitized world. Specifically, they support digital transformation initiatives across three pillars: products & processes (this also includes the business model aspect); technology; and people and organization. While the Digital Office has a big knowledge pool across these areas, they do not blindly dictate a standardized procedure but work with the respective initiative to determine what makes sense for them, which builds trust and prevents a prejudice against the Digital Office as the know-it-all unit. The bigger the initiative, the more experts from the individual pillars will be involved. Expertise provided covers such areas as data science, agile development, IoT, user experience, AI, or blockchain. "I don't like to call us a consultancy – we are an internal unit, after all. We are also no in-house consulting. Sometimes, when it makes sense, we assume the role of consultants and advisors. Other times we assume the role of a challenger, for instance when it's about calibrating the right ambition level and a scope for the project. Generally speaking, my team has all the competencies that are needed to build a digital business – and we lend these to projects where and when it makes sense," Raphael Dölker, co-head of the Digital Office, explains. To determine which experts will actually be staffed on projects, there are two approaches, Dölker continues: "Either projects are so far advanced that they already know 'We need a data scientist now to crunch this data,' in which case we provide that person. Or, which is the case much more often, we are involved very early on in the conception phase of the initiative, in which case we accompany the project across many stages, providing the kind of people and skills most needed for that particular phase." The latter, more commonly used approach is a textbook instrument for bringing 1st and 2nd S-curve people closer together.[38]

Those examples highlight how some organizational setup options lend themselves particularly well to cross-S-curve employee exchange. But even regardless of the organizational design you choose, there are several tools you can always employ to bring two disparate groups of people closer together.

Consider the role of communication alone. While it won't fully substitute for first-hand experience, communication and transparency are some of the bare necessities of a digital transformation. The communication of the "why" for running a digital transformation creates understanding for the new S-curve and helps curb alienation of legacy talent and open gateways for exchange. That communication needs to be repeated frequently, and be consistent in content, accessible to all employees, delivered via as many media and other channels as possible, and reinforced through in-person conversations. We may be preaching to the converted here, though, as many companies have already realized the importance of consistent communication across many channels.

Mercedes-Benz Bank believes in consistent communication, driven by the right tone from the top. They use various internal and external channels to deliver digital transformation messages consistently: the intranet, a weekly internal newsletter that includes highlights, lunch lectures, town hall meetings where employees can ask questions anonymously via iPad, board breakfasts, stand-ups, social media, and several more.[39] To foster exchange between people, leaders need to encourage them to approach one another. They need to communicate the same messages in informal conversations with their team members as they do in official formats. If delivered consistently, messages stick. Mistrust subsides and openness toward the digital transformation – and the people driving it – steps into a place formerly held by skepticism.

Swiss bank Bank Cler relied on other effective tools to spread the news about their new digital bank Zak and to build trust among legacy employees to engage with the new solution. Besides sending monthly project newsletters to keep everybody in the organization informed about progress and to spread a groovy, start-up-like atmosphere, they wanted to get buy-in from employees in the physical branches by conducting roadshows. After Zak's initial success, Bank Cler had made a name for themselves on being digital banking leaders in Switzerland. The next step was to spread the digital spirit beyond the 2nd S-curve onto the 1st S-curve and get people from the core just as excited as external parties, like customers and the media. They went from branch to branch showcasing Zak and illustrating its success, which made even 1st S-curve employees proud. At the same time, it lowered internal wariness of the new product. "And then we had one other element that worked really well," says Matthias Häne, former head of Strategy and Digital Transformation. "In every physical branch, we nominated a super-user – a specialist who knows the product well and spreads that knowledge across the branch, acting as a multiplier."[40] This is a textbook example of getting 1st S-curve employees engaged in 2nd S-curve efforts and building bridges between two formally separate teams.

Reconciling a number of different approaches to engaging employees through tailored communication is what Philipp Leutiger has chosen to do. The CDO of building materials manufacturer LafargeHolcim uses three levers to engage people in the digital transformation. "First, there are the digital transformation teams – my corporate team in the headquarters, leading teams in our subsidiaries like the United States and India, and local teams who run our digital efforts in operations like the Ivory Coast. Second, I have built an online community of a select group of 250 people from across the organization [mostly 1st S-curve units] that I stay in touch with via monthly web conferences, where they can ask questions and get engaged in digital transformation topics, although they actually work in other functions. I call them "Going Digital." Third, the organization as a whole also needs to be taken aboard the digital transformation ship. To stay in touch with everyone, to spread the word about what we do and how digital transformation benefits us all, I do a lot of communication, including on LinkedIn and via keynote speeches and the like," Leutiger explains. His number-one lever concerns 2nd S-curve employees but his second and third levers reach out to the broad group of people who would not otherwise have their fingers on the pulse of digital transformation. Communicating broadly, lowering perceived thresholds to the topic, and making digital transformation tangible through examples and storytelling rather than just sharing KPIs is what he deems most effective in exciting people from across the organization.[41]

Klöckner & Co introduced a new program titled "Digital Experience." This is based on the belief that to bring down barriers between 1st and 2nd S-curve people, it takes first-hand experience in addition to mere communication. When that experience is not inherently woven into the organizational design – like in the earlier cases of ABB and EnBW – introducing a dedicated program is a great option.

"1st S-curve employees understandably will always have reservations toward the 2nd S-curve and 'the digital stuff that's going on over there in Berlin' unless they get to know it better," identifies CEO Gisbert Rühl. To reduce anxiety and thwart prejudices, employees and managers get to see first-hand what's going on in their Berlin-based Digital Lab, who the 2nd S-curve team is, what they do day in, day out, and why what they do is valuable to Klöckner & Co, and even to the 1st S-curve. This program facilitates an exchange between people from traditional business areas and people from the Digital Lab in Berlin. People from the Digital Lab can also join the core business unit for a period of time to see how they work, what their challenges are, how they interact with customers, and – last but not least – how steel products look in real life. This is a textbook example for establishing a link between people of both S-curves, ensuring knowledge is exchanged bidirectionally. Future collaboration between the core and the Digital Lab will be more efficient based on mutual understanding. Lab people learn about how the core business works and can readily use this product and process knowledge in the conception of new products and services. It also injects digital knowledge into the core, when people from the legacy business who partook in the program go back to their units to use knowledge or apply some of the techniques, such as agility, in their daily business.[42]

Taking this model one step further gets us to formal employee rotations – another way to foster exchange and mutual understanding. These are one- to six-month programs that allow workers to join an entirely new department. This format fosters the exchange between 1st and 2nd S-curve employees and is the pinnacle of employee exchange. Given the formalization, potential geographic reach, and the necessity to find someone to cover work in the sending unit for that amount of time, it may not be the swiftest to implement. But its effects will certainly be long lasting.

GET MOVING TO AVOID THE DINOSAUR FATE

Don't forget to observe these best practices related to digital transformation talent when you go about assembling your own digital transformation team:

- Look for digital transformers who have the courage to accept the challenges posed by digital transformation.

- To source these people and build your digital transformation workforce, carefully calibrate a mix of retraining, recruiting, renting, and reconfiguring:
  - Run a strategic workforce planning exercise to quantify how much digital transformation talent needs to be sourced in total and which levers will need contribute how much staff each.
  - With regard to retraining, design large-scale retraining programs that blend on-the-job learning with classroom learning; decide on whether to conceptualize trainings in-house or by an external agency; consider using certifications at the end of learning programs to attest new skills.
  - With regard to recruiting, encourage employee referrals, explore source code repositories when recruiting for developer talent, make your training resources available online to draw talent in, and make sure to use digital tools to aid in the recruiting process.
  - With regard to renting, contract for skills that may become obsolete fast and/or that are not central to what your company does and use university collaborations to get access to fresh talent.
  - With regard to reconfiguring, make use of the three options as appropriate – disassemble and recombine tasks to create reframed job profiles, (geographically) displace workers to new areas or functions, or redesign work processes.
  - Bear in mind the possibility of reducing work or removing workers in select areas by freezing hiring while letting attrition and retirement proceed or by cutting hours.

- Keep in mind that your organizational design will have a bearing on how you can go about bridging the gap between 1st and 2nd S-curve employees:
  - Use digital transformation teams to carry the relevant know-how into core business units (if your organizational setup allows for this).
  - Spread the word and lower perceived thresholds to digital transformation; use a number of diverse channels to convey these messages; use multipliers to spread know-how across traditional 1st S-curve units.
  - Consider introducing employee rotations to formalize the exchange between 1st and 2nd S-curve team members.

GET INSPIRED (BY CLOTHES)

ZALANDO

Many may argue that Rocket Internet–founded Zalando is a 2nd-S-curve-only company and that they are for Europe what Zappos is for the United States. When asked, most customers say the Berlin-based company is an e-commerce retailer. And that is true – to some extent. It was true until 2014 when the company started to undergo a fundamental transformation from being a fashion retailer to becoming a fashion platform. They still operate their online shop but this is no longer the core of their strategy. A key aspect of their transformation was their people strategy. Bastian Gerhard, former head of Innovation and the founder of the Tech Innovation Lab at Zalando, talked to us about their transition and the role of people in this context.

"Until Zalando's IPO in 2014, the primary goal was to break even. Then the vision to become a platform kicked in. We had already grown from a shoe online retail business to a fashion online retail business and now we wanted to transform into a platform connecting a multitude of market players," Gerhard reminisces. The idea was for Zalando to connect designers with factories, factories with the end consumer, or stylists with end consumers. The IPO was heaven-sent in that a lot of money to make this transition happen was available; but it was also a crux because growth needed to be demonstrated quickly.

To make this growth happen, large-scale hiring became necessary. "We had 800 engineers in our tech team in 2015 and needed an additional 1,000 within the next twelve months," Gerhard explains. This was at a time when Zalando had already grown to 12,000 employees in a mere six years. This development is archetypical for a successful start-up undergoing drastic expansion. But there's many learnings also for legacy companies in how they approached hiring along the way."

"We faced three major challenges in our quest to recruit 1,000 engineers in a year," Gerhard remembers. One, quantity: finding that number of skilled people in Berlin alone proved difficult. Two, reputation: Zalando at the time wasn't known as a tech company, especially not among engineers, despite the fact that all their solutions were built in-house. Three, vision: when Zalando was purely an online shop, the direction was quite clear and the focus was on execution. Now that they were venturing into unknown territory, the direction was more ill-defined, with a lack of clarity in what they needed to do.

Several decisions were taken to address these challenges. Hiring was expanded into Dublin and Helsinki where they knew sizeable engineering talent pools lingered. They decided to become a "magnetic employer," exciting engineering talent to join them. To do so and to counter their non-tech reputation, they created their own tech blog, participated in tech conferences, and offered hackathons. They invested heavily in employer branding and started taking part in job fairs. They encouraged employee referrals and did a sizeable amount of acqui-hiring. Becoming a magnetic employer did not stop there. To entice talent to work for them, they trusted in three levers of instilling motivation among employees, based on Daniel Pink's book *Drive*.[43] First, purpose: Zalando needed to have a purpose other than selling fashion goods online. Every team had to define a purpose for themselves. Second, autonomy: they decided to run the tech team as a product organization with full responsibility over their KPIs and end-to-end ownership over all processes (they called this model "radical agility"). Third, mastery: Zalando offered people attractive long-term careers and internal developmental opportunities. They invested heavily in on-the-job training, establishing a comprehensive training catalog that employees could take advantage of. In return, employees committed themselves to staying an additional 24 months – a win-win for Zalando and the employees.[44]

KEY TAKEAWAYS:

- **Understand what your future employees want and deliver on that** – Knowing that engineering talent wants to work at companies with a good tech reputation, actively build up that reputation; knowing that not all talent wants to move to a certain location, expand your footprint to accommodate for that.

- **Be inventive when it comes to recruiting channels** – Take advantage of all the options you can think of, including recruiting at job fairs and conferences, encouraging (and monetarily incentivizing) employee referrals, and acquiring companies to take over their talent (acqui-hiring)

- **Showcase the availability of attractive internal career paths** – Illustrating that developmental opportunities are available and career progression toward more responsibilities is encouraged enhances employer branding – an important characteristic in the battle for talent.

chapter 8

CULTURE: HOW TO GALVANIZE AN ORGANIZATION AND HELP YOUR PEOPLE PULL TOGETHER

The culture of an organization is like a glue that holds everything together. In this chapter, we elaborate on what many think is an elusive term: *culture* is the values, beliefs, and behaviors that govern interactions between members of a company. We go on to talk about what changes to culture are necessary – and which are not – as part of a digital transformation. We then focus on the changes in beliefs and behaviors needed to propel an organization in the digital transformation age. Finally, we close by pointing out how to avoid establishing two siloed cultures (see Figure 8.1).

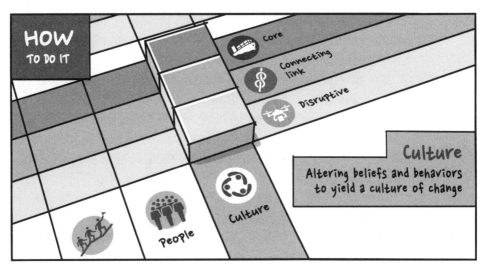

Figure 8.1 Key visual with focus on How/Culture

REALIZE THE CULTURAL CHALLENGES YOUR COMPANY MUST TACKLE

The first pain point related to culture is its elusiveness. As such, many take this to mean culture is just gibberish. Others abuse its supposed vagueness to subsume a plethora of topics under the pretext of culture. Both avenues are wrong. How do you find a middle ground between the two? How can you make culture tangible not only for yourself but for your entire organization to grasp easily? Many companies struggle with steering a middle course between making culture actionable and accommodating its broad implications.

Undisputedly, a cultural change is necessary for a digital transformation to have a shot at being successful. Does this mean a culture and a set of values that permeate an organization – and have for a long time – will be done away with completely? To what extent can traditional values survive – even be fostered – when the environment is geared toward a redefinition of culture? In other words, should old and new coexist, or will one supersede the other?

The current success of the core business is the result of a strong legacy rooted in its cultural DNA. That very company culture would continue to be an important success factor for the ongoing performance of the organization if a digital transformation did not exist. So why bother changing it? After all, the saying goes: never change a winning <culture>.

The effects of digitization on the core business cannot be ignored. There are a series of questions to address. How can the culture of the digitized core business account for technology influences? Is a fundamental change necessary? Can smaller changes to modernize the historic culture of the organization suffice? What role does a modernized company image and a corresponding reputation play in this respect?

How will things look on the 2nd S-curve? Surely a new digital business cannot simply copy and paste a traditional culture. And should it even? To what extent should it cherish its parent company's cultural legacy? Or would this be detrimental to the digital transformation and should it establish its own culture, though disparate from the core? When pursuing a separate culture, how can you avoid forming two siloed cultures, one for each S-curve?

For the change that is necessary, where should it originate from? Are grass-roots movements more effective or are clear directions from the top needed? How do internal company politics impact its cultural transformation? What needs to be done to make the change stick? How can resistance to change be addressed and eventually overcome? How can you even explain to employees that a cultural change is necessary at all when the core business is still performing well? Who needs to be brought in (stakeholders) to motivate employees to be a part of the change? Finally, a cultural change program is a big-ticket item. But quantifying the return or otherwise estimating value is a pickle. Can this even be pursued and, if so, how?

Questions abound, and we attempt to answer them.

DROP THE PRECONCEPTIONS AND INTERNALIZE WHAT CULTURE REALLY MEANS

To grasp what culture means – and specifically what it means in a digital trans-formation setting – let's define it and establish its importance as part of a digital transformation. Then we need to determine to what extent a change in culture is needed when running a digital transformation. Finally, it's necessary to con-ceptualize exactly what kind of cultural change will be most conducive to your digital transformation.

Culture is *not* elusive but instead quite straightforward. It is intricate, for sure, but it is not vague. We define it as the set of values, beliefs, and behaviors that govern the interactions of a firm's individuals – employees and management. This definition is a combined and condensed version of what many of our researcher and practitioner colleagues find culture encompasses.[1] It is also a handy tool for dissecting what exactly needs to be done and changed in a culture when embark-ing on a digital transformation journey.

A sustainable, successful digital transformation needs to be accompanied by – and to some extent rooted in – a cultural change. Consulting firm BCG frames the importance of culture in a digital transformation setting in an article with the catchy title "It's not a digital transformation without a digital culture."[2] We agree. Similar to our definition, they define culture as the values and behaviors that determine how things get done in a company. They list three primary reasons why culture is indispensable in a digital transformation. First, there is a correlation between digital transformation success and culture. Among a number of digital transformations studied, it was found that strong financial performance – both short-term and sustained – was more common among companies that focused on the cultural aspects of their digital transformation. Not a single company that reported having neglected culture as part of their digital transformation reported breakthrough performance. Second, only a culture adapted to the realities of digital transformation allows the digital transformation leaders and talent to succeed. If they bring all their skills to the table, they need this adapted culture to be able to act on their characteristics. Consider intelligent failures: leaders and employees willing to make mistakes and okay with making them is key to a digital transformation. But only if the entire company culture mirrors this failure tolerance and encourages "worst-practice sharing." Third, by implication, this means a digital culture is not only a prerequisite for digital transformers to be at their best but it also attracts digital transformers to the organization. A reputation as a digital leader is a talent magnet. Millennials – and likely Gen Z, once they hit the labor market – are strongly drawn to the big digital brands, promising greater autonomy and flexibility along with a collaborative work environment with likeminded people. MBA graduates are less and less likely to chase after investment banking.[3] Google is the new Goldman Sachs.

We need to speak about where culture comes from and who or what determines whether it needs adjusting. A healthy corporate culture is like a guideline for individuals on how to act. As such, it should be fully aligned with the strategy of the firm. Sometimes the point of departure – the cradle, if you will – of the culture of a company is even its strategy.[4] In a digital transformation this means that a digital culture is born out of the strategy development. As you recall, strategy entails many things, including vision and ambition. These are part of the general strategy formulation process and your digital transformation strategy. Based on the goals you have detailed for your digital transformation strategy you need to evaluate to what degree your current corporate culture supports working toward that strategy and to what extent changes are necessary.

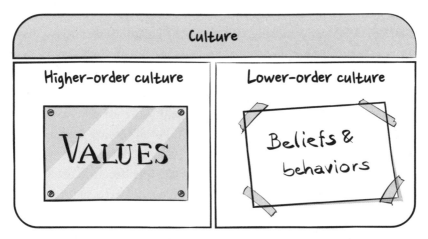

Figure 8.2 Higher–order versus lower–order culture

When we talk about changes to the core company culture, it's important to differentiate between two levels of culture: a higher-order culture and a lower-order culture (see Figure 8.2). A higher-order culture entails, among other things, the values you have determined to be key in your organization. Those values often played an instrumental role in achieving past company successes. They may encompass such noble ambitions like integrity and ethics in work practices, commitment to excellence, and accountability for results. We are decidedly *not* saying that these fundamental company values need changing. They contributed to past successes and it would be disorienting for both tenured colleagues and new joiners if such fundamental guiding principles were abolished. After all, it is often such historic values that make for the good reputation of an organization. A similar credo is being followed at SingPost, Singapore's public postal service. "You need a set of common values to align everyone," says Bernard Leong, former head of Post Office Network & Digital Services at SingPost.[5] He points out the importance of values as guiding principles that have the power to unite people. In short, higher-order values do not necessarily need disrupting in the face of a digital transformation.

What does need disruption is lower-order manifestations of culture – the beliefs and behaviors with which values are being practiced. As such, lower-order culture refers to the more operational aspects of doing business, like ways of working, mindsets, and so forth. They inform specific day-to-day routines reflected in employees' and managers' interactions. Those need updating. Take, for instance, the higher-order value of commitment to excellence. Historically, this may have meant a commitment to designing a 100% solution, having invested weeks and months at a time detailing the specific features and technical specifications needed for a new product. Put differently, the higher-order value of commitment to excellence translated into the lower-order practice of perfectionism in conceptually detailing solutions; this becomes obsolete in the digital transformation age. The higher-order value still has its place but its lower-order counterpart needs to be upgraded to something more conducive to a digital transformation setting. It could translate to rapid prototyping paired with a relentless focus on customers. These principles still tick every box of the "commitment to excellence" definition but are updated with more relevance – and frankly higher chances at being effective at achieving the strategy, which your culture is an enabler for. See how this went full circle? What matters is that the new culture is compatible with the core company values. It's essential that it is *not* compatible with its traditional structure. Or, in other words:

> **❝** 95% of digital transformation efforts in a 'traditional' company have to be focused on culture, and only 5% on technology. It is all about humans. **❞**

Eric Chaniot, CDO of Michelin.[6]

To go back to our house-building analogy: you need something to glue the bricks of your load-bearing and non-load-bearing walls together. It's how you temper the mortar – which ingredients go into it and in which proportion – that has to be redefined.

Values, beliefs, and behaviors – everything that goes into the glue – are broad terms. Culture – especially our definition – is something of a figurative catch all for a number of topics we have discussed in the **HOW** chapters. New processes and governance structures, detailed in the **Processes** chapter (Chapter 5), can only come to fruition if everybody accepts these as the new behavioral standards. The acceptance of failure culture and adaptability to change, as described in the

People chapter (Chapter 7), can only come alive if everyone accepts such beliefs. Transformational leadership can only navigate the VUCA world if leaders accept this as the new norm, as detailed in the **Leadership** chapter (Chapter 6). The same holds true for the new norms of agile software development (**Technology** chapter, Chapter 4) and new organizational forms (**Organization** chapter, Chapter 3). A cultural transformation needs to encompass the organization embracing these constituent elements if the digital transformation house is to withstand all weathers.

There are key factors for the success of the cultural transformation as part of your digital transformation. These are success factors particularly on the 2nd S-curve, where in most cases they are already standard practice. Meanwhile the 1st S-curve may still rely on more traditional beliefs and behaviors. To avoid the two S-curves turning into cultural camps with opposing views, it's best the 1st S-curve slowly and carefully adopts new beliefs and behaviors, one after another, with requisite time allotted in the change process, reducing the risk for backlash. Culture can't go from 0 to 100 in the blink of an eye, and if you try that, the resistance to change will be overbearing. Instead it is a long, staged process.

The 1st S-curve may start with selecting new ways of working in their core operations to get a feeling for what the fuss is about. Only then does it mature to the next stage, adopting more of the digital transformation culture. Slowly and over time the cultures of the two S-curves will meld together, though it is not necessary that the 1st S-curve adopt every single one of the 2nd S-curve's beliefs, if there is a good reason for them not to (production facilities better stick to strict, zero-failure cultures because that's not really the place to take risks). You will still avoid the formation of silos because the two S-curves have enough in common to connect them. Don't force your 1st S-curve to fully adopt all of them, and especially not right away.

To be fair, some of the logic of the necessary cultural transformation that we propose here is highly applicable to large corporations, including publicly listed organizations, and a little less so to family-owned businesses and small- and medium-sized enterprises. A shareholder structure arguably makes the requirements toward a cultural change different from firms that are run by a family, where a cultural change is even more driven by the exemplary behavior from the top than in public companies. But getting a grip on how to culturally transform is necessary no matter the size of the organization.

CHANGE BELIEFS BY MOVING TOWARD A NEW MINDSET – PART I OF THE CULTURE EQUATION

Beliefs are something leaders and people need to internalize and emanate, putting into practice cultural norms in the form of shared beliefs and new mindsets in a digitally transforming organization (see Figure 8.3). A lot of this is reflected in the characteristics of leaders and people driving the transformation; only then can you establish those characteristics as a real culture. That resulting culture – what comes to fruition when you get the right talent on board and have the right supporting (infra-) structure in place – is the snapshot we give.

Figure 8.3 Changing beliefs – shifting toward a new mindset

A new culture rooted in mindsets is something to which Thomas Grübel, CEO of Govecs, the market leader for e-scooter sharing, subscribes. "Technical skills are important, but we try to put more emphasis on the personal attributes and the mindset of our staff and leaders. It's great if applicants have proven their amazing engineering skills in the past, of course. But this is nothing that will make us successful in the future. We try to really focus on the personal characteristics to see if the applicant fits to us, to our company culture – and not just on the skills set alone."[7]

Democratizing customer-centric innovation

Innovation is no longer the R&D department's job. Everyone must take innovation in hand. To work, it takes leaders who empower and inspire people to pursue their own ideas, and who can stand back and have their teams take ownership rather than monitoring every move. Delegation rather than control is the leaders' motto.[8] Cast aside company politics in favor of giving everyone a chance to actively assume their responsibility in the innovation process. It also takes digital transformation talent who have the courage to accept this challenge and the necessary self-starter attitude to put it into practice. They understand that action is superior to planning[9] while their leaders put pragmatism first – another key characteristic. Finally, it takes the requisite process infrastructure to foster decentralized innovation.

The second factor in this equation is a relentless customer focus. Innovation must begin with the customer problem. You think about the customer first and start innovation from there, rather than from the product. This is a cart (product) versus horse (customer) situation. Mind where you put that cart. Instead of thinking of new digital products to offer customers, think about their current journey when using an analog product and then think of ways where digital solutions may be better suited to addressing customers' needs.

Asellion, Covestro's spun-off chemicals e-commerce platform, was developed with the customer at the center. From the beginning, they observed how their customers work and how they get things done in everyday worklife and interviewed them to find out more. Customers were asked open questions like "What solutions do you miss that would be useful for your work? What do you think of this? What does Covestro lack vis-à-vis competitors?" Based on the insights gathered, Asellion developed an idea for a new product. They also came up with other ideas they then tested with customers in the form of mockups but later discarded for lack of merit and significant customer interest in the solution.[10]

Once all aspects of innovation and customer centricity are mixed together, you get a culture that diffuses decision making deep into the organization, supports the need for speed, and encourages employees to look outward to create new solutions.[11] The resulting innovative culture also boasts great external appeal.[12]

SWISSCOM
. . . .

Originally pioneered by US software company Adobe, the "Kickbox" has made its way across the Atlantic where it strikes a chord with Swisscom, Switzerland's leading telecommunications provider. The Kickbox concept you already encountered in the **Processes** chapter is an intra-firm innovation approach that follows the lean start-up method,[13] whereby a decentralized exploration of start-up ideas is orchestrated along a multistage process. As part of this process, intrapreneurs go through a three-stage development approach set up in cooperation with external partners and customers. It is an open innovation process where a network of contributors is used to collaboratively develop new ideas and products. This contrasts with historically closed innovation R&D departments.

The Kickbox approach contributes strongly to the cultural transformation part of the Swisscom's digital transformation. So that employees do not feel overrun by the digital transformation, head of Intrapreneurship David Hengartner's vision was to involve them as much as possible. By allowing every employee the opportunity to turn into an intrapreneur, they become an active part of the digital transformation and carry that message throughout the organization, acting as ambassadors. The program structure gives them maximum autonomy to pursue their own ideas. It also exemplifies how abandoning hierarchical structures can lead to great results despite limited financial investments.[14]

BÜHLER

· · · · · · · ·

Ian Roberts is another advocate for culture being an integral cog in the digital transformation machine. The CTO of diversified tech conglomerate Bühler was one of the masterminds behind the company's Innovation Challenge you also saw in the **Processes** chapter.

At the beginning of each Innovation Challenge, 100 top leaders gather to detail the scope of the problem, always addressing Bühler's customer needs. Teams around the globe then submit and pitch their ideas. The best ideas get published on the Challenge website so everyone can advance the ideas and vote for their favorites. The teams with the highest scores are invited to the corporate headquarters, where they receive additional training and support, before an executive jury eventually decides which ideas get funded and scaled. This Innovation Challenge is another great example for bottom-up innovation that draws in people from the entire organization and spreads a mindset of "let's tackle this together, with the customer at the center of what we do." Not only does it spur on innovative ideas that senior executives alone would not have come up with; it unites people across geographies and functions to jointly focus on customer problems. The combination of these elements makes the Innovation Challenge a strong driver for democratized innovation so essential to a solid digital transformation culture. "I think the most important thing about the Innovation Challenge – other than the business part – is the culture change. I'm convinced that had we not done this and a number of other cultural initiatives, we would have had no chance in the digital transformation," Roberts says.[15]

Internalizing openness to change and instilling a lifelong learning culture

Technology is an inherently restless field in that it advances so fast that believing you can indefinitely rely on established standards is equivalent to digging your own grave. Adaptability is key – being open to (and prepared for) change sets your organization up for success in the face of changing technological realities. The ability to embrace change is a key requirement of digital transformation leaders. Only by departing from historically established norms do leaders even qualify to lead the digital transformation change. As Mark Jacob, managing director of The Dolder Grand and all other businesses of luxury brand Dolder Hotel, puts it, "It needs to be a culture where change is the new normal. Not change after change, but continuous change."[16]

It is not only leaders who need to embrace adaptability. While 2nd S-curve employees typically already bring the requisite change-embracing mindset, the rest of the organization must be brought on board as well. To set them up for success, they need to have access to resources equipping them with the skills needed in an ever-changing digital transformation environment. Upskilling is a reality that a large portion of employees need to face. Promoting a lifelong learning culture accompanied by the requisite learning offerings and making learning an everyday reality is a means to anchoring openness to change. To promote a lifelong learning spirit in your organization, allow people to take time out of their work hours to dedicate to learning. People routinely report a lack of time and space as reasons for not engaging in training programs; institutionalize learning such that employees can engage in learning offerings in addition to continuing to do their core jobs.[17]

You can also nurture curiosity and learning in more informal ways. Reward continuous learning by creating incentives to motivate people to learn. This could be in the form of praising or promoting those who display an effort to learn and develop. More broadly, creating a lifelong learning spirit also means creating a climate that nurtures critical thinking and challenging authorities. Speaking up, even if it means creating discord, is another powerful lever for fostering a learning culture. Giving meaningful and constructive feedback, on both strengths and limitations, helps improve employees' performance. Hiring leaders who practice what they preach, including proving their own adaptability by learning new skills, is a powerful tool as well. If you need entire teams and units to be nonconformists, their leaders better not be sticklers for order and rules. Finally, the general level of motivation for learning can be elevated by hiring leaders and people who are naturally curious. Having curious people in your organization lowers the need for formal retraining because these people will intrinsically pick up new skills. And when they do undergo formal training, it will also stick better, making it more effective overall. High learnability in your team paired with hungry leader minds helps create a strong learning culture.[18]

No one is exempt from having to instill a learning culture in their corporate DNA – not even tech companies credited with being pioneers of such cultures to begin with.

In July 2019, Amazon announced it would invest US$700 million to retrain a third of its US workforce – roughly 100,000 people – by 2025. Amazon's upskilling pledge invests in a range of programs to serve their employees, which not only serves the purpose of transitioning them into growing jobs like data scientists but overall helps instill a learning culture through the introduction of manifold learning formats. The Amazon Technical University equips nontechnical employees with the skills needed to transition into software engineering jobs. Machine Learning University is an institution helping Amazon employees with a tech background gain machine learning skills. Associate2Tech, a fully paid 90-day program, provides fulfillment center associates with the opportunity to move into technical roles. The Seattle-based tech giant will also expand its Career Choice program, which offers prepaid tuition to fulfillment center associates looking to move into high-demand jobs. And the list of levers to instill a learning culture continues, underlining their efforts to make learning a standard across the company. Immersive learning experiences have already created paths to new jobs for hundreds of Amazonians over the last few years, fueling a corporate culture embracing lifelong learning.[19]

Google is another example of a tech company navigating only the 2nd S-curve finding itself needing to adapt a good portion of its workforce and instilling a culture of learning. Realizing that AI is the future of computer science, Google went to great lengths to promote enrollment in machine learning courses and to move employees to embrace this paradigm shift. A fast-paced, practical "Machine Learning Crash Course" was developed by Google's in-house engineering education team. By early 2018, 18,000 Googlers had enrolled in the source, applying lessons from the course to their everyday jobs. That is such a significant portion of its engineering headcount – almost one-third – that it cannot but have an effect on employees' openness to change. This goes to show that in a field that is already inherently susceptible to rapid development, trainings still contribute to strengthening a culture of continuous learning.[20]

SAP's digital business services division started implementing a workforce skills upgrade in 2017. The multiyear learning strategy is designed to support SAP's product mix change toward more cloud-based solutions and digital innovation. Their transformational learning format includes a set of learning journeys featuring bootcamps, coaching, on-the-job shadowing, and online learning. This learning effort was designed to support employees as many roles change and people move into new job descriptions.[21]

What these three examples show is that continuous learning is one manifestation of a change-embracing company culture, and that even in industries thought to be at the forefront of digitization, such learning programs are helpful in having company cultures become even more conducive to employee adaptability and a general spirit of willingness to change.

Promoting a culture of calculated risk and smart failure, not perfectionism

"In a digital world, one of the biggest risks is not taking risks"[22] is a wisdom that digital transformers realize. Unfortunately, this is particularly hard for incumbents to internalize – mostly because they often haven't built the requisite cultures. One in four survey respondents reported that their biggest challenge to digital success is a culture averse to risk and experimentation, and one in five found a lack of common understanding of the company culture a major problem.[23] Realizing risk aversion can be a major impediment to your digital transformation is a good starting point but what matters more is overcoming it. Taking risks does not imply doing so blindly; it means taking calculated risks. While strategic decisions related to the development of the 2nd S-curve made at the highest levels in the organization are not ideally suited to rampant uncalculated risk-taking, bets at middle and lower levels of the organization tend to be manageable in size. Digitization opens the door to experimentation on a smaller scale (for instance, A/B testing) that brings with it a limited downside in cost but a valuable upside in learnings and insights. Take advantage of these smaller scale experiments to normalize a culture of trying and failing. This will establish rapid iteration based on data insights as the new norm, overriding previous obsessions with meticulously tinkering on products, refining them till kingdom come – even before their launch.

Konstantin Speidel, Vice President for Digital Transformation at Allianz Global Investors, is a proponent of calculated risk-taking. "In a large organization, trying things out can be problematic. There's a lethargy to give things a try. Fostering a 'just do it' attitude is important but really difficult. You need to set an example yourself and at the same time create a safe space for your team to make fast decisions without checking. That's a challenge for big organizations but supporting the spirit of risk-taking is still indispensable."[24]

Bühler CTO Ian Roberts has instituted evening get-togethers where people share their failures such that others can learn from them – similar to Klöckner & Co's Failure Nights. He points out that comfort with failure is not only necessary in leaders and employees but is necessary for the entire culture to absorb so the company as a whole becomes fit for the digital transformation. "We introduced this to increase the acceptance of failure and of risks," Roberts says. He is a proponent of the "fail fast, fail cheap" approach, following the lean start-up method.[25] "We do our best to ensure we don't have a culture of punishment. We say failure is experimentation. And if you cannot experiment, then you can never move forward," Roberts declares.[26]

Many companies we spoke with declared their support for the acceptance of risk-taking and failing, of rapid prototyping and experimentation. But many recognize how diametrically opposed this is to the traditional beliefs of the company, rooted in perfect solutions. Deborah Sherry, former CCO at GE Digital in Europe, puts it this way: "It's a clash of cultures. It's a completely different mindset, comparing the safe, slow, deliberate, and perfect launch of something industrial to the fast, cross-functional, trial-and-error, and iteration mentality where failure is fine, and you simply adapt to change."[27] Despite these mindsets being fundamentally different, it's important to embrace them. You just need to be mindful that it will take some time and effort to change long-held beliefs.

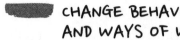 CHANGE BEHAVIORS BY ALTERING STRUCTURE AND WAYS OF WORKING – PART II OF THE CULTURE EQUATION

Besides instilling the necessary beliefs about what is right in a digital transformation context, it is also necessary to anchor such attitudes in structure and ways of working (see Figure 8.4). Reflecting beliefs in modern collaboration models and ways of working apt for a digital transformation makes it easier to practice and live by these mindsets in everyday work. We are creatures of habit, so if cultural change is to stick, then such new behavioral norms need to be turned into habits.[28] Only when deeply ingrained can these behaviors lead to sustainable cultural change. For an account of how to make change stick, even when it's hard, the Heath brother's *Switch* is an amalgam of stories on how to rally entire organizations to change, and how to appeal to each individual's emotional and reflective systems to get them to assume their part in a wider change situation. Such behavioral psychology lessons are highly relevant in a digital transformation context as well, though we will focus on the specific measures to take.

Figure 8.4 Changing behaviors – altering structure and ways of working

Creating an agile organization

In this culture context, the generic way of organizing your people and leaders that is most conducive to digital transformation is an agile organization (not to be confused with agile development). Agility in structure is a new organizational setup paradigm. It can be applied to almost any organization, regardless of their current setup, sector they operate in, or main geographies. Its merits are manifold and its characteristics multifaceted.

An agile organization relies on team-based work, with teams having end-to-end accountability for their assigned projects and being subject to minimal hierarchical burden. They are able to act as speedboats, not bogged down by corporate bureaucracies. Together, the speedboats form a network of teams. These teams are (cross-functionally) mixed teams, consisting of people with many different backgrounds. This is to boost diversity of thought and to prevent silos. Leaders giving guidance supersede managers giving detailed instructions, leaving much autonomy to teams and thus enabling quick changes and flexible action. An agile organization is thus not only a structural element but also represents a new collaboration model.[29]

Adopting an agile structure is not an end in itself. The driving force behind the implementation is that an agile setup can lead to a more efficient use of resources and more transparency over progress and performance.[30] Instead of having multiple hierarchical layers and weeks-long decision-making processes, adjustments can be made quickly and effectively, which drastically reduces decision-making and development time.

The resulting culture is one of diffused decision-making where collaboration is more valued than individual effort. Collective work and information sharing across traditional boundaries of business units and other departmentally organized structures is instrumental for fast-paced digital work. Transparency and interaction are valued higher than in a traditional organization.

One organization that has managed to transform itself and pursue a fully agile-powered model is Haier, the Chinese white-goods company. A series of transformational moves spearheaded by CEO Zhang Ruimin vaulted the company from a little-known refrigerator manufacturer on the brink of bankruptcy to a globally leading white appliances conglomerate. One of the most recent epi-sodes of much transformational efforts includes their moving toward "micro-enterprises," meaning reorganizing themselves into hundreds of start-up-like entities with self-managed teams, typically comprised of eight people. In the course of this transformation toward an agile organization, they eliminated all (yes, all) middle management – about 12,000 employees (rest assured, they were not fired but offered to become entrepreneurs within Haier). In so doing, they went one step further than just relying on self-managed teams; they trusted in an ecosystem of internal start-ups to listen to customers and swiftly act on market feedback. This fundamental overhaul is rooted in Haier's belief that everyone should be allowed to be their own CEO and be fully empowered to make their own (important) decisions, including personnel selection, compensation packages, and distribution of profits (which can go to members of the micro-enterprise). No signatures are needed, nor are there any formal approval processes. The flip-side, however, is the micro-enterprises and their micro-CEOs are equally liable for their failures as for their successes. To prevent failures, exchange among the micro-corporations is deemed key. A global platform connects micro-enterprises with each other to form "micro-communities," allowing them to access relevant resources from Haier's networks around the world. It also enables the micro-enterprises to interact closely with each other, drawing on relevant experience and expertise and sharing in each other's development and production process. This web of interconnected yet autonomous micro-entities – each with their own full mandate to pursue their activities – makes Haier one of the most radical pioneers of agile organizational structures. Through this business transforma-tion, Haier has become more flexible and responsive to customer needs, shifting their organization to better serve and understand their users. They have moved from a mass production company to one that concentrates on mass customiza-tion. And this shows: their market share has grown from 8% to 30% globally. Amid this success, one thing remains important for CEO Zhang Ruimin to stress: it is not Haier that decides the fate of these micro-enterprises but rather the customer.[31]

Agile organizations strike a balance between the start-up world and the established corporate world. Speed and flexibility are just as much a part of an agile organization as are stability and resilience. While a fixed backbone needs to be in place for agile organizations to work, looser dynamic elements complement the backbone to allow for quick adaptability to new challenges.[32]

Taking it a step further, consider experimenting with such agile models as Holacracy, a method of decentralized management where decision-making authority rests fully with the "leaderless" team. Some of our interview partners have done that, among them Uli Huener, Chief Innovation Officer at energy utilities company EnBW,[33] and Thorsten Lampe, CEO of Asellion.[34]

While Holacracy may be an extreme example that relatively few companies would consider adopting on a large scale, making the organization more agile was a common theme in our interviews. Nearly all of our interview partners had at least experimented with agile teams before, if not introduced them more broadly across some units or entire functions.

What we found is it's best to proceed along four steps. First, pioneer this new collaboration model in selected strategic initiatives. Two, showcase to senior executives that this works, using the existing examples. Make the experience tangible for senior executives, for instance, by showing them around team rooms where people from different functions are co-located and work together. Three, having seen that this model works for selected strategic initiatives, establish them as the standard for any new initiatives. Four, roll this out as a standard across the organization, including the 1st S-curve, where applicable. It's important to apply agile organizational principles – and other changes in beliefs and behaviors – where it makes sense. There are few companies that have switched over their entire 1st S-curve operations to agile principles. When it does not make sense, refrain from doing this. And if it does make sense, take the time to transition the 1st S-curve peacefully, accompanied with a solid change program. Shifting to an agile organization constitutes a major change for employees and you should strive to make that experience as smooth sailing as possible for them.

A welcome side effect of agile organizations (including extreme forms of it, such as Holacracy) is that they nip company politics in the bud. Giving everyone equal say is an inherent benefit of this altered organizational structure. Decentralizing decision making and empowering (and holding accountable) all talent to contribute to team success makes an organization more equitable, thus robbing company politics of taking over. It is much simpler for nepotism to take hold in a hierarchy than it is in an agile organization. While hierarchies more easily allow for the passing along of select people or opinions, the inherently decentral setup of an agile organization robs protégés of their ability to influence the organization broadly. Extra points for the agile organization.

Relying on new ways of working

Picture yourself having the senior executives of your firm over for a visit of your team room, where people from different backgrounds work together on solving a digital transformation challenge. If you want to show your senior management how agility looks, it's not enough to just illustrate what the team structure will look like, but you can draw them in further by showcasing how these teams get their work done. Luckily, for many new ways of working, this can be illustrated with a multisensory experience.

Agility also applies to innovation and work methods, of some of which you have heard in the **Processes** chapter (Chapter 5). Originally used in product development, agile methodologies were instrumental for the iterative and incremental development of a hypersonic jet in the 1950s. Scrum, a process framework for effective team collaboration on complex projects or products along repeatable work cycles called "sprints," was codified and first presented to the public in 1995. "Lean thinking" has proven similarly popular. First studied in Japanese manufacturing systems, particularly the Toyota production system, the term "lean" was coined to describe methods of improving productivity by eliminating waste. Formal lean and Kanban software development systems emerged in the 2000s. Meanwhile, lean methodologies, Kanban, and any hybrids (like Scrumban and lean scrum) are understood as applications of agile values that can reach far beyond the sphere of software development.[35] Another approach that's rapidly gaining popularity is design thinking. A human-centered process for solving complex problems, it puts user needs at the center and trusts in rapid prototyping and practical results.[36]

And then there's a wide array of tools to support these new methodologies and collaboration models. Consider Slack, the cloud-based, online team collaboration tool that aids in orchestrating team coordination and communication, or its competitor Microsoft Teams. Or there's Yammer – also a Microsoft product –

a social networking service for private communication within companies. Such tools are not only examples of solutions to modern problems in and of themselves, but they also serve as integrators of a variety of other tools, embedding in one interface a number of other more specialized tools – like Trello and Asana, collaboration tools that organize work projects and tasks online.[37]

These lists are not exhaustive. This is just to give you a glimpse at the breadth of methodological options and supporting tools to consider putting in place as part of your digital transformation. We aspire to motivate you to look into these new ways of working and adopt what works for your organization's digital transformation.

There are many approaches and tools that can be demonstrated to non-believers. Being able to easily observe such manifestations of new ways of working can significantly lower perceived thresholds to adopting them. When you take your senior executives on a tour, demonstrate the methodologies and tools you employ. You will be more likely to convince the illustrious group of visitors if they see first-hand what these things mean and where their power comes from.

Agile ways of working should not be just another creative thinking or iterative testing approach. Instead, it's a well-crafted holistic approach to work that can help organizations achieve better outcomes, faster, and more efficiently than with traditional methods.[38] Using a test-and-learn approach, companies can reduce the risk of failure that's associated with digital initiatives. Although many executives are afraid of losing control and fear that everything might end up in chaos, regular monitoring and the prioritization of tasks can in fact ensure that self-managing teams are working continuously toward an overarching goal in line with the strategy.[39]

The main benefit of agile ways of working is that they allow for an increased focus on things that really matter for customers while at the same time delivering solutions faster and more efficiently than with other methods.[40] The foundation of this is formed by a well-run iterative process that allows the detection of flaws and errors much earlier in the process and makes adjustments on the basis of new learning possible.[41] Thus, instead of long planning cycles, multiple levels of decision-making, and many layers of separation between the customer and the developer, reviews and decisions are made quickly on a regular basis, and plans and assumptions are replaced with hard data and customer feedback.[42] On this basis, small-cross functional teams can experiment with prototypes, learn quickly from early customer- and market-tests, and ultimately deliver innovations within days or weeks, not within months, or even years. And the best thing about it: research shows that organizations where agile ways of working have become a standard see substantial improvements along a number of dimensions. The customer satisfaction and the return on digital investment is three to four times higher, and development costs decrease by 15–20%. Employee engagement improves, too.[43]

Agile ways of working can be applied pretty much everywhere, as the example of Klöckner & Co, the German steel distributor, shows.

❚❚ With our old waterfall approach, development took several years and resulted in very high costs and complex products. The new world approach - ideation process, the rapid prototyping and testing with customers - convinced me immediately. Since then, we are doing everything around the digital transformation in an MVP-like approach. **❚❚**

Gisbert Rühl, CEO of Klöckner & Co[44]

Many of our interview partners agree that such modern ways of working are indispensable in their digital transformation efforts. Scrum, design thinking, and various agile methods are used at REHAU.[45] The lean start-up methodology is on everybody's lips at Bühler.[46] Scrum meetings, Kanban boards, and sprint backlogs are a common sight at Asellion.[47] Scrum, design thinking, and the lean start-up methodology were core processes of what Bank Cler did when they established Zak.[48] Osram Innovation uses Slack.[49] CEWE trusts in lean management.[50] Wastebox was developed in sprint cycles.[51] You get the picture. This is just to name a few, though. The list is a lot longer – in fact, nearly everyone we spoke with had introduced one or multiple new ways of working to their organization, attesting to their critical importance for a digital culture and the digital transformation as a whole.

290

CONTEXTA

Consider becoming a creative nomad like communication agency Contexta. Founded some 50 years ago, Contexta currently has around 30 employees. As such, it is not a lethargic, corporate behemoth. It is smaller and more flexible than most other companies we spoke with, just owing to its size. This story can still serve as inspiration for what it means to think outside the box. So far outside the box that the box is a dot to you.

Contexta decided to abandon their fancy offices in the Swiss capital Bern in exchange for – nothing. Well, not nothing. In exchange for changing locations in nontraditional places. Since August 2019, Contexta no longer has a permanent mailing address. What they do now is lodge in places that bring them closer to people than an office could. Every few months they change locations. The zoo, a café, a public pool, charity organizations – the sky is the limit. Switzerland is relatively small so employees commute daily to whatever the current location is. Minimalism rules – they have abandoned most physical corporate baggage, focusing only on the essentials. The office equipment they do need (like desks) are standard pallets, such that the entire infrastructure can be set up and taken down in a matter of hours. In return they get a closer connection with individuals they want their communication to speak to. Inherently the new design also does away with hierarchies – no visual or other distinctions are being made between Creative Director and rookie. They also get a reputational boost, leaving behind their "mom-and-pop agency" reputation and building an image of an innovative communications thought leader. All of this is part of Contexta's ambition to become a more strategic partner to their clients, not only implementing briefs but contributing real insights and helping drive strategy.[52]

The case of Contexta is also a perfect example for the process of matching your strategy with your culture. The first step in determining cultural changes is to define your strategy and see how well it is aligned with your current beliefs and behaviors. For Contexta, there was a clear mismatch between strategic ambition (become a thought leader for their clients) and the infrastructure in place to support that (traditional office). Contexta abandoned long-held beliefs of what a standard structure should look like.

Belief- and behavior-related characteristics enable the fundamental shift in corporate culture needed to pave the way for digital transformation success. This modern, change-embracing culture will also yield significant reputational spillover effects that in turn will attract talent and leaders and boost investor confidence. Promoting a culture of encouragement to innovate, instituting a supportive work climate where failing is okay, and providing lifelong learning opportunities are must-dos. A change in structure and ways of working will be necessary, including the departure from siloed bureaucratic hierarchies and long development cycles and a move instead toward a new collaboration model based on cross-functional teams. But the crux of the matter is the internal resistance to change – particularly from middle management – that requires senior leaders to skillfully navigate by authentically leading the cultural change. Only if the cultural change pervades all levels, functions, and geographies does it stand a chance at establishing itself as the new norm.

MANAGE THE CULTURAL TENSION BETWEEN THE 1ST AND 2ND S-CURVE

The 1st and 2nd S-curve will likely adhere to different daily practices for a while before the changed beliefs and behaviors take effect across the organization. The practices and mindsets discussed likely are standard on your 2nd S-curve already while your 1st S-curve will introduce them reluctantly, slowly adding more and more over an extended period of time until they eventually catch up. It's worth stressing again that your 1st S-curve should select those that make sense for the respective setting and warmup to the 2nd S-curve through shared beliefs and behaviors in these select areas.

The 1st and the 2nd S-curve cultures are still united by the values they share. Values endure times of change, including digital transformation. So, unless they are fully detrimental to the new strategy, they would remain untouched, meaning 1st and 2nd S-curve cultures have a significant common ground to draw from. Only in the manifestations of their beliefs and behaviors will they initially deviate. But as we have described, slowly introducing the new, digital-transformation-friendly beliefs and behaviors to the 1st S-curve is the best strategy of eventually uniting them both. Let's look at some success factors for doing just that.

Backing by senior management

Cultural transformation needs to be supported by C-level management who have an understanding of the long-term history of the organization and a vision for its future. Senior management needs to set the right tone and embody the motivation they want to see in everybody else. The effect will eventually trickle through to middle management, although permeating this level will be where most time needs to be invested.

Many of the senior leaders we spoke with follow this logic.

> Digital transformation is nothing you can delegate – this has to be a top management priority. Otherwise you will not achieve a real impact in a large corporate.

Philipp Wetzel, Managing Director, AMAG Innovation & Venture Lab[53]

Several pointed out the importance of communication and of their own authenticity and availability to talk to employees as key to navigating the cultural change.

❝ It is absolutely decisive that the c-level team makes the priority of the topic clear to the entire organization, and authentically so. Emails, newsletters, and pretty slides do not suffice. The message has to be spread across the organization day in, day out. You need to talk to everybody who has doubts. Senior leaders must not think themselves too good for answering questions and addressing employees' concerns in frequent, direct conversations with them. **❞**

CDO of a large discount retailer[54]

❝ It is about communication: How do you communicate, are you approachable? For myself, I have an open-door policy. Everybody can come, have a chat, ask questions. We have created particular formats; once a month, I have a format where people can register and pretty much ask any question that's on their mind, private, professional, on the marketplace. I'm not saying that I'll have an answer to everything, but it is just about openness and taking the barriers down. When you are trying to drive a cultural transformation, that is absolutely crucial. **❞**

Former CDO, chemical and consumer goods company[55]

Some made clear that change takes a while, so one must not be impatient.

❝ Transformational change is not an overnight business. Convincing employees to embrace a new culture needs to be moderated by a continuous communication process, which can be intense. It takes a lot longer than you might originally envisage. You might even think 'Why isn't this proceeding faster? It should be clear to everybody that ordering with a fax machine is outdated.' And people do know that. But that still doesn't mean they immediately jump ship and do everything online. **"**

Gisbert Rühl, CEO, Klöckner & Co.[56]

There is a silver lining – especially when you can find multipliers willing to spread the digital transformation culture throughout the organization.

" Usually, people ask themselves 'If everything is going well, why should I change?' Usually, human nature is not about 'I want something new every day.' So, if you want people to join the cultural transformation, you need to explain the value of change, the 'Why?' and 'What's in for me?' And you need to find the excited ones and use them as multipliers to motivate others. You will need multipliers and buy-in at all levels, otherwise you will fail. **"**

Katharina Herrmann, Global Head of Platforms and Beyond Banking, ING[57]

The bottom line is, senior leaders need to navigate the cultural change and give reasons for it. They need to prioritize communication and be available to the entire organization for any questions or concerns. Ideally, they create allies and disperse them around the organization to act as agents of cultural change. Cultural transformation is a marathon, not a sprint.

Bottom-up movement

Communication from the top is best paired with a bottom-up approach to reach maximum impact. When grassroots movements that embrace the new culture emerge in parallel to change being driven at the top, the new culture has a shot at permeating much faster throughout the organization. New 2nd S-curve recruits can help propel the change by bringing in new spirit paired with the necessary expertise and credibility, so long as they internalize the new DNA of the organization. But change can also be driven from more tenured colleagues, assuming they are 2nd S-curve enthusiasts.

> At AXA Switzerland, we started to work in agile mode in 2016 and it was very much a grassroots movement out of our IT department. It kick-started our successful, enduring transformation and helped to accelerate our digital and data initiatives. I fundamentally believe that it was successful because it was not a top-down, "Big Bang" approach, where the CEO gets inspired, and tells the Executive committee to go ahead and implement agile. Innovation is a delicate little plant. Giving it time and space to grow is key. That's what we did with our teams and agile methods. Often when things are being turned into a big deal, there is so much attention on them that the whole hype might do more harm than good. It's like an ugly baby - it unsettles everything, needs a lot of attention, keeps you up at night, and takes a long time until it grows into something meaningful. For the longest time, only the parents think it's pretty. We wanted to avoid that ugly baby and instead let parts of the cultural change happen under the radar.

Carola Wahl, former CTMO, AXA[58]

Outside-in approach

Another powerful lever for establishing a culture is an outside-in approach. Bringing in people from other companies and industries can weigh heavier than internal managers' repeated messages after a while. Credibility earned externally can add extra motivation for the cultural transformation.

 Every time we work on a new digital transformation initiative, we check whether there's some people who are ahead of us in other industries, so we can learn from them. Especially players in the banking, insurance, and travel industries would be dead by today if they hadn't successfully mastered digitization. So, we meet up with these people to hear about their successes and failures. We've had executives from Schneider Electric, Veolia, and Total come over. They are much more effective in delivering a message than when I continuously preach the same thing. This outside-in perspective is really driving our cultural transformation.

Eric Chaniot, CDO, Michelin[59]

GET MOVING TO AVOID THE DINOSAUR FATE

We suggest keeping the following best practices in mind when you think about the cultural transformation of your digital transformation.

- Revisit your strategy and its components (ambition, vision, and so forth) and check to what extent this is aligned with your current culture (values, beliefs, behaviors):
  — Refrain from disrupting your historic company values unless they are diametrically opposed to your strategy.

- Shift your mindset in three ways:
  — Democratize customer-centric innovation – open up innovation management from the R&D to the entire organization; prioritize the customer.
  — Internalize openness to change and instill a lifelong learning culture throughout your organization – have leaders and people demonstrate their adaptability; normalize learning and training.
  — Promote a culture of calculated risk-taking and smart failure, rather than a culture of perfectionism – value rapid prototyping and fast iterations more than perfect solutions; make failing okay.

- Change your behaviors by altering the structure of your organization and its collaboration model, and by introducing new ways of working and supporting tools:
  — Create an agile organization relying on a network of (cross-functionally) mixed teams; minimize corporate bureaucracies; trust in the power of networks as opposed to hierarchies.
  — Introduce new ways of working; make sure to introduce new tools alongside.

- Unite your organization under one culture:
  — Have C-level executives set the tone for the cultural transformation.
  — Create allies across the organization who can act as agents of cultural change.
  — Allow for grassroots pro-digital-transformation cultural movements to flourish.
  — Consider bringing in people from other companies to share how they have managed their cultural and digital transformation.

GET INSPIRED (BY POSTAL SERVICES)

SingPost

SingPost is Singapore's public postal service provider. When it embarked on its digital transformation, Bernard Leong – at the time head of Post Office Network & Digital Services – prioritized the role of culture in the overall transformation. "The most difficult part of the digital transformation is the cultural transformation because implementing and sustaining culture change is a challenge." He came to realize that people like the idea of a transformation, but they do not want to change. Often, in fact, they refuse change and actively work against it.

To make cultural change stick, Leong considered his options. He recognized the usual procedure for a cultural transformation was to cascade the change from the top down, with senior management leading the conversation. But SingPost decided against this approach because they thought it would take too long. Instead, they opted for a combined approach. This consisted of top management pushing the message from the top down but at the same time educating and enabling front-line staff in digital capabilities, thereby planting the seeds for digital transformation acceptance through a bottom-up method.

In retrospect, Leong recalls two key learnings. One, CEO buy-in is a must. The CEO and his management team need to be authentic promoters of new digital solutions. Digitization must be at the top of their agenda. Two, listening to people and taking their feedback and concerns seriously is paramount if you want to get their buy-in as well. "In fact, you should seek out feedback not only from customers but also from internal employees. The customer may be king but the employee sure matters, too," Leong explains.

Leaders needed to understand the pain points at the front line. To provide top managers an authentic glimpse into everyday problems staff faced, they had to spend several days as "service ambassadors" in the postal office. This newfound understanding of processes and people helped them redesign the postal office, equipping it with relevant digital tools and services.

"If you ask me, culture is even more important than technology in a digital transformation. Technology will always be there, but you need to get the people to transition to a new culture if you want to succeed with your transformation," Leong concludes.[60]

KEY TAKEAWAYS:

- **Consider implementing a dual top-down/bottom-up approach** – CEO support is indispensable, but it is most effective when complemented with a grassroots movement.

- **Have leaders understand their employees' pain points that hinder them from welcoming the cultural change** – Placing leaders in frontline staff shoes builds understanding and can help produce better solutions.

- **Take employee feedback seriously** – Feedback is a gift, not only when the source is customers but also when it is your own employees.

Part 4
WHERE TO SEE RESULTS

chapter 9

BECAUSE YOU'RE NOT DOING THIS FOR FUN BUT FOR RESULTS

Congratulations, you're almost done (we'd love to say "with your digital transformation" but really it's only "with this book"). In this last chapter you will learn how to define the right KPIs, that is, how you determine which parameters matter for which S-curve at which point in time, and set objectives for these parameters and how you should go about business case building. (Mind that there is a distinction between which parameters you deem relevant ("the right KPIs") and what kinds of aspiration levels you wish to achieve for each of them ("the objectives").) We will also deep dive into how to ensure transparency and documentation, and whom to assign accountability to, before we end with some closing notes on back-coupling effects between your 1st and 2nd S-curve, and between digital transformation payoffs for organizations and for the greater public good (see Figure 9.1).

Figure 9.1 Key visual with focus on Where.

REALIZE THE "WHERE" CHALLENGES YOUR COMPANY MUST TACKLE

Once companies have tackled the *why*, *what*, and *how* of their digital transformation, the next thing is to look for results.

When faced with the task of success measurement of a digital transformation, pain points and question marks abound. The most fundamental point of departure may be the question, how do you even measure success? We argue a digital transformation is a fundamental overhaul of a business across two S-curves. It is thus only natural that it should enter the books of both S-curves because its effects will be reflected in the performance of both. Managers then need to ask themselves, what success parameters matter for the 1st S-curve? And which ones are relevant for the 2nd S-curve? How do these differ and do they ever converge? Are there any back-coupling effects between the two, that is, could efforts on the 2nd S-curve potentially translate into performance on the 1st S-curve? If so, how shall this be accounted for?

We will preemptively address one thing: different KPIs (and objectives) matter for the 1st S-curve than do for the 2nd. It is likely that legacy-driven companies will not have such an easy time switching from traditional 1st S-curve KPIs to the KPIs that matter on the 2nd S-curve. Which KPIs are the hardest for them to transition to? How can that transition best be facilitated? They may have a particularly hard time accepting potentially high failure rates of innovative business ideas on the 2nd S-curve. (After all, 9 out of 10 start-ups fail.[1]) How, then, can legacy companies deal with such drastically lower success rates on the 2nd S-curve?

Also, how will success factors change over time depending on the stage a digital transformation finds itself in? How relevant are qualitative KPIs versus quantitative KPIs? How do you go about setting objectives? Or, more fundamentally, should objectives be set at all? If so, who should be held accountable for achieving these objectives? And who should know about the status quo of the KPIs, run rates, and other preliminary rather than final performance indicators?

While the "Where to see results" may be the last chapter in the sequence of the digital transformation framework in this book, it certainly shouldn't be last thing you think about. In reality, an aspiration level for results should be set early in the process. Think about it this way: Why would any sane person or company want to embark on a fundamentally disruptive journey, like that of a digital transformation, if it wasn't expecting positive bottom-line effects? So it's only logical to start the digital transformation with an end goal (however vague or concrete) in mind. Not least because also in a digital transformation context does the age-old saying hold true: only what gets measured gets done.

Digitization does not change the fact that we need to steer businesses based on KPIs. Digitization not only makes this latent necessity even more pronounced; it also renders it infinitely easier. A digital representation of any activity allows the easy, real-time capture of manifold parameters that can be used as a means for impact measurement. But just because digitization equips us with that ability, it doesn't mean it automatically tells us what to focus on. The brainwork of capturing the right KPIs in a veritable ocean of data is still on the digital transformation practitioner. Your strategy dictates how you achieve your goals. The goals dictate what parameters you should measure. These parameters tell you whether you've been successful in achieving your vision. This is to say, it's necessary to think about the kind of results you want early on during the strategy development, or else your digital transformation efforts will be misguided and will not yield what you are after, or they may even be altogether futile. Giving thought to what you want to achieve with your digital transformation, you will be well equipped to reap the associated measurement benefits.

 MOVE FROM KPI LAUNDRY LISTS TO STRATEGIC KPI SETTING

Is this what comes to mind when you think "three horizons" (see Figure 9.2)?

Figure 9.2 Three Horizons

Or are you potentially thinking of stunning landscape idylls against the backdrop of gorgeous sunsets along the Ligurian Riviera, Santorini, and Ipanema Beach? If either of that, then unfortunately we have to disappoint you. These are not the kind of three horizons we mean. If, on the other hand, you are thinking about an approach for how to manage current business performance while maximizing opportunities for growth in the future, then you have likely been to business school and/or followed management literature around the millennium to know what we are referring to.[2]

The Three Horizons model describes innovation as occurring on three time horizons: continuous innovation, expansion of the existing business model, and the creation of new digital business models. While some view the Three Horizons model as an enduring idea with much relevance today,[3] there has also been criticism that the traditional timelines associated with the three horizons are no longer realistic.[4] What does remain relevant, though, and where the similarities between Three Horizons and the two S-curves come in, is that the different Horizons and S-curves need different types of performance metrics to adequately account for the arguably different goals each of them pursues. Horizon 1 focuses on traditional financial metrics such as profit, return on invested capital, and cash flow. Horizon 2 uses more customer-oriented, entrepreneurially driven metrics such as revenue and net present value, both focused on customer feedback in the form of sales generated. Finally, Horizon 3 centers on more milestone-based, market-oriented metrics, evaluating the commercial progress of the initiatives. This logic of differing metrics depending on your S-curve holds true in the context of digital transformations as well.

This is a long-winded way of saying that the "right KPIs" will differ by S-curve. And, having spoken to many executives at companies from different industries about their approaches to results measurement, we find that there's a few other things to consider when determining your KPIs. Figure 9.3 is your "KPI to-do list."

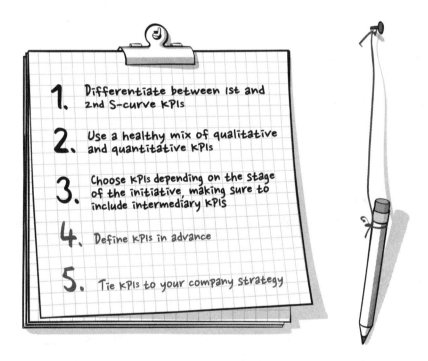

1. Differentiate between 1st and 2nd S-curve KPIs

2. Use a healthy mix of qualitative and quantitative KPIs

3. Choose KPIs depending on the stage of the initiative, making sure to include intermediary KPIs

4. Define KPIs in advance

5. Tie KPIs to your company strategy

Figure 9.3 KPI to-do list

Items (1), (2), and (3) may be easier to grasp referring to the handy cheat-sheet in Figure 9.4.

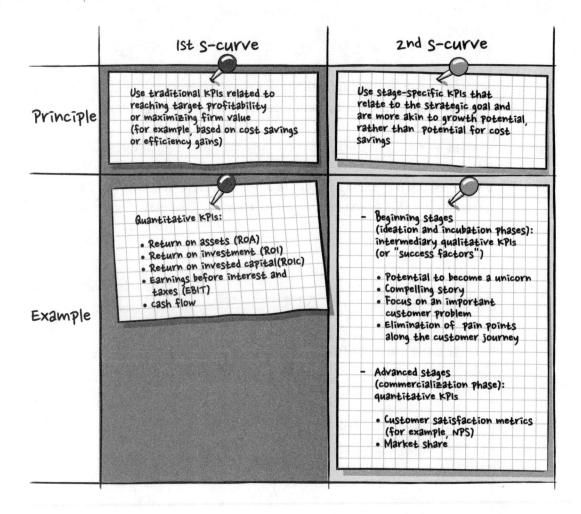

Figure 9.4 KPI cheat-sheet

The fact that traditional 1st S-curve KPIs are ill-suited to account for 2nd S-curve performance and that a new approach to evaluation criteria is needed for the 2nd S-curve (1) is something AMAG, the Swiss car importer and dealer, told us.

AMAG

· · · · · ·

Do 2nd S-curve initiatives need a different evaluation governance, and, if so, what should that look like? This is what Philipp Wetzel, managing director of AMAG Innovation & Venture Lab, asked himself as he reflected on the initiatives his Lab was pursuing. These initiatives were grouped into three buckets: "Now" initiatives (pursued immediately), "New" initiatives (usually an investment horizon of three to no more than five years), and "Next" initiatives (positive returns expected in five to ten years). Now and New initiatives correspond to the 1st S-curve with stable projected developments, building on a 30-year-old business. Next initiatives corresponded to 2nd S-curve efforts with expected volatility in sales and profits.

Wetzel decided to record the development of Next initiatives along classic KPIs. But he firmly pointed out that while these KPIs were being tracked for good measure, they were neither seen as relevant indicators of performance nor as what the business was optimizing for. Instead of chasing after EBIT (earnings before interest and taxes), alternative measures of success (such as building reputation for the AMAG brand in a new area) were deemed worth striving for. This was based on Wetzel's realization that even if the Lab burned money within the first years, it still made an important contribution to the entire organization that was less quantifiable but the qualitative impact was no less relevant. The value of the Lab being an innovation scout and incubator for new ideas and the initiatives bore important signaling effects to the outside. Another important qualitative measure for the success of the 2nd S-curve was the extent to which it fueled a cultural change. Indeed, its contribution as a driver for new ways of thinking and working not only on the 2nd S-curve but with spillover effects into the behavior in the core business were value-adding side effects worth registering.[5]

Now that you've seen how AMAG approaches addressing item (1), and that a guiding principle for tackling item (1) in your "KPI to-do list" is for your 1st S-curve KPIs, you are free to rely on your proven project management KPIs. Your 2nd S-curve KPIs should reflect a less rigid approach to assessing impact as you should choose them following a VC-like approach, with intermediary KPIs paving the way toward longer-term success factors in line with your strategy.

Let's look at how the other elements of your "to-do list" play out in real life. Consider Volkswagen, the German car company, which successfully tackled achieving a mix of qualitative and quantitative factors (2), specific to the respective stages of initiatives (3), which they defined in advance (4) while making sure to tie them directly to the company strategy (5).

VOLKSWAGEN

The ultimate KPI, the ultimate question for Falke Bothe, director of the Digital Transformation Office, is "Are we earning enough money with our cars sold to finance our transformation?" Secondary questions include: Which customers are we selling these cars to? Via which dealers? Where? Which models? Which configurations (panorama windows, A/C, and so forth)? Thankfully, all these corporate KPIs are clear-cut, quantitative, and easy to measure. But digital transformation KPIs also need to be qualitative in nature, Bothe argues. They need to include questions such as: Do we even have digital business models in place? What is our plan to pursue them? What do we eventually want to offer the customer? By extension, one also has to think about how to go about the internal upgrading of skills necessary to deliver on these business models. A related KPI could also be: What training programs am I offering my employees to upgrade their skills? Eventually all of these qualitative questions will need to translate into quantitative KPIs (for example, how many miles on average do users use our alternative mobility solutions (per day/year)? How effective are our training programs in upgrading our employees' skills?).

While the classic quantitative KPIs seem quite different from the more qualitative digital transformation KPIs, it's important not to fall into the trap of parallel reporting. Instead a change or extension of your usual reporting is necessary. Maintaining different reports is overbearing, adds complexity, increases the sources of error, and simply does not do the importance of your digital transformation KPIs justice.[6]

Generally, having established that success parameters need to differ by S-curve (1), let's consider how qualitative and quantitative KPIs can best be specific to the two S-curves (2).

First, stop #1: quantitative KPIs.

For initiatives on the 1st S-curve, quantitative success measurement can be based on your classic KPIs and may include return on assets (ROA), return on investment (ROI), return on invested capital (ROIC), and earnings before interest and taxes (EBIT). Sound familiar? This is nothing new.

Initiatives on the 2nd S-curve need to be evaluated less based on short-term quantitative criteria and instead more on quantitative KPIs that relate to your long-term strategic goal of the 2nd S-curve (5). These KPIs hinge more on growth potential rather than on target profitability. They may include customer satisfaction metrics, such as NPS, or other KPIs from the lean start-up method (that is, actionable metrics that tie specific actions to observed results, such as funnel metrics (for example, number of users) or SEM metrics).[7] In this context, it is advisable to put a focus on market-based criteria, where possible (for instance, how many customers are willing to pay for a new product instead of how many click on a banner advertising that product). One useful guiding concept for relevant, quantitative, market-based KPIs for 2nd S-curve initiatives is so-called digital traction metrics. They provide proof a customer is actually interested in a company's products or services. A combination of behavioral metrics (number of unique users, user engagement, conversation rates), they gauge not only the popularity but also the momentum for potential market adoption of a new product or service.[8]

As you determine these quantitative KPIs, be mindful that once the 2nd S-curve initiative has matured to a market-ready stage (for example, when you

311

are full-launching your product or service), KPIs can transition toward those of the 1st S-curve (for example, profitability) – item (3) on your "KPI shopping list."

Next, stop #2: qualitative KPIs.

Quantitative KPIs change over time and those of the 2nd S-curve will start to assimilate those of the 1st S-curve. The same logic holds true for qualitative KPIs. Qualitative metrics initially prevail on the 2nd S-curve because they better reflect the long-term, growth-oriented success indication needed for a proper and fair evaluation of 2nd S-curve initiatives. In practice this means in the initial stages of an initiative (especially in the ideation and incubation phases), qualitative KPIs are best suited for the 2nd S-curve. One might even deviate from the strict definition of KPIs and instead focus on success factors, ticking off whether or not they are in place. These can include whether the business has the potential to become a unicorn, whether the story is compelling, whether a significant problem is being tackled and pain points are being eliminated along the customer journey, whether an emphasis is put on the key things, whether support from the Board and the remaining environment has been achieved – all to be answered with either yes or no, and not measured quantitatively. In addition, initial phase 2nd S-curve qualitative KPIs can also include milestones along a time plan (such as establishing a prototype or doing alpha/beta launches). Only later, particularly in the scaling/commercialization phase, does it make sense to move to using more traditional KPIs for the 2nd S-curve. As you determine these KPIs be mindful that all of them, including the transition point from 2nd to 1st S-curve KPIs, should be defined in advance (4) and communicated clearly to all relevant stakeholders for maximum transparency and goal alignment. Make no mistake: eventually all initiatives, including those on the 2nd S-curve, need to contribute positively to your P&L and deliver value in the more traditional sense. The point of combing your items (1) and (3) – choosing KPIs that are specific to the S-curve and the respective stage of the initiative – is that you cannot use traditional KPIs right from the start because this would literally thwart all your 2nd S-curve efforts in their fledgling stage.

To expand on the importance of (3), including the necessity to work with intermediary KPIs, consider a German technology company we interviewed. They use softer intermediary objectives rather than strict revenue-related ones for the initial assessment of their 2nd S-curve efforts. For instance, they work toward a number of connected machines per year rather than toward a revenue share generated from digital businesses. The latter would just be discouraging, as digital revenues for the time being continue to remain negligible in size compared to revenues from core businesses. As a consequence, softer intermediary KPIs are needed to pave the way toward digital revenues. Why follow this approach? The only predicament is that the market isn't there yet. The projected value pool that underlies this opportunity has been deemed large enough (most likely in the strategy building process) to go after this new growth opportunity. For the time being, the number of connected machines are a useful intermediary KPI, paving the way to using other KPIs once ready (including revenues and profit).[9]

No matter the type of KPI (1st versus 2nd S-curve, qualitative versus quantitative, intermediary versus final), remember all success factors should be defined in advance and it should be clear from the start how and when evaluation will take place, and what any consequences (including the potential termination of initiatives) will be.

It may seem like we are cutting the 2nd S-curve a lot of slack. "Use more qualitative KPIs. Use even nontraditional qualitative KPIs. Only transition to quantitative KPIs later. And only contribute to real company success quite late in the process." We acknowledge a double standard here, using different success factors for different initiatives. But that's okay. Frankly, more companies need to start doing this while investors have long adhered to a double-standards treatment of traditional versus digital companies.

Consider Twitter, which reported a loss of US$79 million before its IPO in November 2013, yet commanded a valuation of US$24 billion on its IPO date. Facebook paid US$19 billion for WhatsApp in 2014 when it had no revenues or profits and Microsoft paid US$26.2 billion for LinkedIn in 2016 when it was reporting losses. By contrast, in 2017, industrial conglomerate GE reported losses of US$9.8 billion – its first losses in five decades – and was met with a 44% decline in share price. It's quite astonishing that investors would punish an industrial company so severely for a lack of financial performance when they seem to skillfully brush aside such information for digital firms. Or is it? Not when you realize that traditional financial reports and accounting earnings are almost irrelevant for digital companies because they cannot account for the main value creator for digital businesses: increasing returns to scale on intangible investments.

The balance sheet usually gives a reasonable picture of productive assets and goods, but this has very limited relevance for digital companies. Also, traditional reporting is backward-looking while digital companies usually report forward-looking KPIs. Balance sheet reported assets have to be physical and owned by the company. But Airbnb doesn't own the properties it lists and Uber doesn't own its drivers' cars; hence there are almost no physical assets or inventory to report. What matters for a digital company are R&D, ecosystem partners, data, human capital, and so forth. Investments in these intangible success factors, which actually are enhanced with use (as opposed to depreciating with use, as is the case with physical assets), are not capitalized as assets but treated as expenses in the calculation of profits. So the more that is invested in the future, the higher reported losses are going to be.

The core ambition for many digital companies is to create network effects (for example, the more users Facebook has, the more valuable the whole platform becomes to the individual user) and command a winner-take-all profit structure once they have achieved market leadership (as Facebook has). However, there is no place in traditional financial statements to account for the concept of network effects or the increase in the value of a resource with use. Instead, this leads to depreciation expenses. Hence the core functionality behind the success of many digital companies – increasing returns to scale – violates the basic tenets of traditional accounting – depreciation of assets due to usage. As a result, investors have no choice but to discount the meaning of traditional financial KPIs when making their investment decisions.[10] When skilled investors willingly overlook classic performance metrics for digital companies, company internal decision makers evaluating the success of 2nd S-curve initiatives should follow suit and employ more appropriate evaluation criteria than your run-of-the-mill EBIT to assessing the impact of such efforts, at least during the beginning phases.

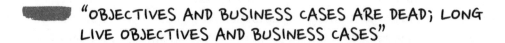 ## "OBJECTIVES AND BUSINESS CASES ARE DEAD; LONG LIVE OBJECTIVES AND BUSINESS CASES"

Once you've defined the right KPIs, the next challenge is how do you go about objective setting? In a similar vein of thought, how do you approach business case building? As you ask yourself these questions, remember the distinction: KPIs refer to the metrics that matter for determining your impact; objectives refer to your ambition level along those previously determined metrics.

Let's look at the 2nd S-curve first. There's really only two ways to approach objective setting, Falk Bothe of Volkswagen, points out: "Either you set an objective for the 2nd S-curve, often expressed as the share of revenue you expect to come from the digital business by a certain point in time (for example, 40% of total revenue to be generated from digital businesses by 2030), or you don't because you really can't, given the unpredictability of the environment – and instead of setting a concrete objective, you just monitor the digital business along the KPIs you have defined, see how those develop, and whether the new digital business bears any chances of success."[11]

A similar logic applies to building a business case because the same reasons for *not* doing it apply – namely the sheer unpredictability of the market makes it hard, and to some degree pointless, to quantify an objective or a business case. The many moving parts (including unforeseeable technological progress, competitive moves, regulatory developments, and customer acceptance), if accounted for properly and in real time, might just lead to very different outcomes at different (yet relatively close-to-each-other) points in time.

Let's stay in the automotive sector and imagine how all of these constraints to building a solid business case, say related to autonomous driving, play out. Technological progress: Can you really predict the state of autonomous vehicle technology over the next 10 years? If you're thinking yes, be honest and reconsider – would we really have been able to predict 10 years ago that driverless cars on Pittsburgh roads would be a common sight?[12] Competitive moves: Given the lack of knowledge of where your own company will be in 10 years, how can you possibly predict what your competitors (including any new entrants) will be up to? Even if you were engaging in corporate espionage (which we are, of course, not condoning), you would have no way of knowing what they will have achieved by then, seeing each and every one of them is again subject to as many unknowns as your own company is. Regulatory developments: Do you believe in your prophetic abilities insomuch as you know how accepting and encouraging governments will be of Level 4 (fully automated) or even Level 5 (full automation)[13] autonomous driving? Let alone the ethical dimensions which have yet to be resolved. Customer acceptance: Do you have a solid methodology for forecasting how welcome driverless cars will be among all age groups between 16 and 100 in 10 years? And even if you knew that, the vast majority of these people will own regular cars at that point in time. Do you have a way of predicting the sales price of the car, customers' disposable income, and their willingness-to-pay to determine whether they would even be able and willing to exchange their old car for a new one? You can surely make assumptions about all this and build a nice-looking model. But if you tweak only one of your arguably not-so-well-founded assumptions, your output will look very different.

In the absence of all this information, is it then realistic, or helpful, to set quantitative objectives and build a business case for your 2nd S-curve initiatives, when the underlying hypotheses for both are so ambiguous? Wouldn't you just be better off packing up your crystal ball and going home, un-business-cased?

AMAG would answer this in the affirmative. They realized it was illusionary to calculate a solid business case for the 2nd S-curve that would reliably hold. But their conclusion was that calculating a business case nevertheless was helpful, at the very least for confronting yourself with all the assumptions that influence the outcome of your venture, for generating learnings from doing that exercise and using these to calibrate a rough estimate during the testing phase. The key for them was to be open to and fully embrace iterating the business case, using it to better understand and even stress-test the business model and underlying revenue and cost drivers. Insights from reiterating the business case thus reduced uncertainty, and they were eventually used to inform the commercialization phase.

The key takeaway for 2nd S-curve initiatives is that you can and should calculate a business case, but not take it too seriously. Going through the process of identifying all the factors influencing the commercial viability of your venture and trying to quantify their underlying levers is a helpful exercise for sure. Quite likely, you will actually have thought of the potential underlying value pool as part of your strategy. This will be the base on which you will build your additional business case assumptions. Again, be mindful that all the input factors in such a model are often vague assumptions where the slightest tweaking fundamentally alters the outcome. Given the unpredictability of both your internal capabilities and external developments, a business case should be seen for what it is – a helpful and sometimes necessary exercise but not a fully reliable predictor of success.

Of course, there are situations where you will need a business case – for instance, when you are pitching to the board and they need to decide among a number of ventures to potentially pursue. It's likely they will want to see a business case, and that is only fair. Run those numbers while retaining the humility to know that these are only projections. A similar logic holds for objective setting. You will likely be asked for the goals your venture is working toward and that is a fair question. Having an answer ready will at the very least soothe concerns. So set these objectives in line with your business case. Embrace changes and adjust your business case, its underlying assumptions, and your objectives continuously to reflect your latest level of knowledge. The exercise of going through this thinking alone will help further sharpen your own understanding of the venture.

There are several companies that practice this more "fluid" approach to objective setting and business case building in real life. Alpiq, the Swiss energy service provider, uses a phased approach whereby objectives in the beginning phase are merely intermediary milestones to be reached by a certain date. This phase is also used to gather as much data as possible to later inform building a relatively solid business case whose assumptions are well-grounded and that can be used to derive objectives.

All of this so far concerns only objective setting for the strategic, long-term initiatives on the 2nd S-curve, which often build on forward-looking bets related to AI, IoT, and similar. It should be clear for companies that they cannot be expected to break even in the short term, but they are still worth investing in.

Let's now move to the other end of the spectrum where the more short- and mid-term-oriented initiatives of the 1st S-curve reside. Efforts related to the digitization of the core business are typically aimed at either efficiency improvements or customer experience upgrades. Particularly for efficiency improvements should (ambitious) objectives be set and a clear business case be calculated. Classic return expectations are expected and proven project management approaches will pave the way to success. This should be a road much taken. For customer experience enhancements you should set objectives and calculate a business case as well. But these objectives and the underlying KPIs need to be very different from those of an efficiency improvement initiative. The KPIs should be market-based criteria and the objectives should be ambitious, reflecting customers' real willingness-to-pay. If these objectives are not met early on, do your best not to shy away from pivoting or terminating the initiative.

Again, you may think we are cutting the 2nd S-curve a lot of slack by allowing it to go almost objective- and business-case-free while the requirements of the 1st S-curve are a lot stricter. But don't forget: the 2nd S-curve will eventually also need to meet targets, just later in the process when it has morphed into something more closely resembling a new 1st S-curve. This is not an infinite pardon but momentary relief. Cutting the 2nd S-curve some slack in terms of objectives is practiced by many leading organizations.

One big issue related to objectives and particularly business cases has not yet been addressed. In the words of a popular Swedish band from the 1970s: [it's all about] money, money, money. For our purposes, this translates into the viable question: How much money should even go into the 2nd S-curve to begin with? We've talked mostly about the unpredictability of the income side (Can you really set an objective, say, for revenue, when your parameters are highly volatile? Does it make sense to calculate a business case when market acceptance of your product or service is so unpredictable?). But we must also look at the other side of the equation, or the business case: expenses. A question equally intriguing as that of financial income is that of financial output. How much money do you need to pump into the 2nd S-curve? What is a reasonable expense figure for your business case, should you build one?

A helpful rule of thumb is to set aside 1 to 2% of revenues (from the 1st S-curve) for your radically new business; 1 or 2% is not nothing. How can an established business handle that significant extra financial outlay? There's a couple of ways. One option is to partner with direct competitors or tech companies to alleviate the financial burden from the single firm and spread risk across multiple parties. The preferred option for most companies, however, is for their own 1st S-curve to pick up speed and generate more revenue. The extra income generated then goes into financing the 2nd S-curve, which will operate at a loss for the time being. This mode ensures that total EBIT (that is, across both S-curves) can be kept relatively constant. If neither of these is possible, the last resort and least popular path (especially from a shareholder perspective) kicks in. In this scenario, additional revenue to offset the extra

2nd S-curve expenses cannot be generated, so total EBIT (across both S-curves) drops. The best thing to do in this world is to know this early on and to communicate it preemptively and proactively (rather than retrospectively) to the Board, which is then in a better position to prepare for and accept that scenario, though investor backlash may still ensue.

This very reality yet again illustrates why legacy companies face such a different challenge when it comes to digitization and digital transformation compared with start-ups. The latter receive funding for their 2nd S-curve business (in most cases, the only business they even have, given their lack of history) from venture capital firms – and sizeable amounts of funding at that. In fact, these funding rounds are often so substantial that no corporate start-up could ever compete (let alone the fact that VC funding is no viable option for incumbents to begin with). Many large firms work tirelessly over many years to achieve significant revenues. Imagine suddenly having to generate US$50 million out of nowhere because a new business venture needs the money, and thus not even being able to reap the benefits of the extra generated cash because it is immediately pumped into something else. No wonder the (1st S-curve business of a) legacy company easily gets frustrated. Meanwhile, getting US$50 million in a funding round from a VC? Oddly, often not such a big deal.

FAIL, FAIL AGAIN AND BETTER

You have done everything right and still something went wrong. You determined the right KPIs, making sure to follow your five-point to-do list. You set reasonable objectives and calculated (and recalculated) a sound business case. Still, the brutal reality is that not all digital transformation-related efforts will avail, as your success measurement surely will demonstrate. Understandably, accepting this is hard for businesses so they'd best brace themselves for the eventuality that, while some digital transformation initiatives will yield results that need to be accounted for, others will be of little or no success and will need to halt. This means the overall success rate across digital initiatives will be quite a bit lower than the utopian (yet always hoped for) 100%. One company that faced this very challenge is Munich Re, the globally leading reinsurance company.

MUNICH RE

Imagine having to place several bets and knowing that only a few of them will prove successful. This is what Olaf Frank, head of Business Technology, had to do when tasked with evaluating the digital initiatives Munich Re had been running for the past few months.

What made this particularly hard was that Munich Re – like many other traditional companies – found it hard to stop initiatives that were failing to deliver results. "There were several reasons why this was so difficult," Frank explains. "First, at Munich Re [and in traditional companies in general; authors' note], failure is something that everyone tries to avoid. If you fund an initiative and put resources into it, you want it to succeed and earn money; if it fails, that is just hard to accept. Second, it's generally uncommon to write off R&D costs. Third, you don't want to discourage motivated employees – those working on digital initiatives are usually very driven and you don't want to risk taking the wind out of their sails. Fourth, you don't want to be overly critical and stop an initiative that just needs more time or a little twist. Fifth, the idea you are about to stop is one that you initially found promising, so departing from your gut feeling is another mental barrier. Sixth, with the initial funding of that idea you made a commitment (financially and otherwise), so to stop the initiative before it has reached its goal is painful simply because of sunk cost. And finally, it's usually a whole committee of people (potentially the decision-making body) that decides about such go/no-go decisions. This does not really make things easier, because the criteria for evaluation are not set in stone. Instead what ends up materializing are a lot of debates based on differing opinions between the members of the decision-making body. The result, in the end, is not always clear-cut."[14]

It can be hard to cut initiatives short when you had high hopes for them. Nevertheless, it's critical that companies learn to do so. One thing that helps to get there are clear evaluation criteria from the get-go (item four from the earlier list). These should be akin to the ones we described earlier; at the same time there is no harm in broadening the definition of success to include noneconomic concepts that are more optimistic. For instance, did this initiative generate new learnings? Did we gain experience and market access in a new segment thanks to this initiative? Finding the silver lining may be an important lever to further employee morale.

When we talk about measurement and criteria to evaluate success on the 2nd S-curve, we also must talk about the inherent uncertainty and the higher level of risk associated with these efforts. For established organizations, this often means breaking new ground. Everybody involved needs to internalize that a departure from the current business invariably entails an uncertain and risky endeavor. The level of risk depends on how far your organization moves away from its core. Because of these uncharted, uncertain waters that are not guaranteed to translate into traditional business performance metrics immediately, understanding and buy-in from everywhere in the organization is essential. The digital unit will, of course, do everything in their power to generate a return and make the investment a success, but a certain degree of risk persists, especially in the beginning stages. First, to limit that risk, decision-making bodies can agree to take a calculated risk only (for example, set a max of US\$2 million per initiative – this number should obviously vary based on the firm in question). Before the initiative kicks off, expectations should be clear: if the initiative fails, the plug is pulled after running out of the US\$2 million. Bottom line, though, is that the will to go through with the initiative outweighs the potential sunk cost of US\$2 million. Second, a stage gate development process additionally aids in the limitation of costs and reduction of uncertainty early on. That's because small development teams and rapid prototyping usually do not cost enormous amounts of money. Plus, clearly defined stage gates allow a solid overview of costs, easily keeping track of investments and pay-offs. Third, testing and iterating ideas with customers early on provides extra help in ruling out uncertainty. At the point where significant investments in scaling become necessary, you already know how your customers will react and have a handle on potential performance, which warrants the investment in the first place.

TRANSPARENCY TRUMPS THE TELEPHONE GAME

The core message here is easily delivered: maximum transparency is critically important for establishing the importance of digital transformation KPIs and for the success of the digital transformation as a whole.

Some digital transformation leaders are happy to take this quite literally.

> If it were up to me, I'd put up a screen displaying the most important KPIs in the entrance hall of the building so everybody would know where we stand on a daily basis. Better yet, I'd display those KPIs in the canteen where both board members and regular staff from across the organization - Sales, Finance, and so forth - dine daily. I'd make the screen an infotainment center, blending information, like the latest news from the mobility sector, with entertainment. This is a great way to nudge employees to stay abreast of the latest developments. If you wanted to take it to the extreme, a heightened nudging lever may even be to display people live waiting at bus stops. This could increase the accountability of everybody involved in developing alternative mobility solutions for improving results and bringing solutions to market quicker

Falk Bothe, Director of Digital Transformation Office, Volkswagen[15]

What would you show on your screens? Best is to build dashboards, using business analytics and visualization software you likely already employ (such as Power BI or Tableau), showing your KPIs. These dashboards should not only be available on-screen but centrally as well (a quick link to your intranet).

If you want to circumvent having to determine your own KPIs, setting up your own dashboards, and so forth, do as BNP Paribas, the French banking group, did.

BNP PARIBAS ASSET MANAGEMENT

"If you're not in the retail banking business, impact measurement is difficult. In B2C banking, your digital transformation impact measurement will naturally follow your customer journey, and your metrics will be directly related to your customers. That's because a digital transformation in retail banking is about digitally transforming the relationship with your customer. In B2B banking, like BNP Paribas' Asset Management, it's hard to nail down how to best measure impact," Arnaud Zeitoun says.

Zeitoun is now the Deputy CEO in charge of Transformation at BNP Paribas Switzerland and previously was the Global Head of Transformation at BNP Paribas Asset Management, running their Transformation Management Group, which includes their digital transformation efforts. The Transformation Management Group was established to be a three-year program. For their digital transformation efforts, they realized early on that impact measurement was a tricky one. They partnered with market research firm Gartner to use its proprietary Digital Business Benchmark and Maturity Assessment. This standardized framework gives the digital transformation team a solid 12-dimension model to assess their digital readiness and a useful external benchmark against other asset managers. It includes both qualitative and quantitative dimensions, including many that we cover in this book (for instance, leadership, digital culture). Besides the inherent credibility of the framework, Zeitoun particularly appreciates that it is an unbiased, external view of what matters.

At the same time, he cautions, such an external grid should not dictate the whole digital transformation strategy. It serves as a helpful lifeline, a guide toward the implementation of the strategy, but it's not equivalent to the strategy.

Regardless of where the KPIs come from, transparency always matters. The Gartner report is shared among the digital transformation community on a monthly basis because, as Zeitoun points out, "it's important not to make it a secret."[16]

Naturally there are different appetites for information sharing and transparency. But in the context of a digital transformation, the way to go is all-in. Everybody who has a stake in the digital transformation needs to know what KPIs the digital transformation is working toward and how it is performing. No need to spill trade secrets but no harm in being open, either. At the very least, seeing the 2nd S-curve perform well along their own KPIs may dampen skeptical vibes coming from the 1st S-curve.

And if something does go wrong, which it inevitably will, how do you document a terminated initiative? Code word: postmortem (or graveyard, which is what WACKER Digital, the digital program of chemicals conglomerate WACKER, calls it). More nicely phrased, closing memo.

In this context, a postmortem is a written account of learnings from a terminated digital transformation initiative. It helps to "fail better" the next time because it documents what happened, why the initiative potentially failed, how any issues were mitigated or potentially resolved, how much was invested to yield what kind of impact (including any relevant KPIs), and what any learning is from this occurrence. First, this serves as an important written reference to go back to when needed. In the agile digital transformation world, documentation is often overlooked and for good reason. A post-mortem can be instrumental in building resilience and preparing for issues that may arise in other strategic initiatives. Plus, it has a positive effect on culture building: sharing failures openly and without fear for repercussions and maintaining a constructive dialog of jointly making this better the next time around is key to establishing a culture conducive of digital transformation work.[17]

Of course, both transparency on the current status and documentation of past results need to be delivered on a relatively aggregate level with a reasonable clustering depth (for example, by geography). It must not be broken down too granularly. In countries with strong unions, this would not be possible anyway due to worker protection. Regardless, it should be avoided everywhere to prevent finger pointing.

DON'T PLAY THE BLAME GAME BUT DO HOLD PEOPLE ACCOUNTABLE

Who is accountable for digital transformation KPIs and any potential objectives you may have set usually follows the governance structure of your digital transformation or of your organization as a whole.

While every team member needs to feel accountable for achieving predetermined goals (particularly those on the 1st S-curve), it's best to anchor the reporting accountability for the defined KPIs on maximum seniority – ideally CEO-1, such as Chief Digital Officer, Chief Transformation Officer, Chief Innovation Officer or Chief Technology Officer, or anybody skilled and experienced in the digital transformation space and directly (or as directly as possible) reporting to the CEO.

A close connection to the CEO is helpful to underscore the importance of digital transformation efforts, making clear to the whole business that this is a fundamental overhaul of the organization that commands senior attention.

While such senior executives may hold the reporting accountability, the accountability for achieving the defined KPIs should sit with the digital transformation team – the *entire* team. The same logic as with transparency and documentation applies: everybody should know how they are jointly doing so there is maximum buy-in and commitment to the cause from all, but avoid finger pointing at all cost. If one KPI is not doing well, then the team should jointly brainstorm for how to improve rather than siloing it with a single person.

Another reason to share KPI accountability among a team is that in a digital transformation environment, team member turnover is often high. This doesn't mean team members often leave; it just means they regularly rotate positions as work packages change and initiatives evolve. Having the responsibility for a certain KPI resting with only one person makes team member transitions more difficult, potentially increasing the burden on the new team members.

BEWARE OF THAT BOOMERANG

The beauty of digital transformation efforts on the 2nd S-curve inter alia lies in the potential for positive spillover ("back-coupling" or "boomerang") effects into the core business. These are twofold, being qualitative or quantitative in nature.

Picture this: your company is successfully engaging in 2nd S-curve initiatives. You are earning a lot of positive press coverage for that. Your whole corporate reputation experiences a renaissance given your "visionary foresight" and "zealous perseverance" in the pursuit of a digital business that could "shake the non-fruit Apples of this world," as a business magazine puts it. College graduates flock to your headquarters and line up outside your gates carrying banners. "I want to dedicate my work life to you." These are clearly qualitative back-coupling effects of your 2nd S-curve initiatives creating a positive momentum for your company as a whole, thus rubbing off on your 1st S-curve.

Eventually this favorable media coverage and the resulting positive aura of your company will translate into investor confidence. Suddenly we find ourselves in a very quantitative corner because investor confidence can usually be observed in real share price value. If you're not looking to build a discounted cash flow (DCF) model, refer to your market capitalization for a shortcut to your market value. Very likely you will see this spike following such positive press coverage around the long-term viability of your company. Nike experienced this. CEO Mark Parker attributed much of Nike's earnings run and share price increase in their fiscal Q3 2019 results to their successful digital transformation and emphasis on digital initiatives, with NIKE Digital achieving a growth rate of 36% during the quarter. While the SNKRS and NIKE apps clearly stole the brick-and-mortar shops, thunder, increased investor confidence from digital initiatives benefits the core business.[18] A strong market position allows Nike to reinvest in its core business again, for instance, by boosting its women's wear portfolio.[19]

Aside from share prices, which, in all fairness, can be a bit of a show-and-tell game, the core may also benefit from such more predictable and durable back-coupling effects as increased sales in the core through cross-selling from the new digital business or a better utilization rate of core sales staff as they take on serving 2nd S-curve customers as well.

It is understandable there can be animosities between the 1st and 2nd S-curve – particularly from the 1st toward the 2nd. Yet the 1st S-curve is not only a giver but can also be on the receiving end of things. The positive effects the 1st S-curve can gain from the 2nd S-curve shall not be understated, and they should be called out as such.

Get to the bottom of these effects by investigating them thoroughly before mirroring what you find to your core organization. In interviews with those college graduates lining up outside your gates, ask them what motivates them to join your company, and the answer "reputation for innovative corporate culture" should ring a bell. You can do the same with investors and inquire about their investment reasons. Collect these feedback points and present them to your 1st S-curve organization, showcasing how skilled workers and willing investors benefit them, and not only the 2nd S-curve. Ideally lay out your plans for reinvestments in the core, illustrating exactly which areas of the 1st S-curve will see increased investments flowing their way. At all times, make clear that the workhorse (1st S-curve) and the striped unicorn (2nd S-curve) work in unison – making the same company successful. Give-and-take is commonplace, and it will go both ways.

To conclude, we add a somewhat more philosophical side-note. We extend the concept of back-coupling from between 2nd and 1st S-curve to between digital transformation payoffs for companies and payoffs for the public good. This purpose-oriented lens comes full circle in this last chapter of our framework.

In this book, we deliberately focus on how legacy companies best approach a digital transformation. However, particularly as it pertains to impact, it would be grossly negligent not to bring a broader societal perspective into play. The digital transformation of for-profit firms has fundamental effects not only on themselves and their justified pursuit of corporate longevity and continued financial returns. Beyond its effects on industry, it also impacts individual consumers and society as a whole, as well as the environment. One entity that is dedicated to understanding digital transformation in this way is the World Economic Forum.

WORLD ECONOMIC FORUM

Launched in 2015, the World Economic Forum's Digital Transformation Initiative has made it its aim to investigate the potential digital transformation has to impact individual people's lives, create benefits for society in general, and unlock value for companies. It is also meant to serve as a hub for discussions around the latest developments in the digitization of business and society.

Related to impact measurement, the Digital Transformation Initiative has advanced with great strides and made a seminal contribution to quantifying the benefits of digital transformation on industry and society. Cristian Citu, Digital Transformation Lead at the World Economic Forum, says that there is an estimated US$100 trillion of value that digitization could create over 10 years (2016–2025). These numbers are the result of a two-year effort, during which time the Digital Transformation Initiative developed a unique value-at-stake model to assess technology's impact on business and society. This framework analyzes the impact of over 130 digital initiatives (bundles of innovative digital technologies such as AI, big data analytics, and cloud computing) from 11 different industries. An individual initiative's potential impact, Citu explains, is the sum of two components: the digital value to industry and the digital value to society. The digital value to industry comprises the potential impact on an industry's operating profit (value addition from new products and services) and operating profits that shift between industry players (value migration from shifting profit pools). The digital value to society encompasses consumer benefits (the gain to customers from cost and time savings), effects on society (financial and nonfinancial gains, such as productivity gains, lives saved, life expectancy increase, net job creation), and the impact on the environment (savings of emissions of CO_2 and other gases).

Consider the travel and tourism industry, where US$380 billion could be generated until 2025 alone. This is thanks to the dispersion of access-based platform business models enabling the sharing and exchange of assets in the travel ecosystem. As a result of such new business models, costs of ownership are reduced for the owning party (US$182 billion), savings are generated for the borrowing party (US$193 billion), and a potential reduction in CO_2 emissions of 107 million tons (valued at US$5 billion) can be achieved if new aircraft sharing models are adopted in commercial aviation.[20]

This goes to show that besides additional value to individual businesses, positive impact from digitization and digital transformation can be accrued on the part of societies and the environment, too.

 GET MOVING TO AVOID THE DINOSAUR FATE

To set you up for success when devising your impact measurement strategy, be sure to follow these best practices:

- Determine KPIs that are specific to the respective S-curve and the stage that the digital transformation finds itself in:
  - On the 1st S-curve, use traditional KPIs such as metrics related to reaching target profitability or maximizing firm value (for example, ROA, ROI, EBIT).

— On the 2nd S-curve, use KPIs that relate to your strategic goal more akin to growth potential rather than cost savings (for example, customer satisfaction metrics such as NPS).

— In the beginning, choose mostly qualitative KPIs for the 2nd S-curve, or, more simply, check (yes/no) the presence of success factors (for example, compelling story, potential to become a unicorn), or use the timely achievement of milestones.

— Later on, move over to using more traditional KPIs also for the 2nd S-curve (for example, market share).

● Build a business case and set objectives for your 2nd S-curve initiatives (simply because you will likely be asked for them); test your assumptions and adjust both your objectives and your business case continuously based on latest learnings; for your 1st S-curve initiatives, set up a diligent business case and do track against ambitious targets.

● Be mindful that success rates on the 2nd S-curve might be dramatically lower than for "safe bets" on the 1st S-curve, and include alternative success metrics that do not fit the "economic success" bill (for example, learnings, new market access).

● Anchor the reporting accountability for the defined KPIs on a senior level to ensure their full commitment to the cause, and anchor the accountability for achieving the defined KPIs on a team level to ensure buy-in from the entire team.

● Ensure maximum transparency on (and proper documentation of) KPIs but make sure to break it down on an aggregate level to avoid finger pointing.

● Nudge people to stay abreast of latest numbers and account for the fact that the 2nd S-curve will eventually (have to) contribute to traditional 1st S-curve KPIs (for example, EBIT), and track 1st and 2nd S-curve contributions to these KPIs separately, where possible.

GET INSPIRED (BY BANKING)

SCANDINAVIAN BANK

When a Scandinavian financial institution decided to transform their largely analog mortgage and loans business into a digital business in 2018, KPIs were top of mind for the team. "In the old process, when a customer applied for a consumer loan, they could in theory do it online. But the application was then still handled manually in local bank branches, making this a long, cumbersome process that was anything but a pleasant experience," a former bank executive explains. "The median time for processing such an application was around 2.5 days. Now we have introduced a digital process that does this in real time, bringing the processing time for an application down to zero," he explains. Now we're talking KPIs.

"You cannot go from zero to 100 in three months. We used KPIs to slice down the problem," the executive says. He hints at the importance of intermediary KPIs. These were also instrumental in setting expectations for senior management. They, too, must understand that Rome wasn't built in a day and that during Rome's construction, the guiding KPI was not to finish the city – instead a staged approach (building streets, buildings, and so forth) was employed. Modern corporations are no different. At the bank, the initial KPIs included the number of banks using the new digital solution and the technical coverage the solution supported.

"We started out with a few individual branches only, then expanding into almost 20, and more from there. We also started with one type of applicant, which accounted for approximately 10% of coverage of all submitted applications," we are told. Making these parameters visible – a certain number of branches and only 10% of all applications – was important to set expectations. It was equally important to stress that the aspiration level for coverage was 100% by the end of the same year.

The ultimate KPIs for the head of this transformation were the cost-to-income ratio, NPS, and market share. But all were influenced by the intermediary KPIs, which is why they were tracked and reported more rigorously and seen as more telling of the performance.

In general, there was a lot of attention on this fundamental digital overhaul of the credit and loans business. A part of a larger overall transformation of the bank, transparency of progress had to be ensured at all times. Accountability for KPIs rested with tribes – agile organization jargon for a collection of squads (the smallest group in the organizational structure, led by a Product Owner). Documentation requirements were high. Given its highly regulated nature, the mortgages and consumer loans market was subject to regulations from national and international supervisory authorities. There was, however, some flexibility in target setting as this was done as a bottom-up approach to ensure that while the transformation was ambitious, performance indicators were set at a realistically achievable level.[21]

KEY TAKEAWAYS:

- **Set expectations using intermediary KPIs** – It needs to be clear to senior management that the end goal will only be achieved with a time lag and that intermediary KPIs bear more descriptive power over current performance.

- **Determine guiding KPIs into which intermediary KPIs feed** – Think of it as an issue tree where the ultimate goal is determined by a number of lower-order factors that can be influenced more readily and where changes translate into effects quickly.

- **Setting objectives bottom-up makes way for realism in addition to ambition** – Top-down target setting can be overly ambitious; use a more democratic approach to setting objectives.

conclusion: Reinvent Your Organization by Putting the Pieces Together

After a few hundred pages, you have reached your final destination. There is no holy grail here, no hidden golden nugget for you to discover. Only a wrapup of what you have heard – in the form of a story unifying the concepts presented throughout this book.

We hope that this and all the other stories we shared inspire you to turn your organization into a digital transformer that masters balancing the continued success of your core business while setting up a digital business.

BTPN
......

Why: The point of departure for the bank, a leading Indonesian financial institution, was to grow and open up new business areas (specifically, consumer banking) beyond the historical focus on pensions. They soon realized this was not possible with a traditional brick-and-mortar presence for a number of reasons, including the distinct geographical makeup of their home market, given Indonesia is the world's largest island country with more than 17,000 islands, the seventh largest country globally in sea and land area, and the fourth most populous. Growing through digital means was thus seen as the only viable way to expand into a new business area. Paralleling these motivations, management also realized that a broader overhaul of the traditional core as part of a longer-term transformation was necessary to not be left behind as competitors were also upping their game.

What: The mission to establish a best-in-class digital bank rooted in a purely digital business model was set early on. With regard to defining the actual digital strategy, the team focused on the specifics of the business opportunity at hand to determine a path forward. They detailed what goals they wanted to achieve, who the most attractive target customer segments were, and where the revenue potential lay – all elements part of any strategy development process. What set their digital strategy apart from a typical strategy, though, were two factors: (1) the importance of capability building, which in typical strategy development is seen as a negligible implementation issue but here really took center stage, and (2) the relentless focus on the customer and the value proposition, which in typical strategy development is a more subordinate thought but here really determined the strategic course of a new business.

How: Regarding **technology**, the bank set itself a very high bar because digital is so much at the core of the business (digital IT is in fact part of the product) and not just a channel. The majority of customer-facing digital components were built from scratch in-house, partially because the systems needed to fulfill the customer proposition didn't already exist in the parent organization. The digital business now relies on a state-of-the-art tech stack, fully microservices-based, similar to that which any modern tech start-up would pursue, while select systems are still shared with the core bank and integrated via APIs. The **organization**al setup since beginning has been that of a start-up, with the Board of Commissioners acting as early investors. This also meant that, in terms of **processes**, virtually everything was designed from scratch (aside from few exceptions) and the digital bank also had full control over the rollout. This followed a staged approach with the soft launch of the unbranded app minimum viable product (MVP) first and a full launch several months later, with features being added on a rolling basis since then.

In terms of **leadership**, the bank looked for profiles combining three criteria: experience in the digital arena, financial services knowledge, and a proven leadership track record. Turns out that demonstrated leadership experience was ultimately the most crucial factor and the hardest to find. As a result, the remaining criteria were somewhat relaxed, also for the remainder of the **people** who joined the digital bank—experience in digital was substituted with excitement for digital and, especially on more junior levels, an industry-agnostic view on past experiences was adopted. Given the relentless focus on the customer, people from customer experience–centric industries (like hospitality or retail) were proactively sought out because it was trusted that they would bring the necessary customer centricity to the table. As far as sourcing both leaders and staff were concerned, the bank relied almost exclusively on external hires, which today account for around about 95% of the headcount. Establishing a fruitful **culture** in the newly created business turned out an easy exercise given the digital bank was fully aligned on a "start-up feel," where wearing T-shirts is welcome. The ways of working rely on a squad chapter model, where multifunctional teams cooperate in agile ways. Reconciling this with the traditional bank was the real challenge. The guiding principle of customer centricity ultimately helped unify the two worlds as both had committed themselves to subscribing fully to this mission.

Where: Given that the digital bank constitutes a completely separate and new business that was motivated by the intent to venture into a new business area, the KPIs that are tracked are fundamentally business-focused instead of digitally specific (for example, customer numbers, customer balances, cost of acquisition), and impact measurement in the digital bank is really equivalent to general business tracking. One significant difference to a brick-and-mortar model is, of course, the customer journey and the analysis of dropout rates along that journey (for example, app downloads, in-app registrations, completion of know-your-customer (KYC) process). Tracking is fully automated and visualized in Tableau dashboards. How new KPIs can be tracked (for example, how the necessary information can be transferred into the data lake) is always an inherent consideration. Besides the focus on such quantitative KPIs, softer and more qualitative evaluation will be explored in more detail going forward. For instance, monthly nominations for outstanding customer focus have been introduced.[1]

Striking a balance between two very different worlds remains a central topic for BTPN now and in the future. And it should be for every organization. Irrespective of size, the digital transformer's dilemma is one that firms cannot evade. What we describe in this book is just as applicable to a five-person company, as it is to a 500-person company as it is to a 50,000-person company. Granted, for a five-headcount firm, the role of external partners will be even more pronounced simply because they have such limited in-house capabilities, necessitating employees to each wear multiple hats as it is. But the logic of how they need to transform is still the same. Similarly, for a 500-headcount firm, the realities of this book will be the same. They too need to rely more strongly on partnerships to make the digital transformation happen. That's because they only cover a small piece of the value chain and collaborators chip in to make change happen along the shared value chain. In our interviews we found that smaller companies tend to focus their efforts on the 1st S-curve, not realizing the potential (and ability) to act on the 2nd S-curve. These differences aside, though, digital transformation and the digital transformer's dilemma is as applicable to your "mom-and-pop" store as it is to the Fortune 500 companies of the planet.

Notes

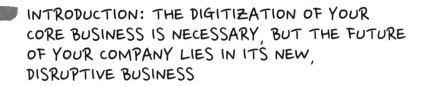

INTRODUCTION: THE DIGITIZATION OF YOUR CORE BUSINESS IS NECESSARY, BUT THE FUTURE OF YOUR COMPANY LIES IN ITS NEW, DISRUPTIVE BUSINESS

1. BBC; https://www.bbc.com/news/business-47332805
2. *The New Yorker*; https://www.newyorker.com/business/currency/where-nokia-went-wrong
3. *Harvard Business Review*: https://hbr.org/2016/07/kodaks-downfall-wasnt-about-technology
4. *Harvard Business Review*; https://hbr.org/2018/03/why-so-many-high-profile-digital-transformations-fail
5. McKinsey & Company; https://www.mckinsey.com/featured-insights/future-of-work/jobs-lost-jobs-gained-what-the-future-of-work-will-mean-for-jobs-skills-and-wages
6. Schwab, Klaus. *The Fourth Industrial Revolution*. New York: Crown Business, 2017
7. Iansiti, Marco and Lakhani, Karim. *Competing in the Age of AI: Strategy and Leadership When Algorithms and Networks Run the World*. Cambridge, MA: Harvard Business Review Press, 2020
8. Forbes; https://www.forbes.com/sites/shephyken/2018/08/19/uber-your-business-before-it-gets-kodak-ed/
9. Fortune; https://fortune.com/2020/03/23/coronavirus-economic-impact-predictions-great-recession-2020-markets-imf/
10. Forbes; https://www.forbes.com/sites/alexkonrad/2020/03/13/zoom-video-coronavirus-eric-yuan-schools/#754d19204e71
11. CNBC; https://www.cnbc.com/2020/03/19/dominos-expects-to-hire-10000-workers.html
12. *Washington Post*; https://www.washingtonpost.com/business/2020/03/26/unemployment-claims-coronavirus-3-million/
13. *Business Today*; https://www.businesstoday.in/current/corporate/coronavirus-dominos-switches-to-contactless-delivery-heres-how-it-works/story/398381.html
14. *New York Times*; https://www.nytimes.com/2020/03/23/technology/coronavirus-surveillance-tracking-privacy.html
15. *New York Times*; https://www.nytimes.com/2020/03/19/us/coronavirus-location-tracking.html
16. GovTech Singapore; https://www.tech.gov.sg/digital-government-transformation/
17. *Wall Street Journal*; https://www.wsj.com/articles/airbnb-bookings-plunge-amid-coronavirus-pandemic-11584032412
18. Robinhood; https://snacks.robinhood.com/newsletters/3GrDekUbeSUHNRq33vbDag/articles/3rC0C91lB3jKOjyrZfutDP/
19. *The Guardian*; https://www.theguardian.com/commentisfree/2020/mar/03/overhyped-overvalued-tech-startups
20. Bloomberg; https://www.bloomberg.com/news/articles/2020-01-02/private-equity-is-starting-2020-with-more-cash-than-ever-before
21. EY; https://www.ey.com/en_gl/news/2020/03/ey-report-reveals-private-equity-industry-is-well-prepared-to-endure-the-next-downturn
22. *The Independent*; https://www.independent.co.uk/life-style/health-and-families/coronavirus-home-workout-exercise-class-yoga-dance-kids-elderly-joe-wicks-a9421126.html

23. McKinsey & Company; https://www.mckinsey.com/industries/financial-services/our-insights/leading-a-consumer-bank-through-the-coronavirus-pandemic

24. *Wall Street Journal*; https://www.wsj.com/articles/nyse-to-temporarily-close-trading-floor-to-slow-coronavirus-11584568565

25. CNN; https://www.cnn.com/2020/03/09/us/coronavirus-university-college-classes/index.html

26. Fortune; http://fortune.com/2013/05/17/ginni-rometty-reveals-the-future-of-watson/

27. A template for developing or documenting business models along nine elements. Based on: Osterwalder, Alexander and Pigneur, Yves. *Business Model Generation: A Handbook for Visionaries, Game Changers and Challengers*. Hoboken: Wiley, 2010

28. Courtesy of Andreas Opelt, Saubermacher, personal communication, 23/10/2018; Courtesy of Christof Stromberger, Denovo, personal communication, 14/11/2018

 # CHAPTER 1. ACT OR DIE, PRETTY SOON

1. McKinsey & Company; https://www.mckinsey.com/business-functions/digital-mckinsey/our-insights/how-digital-reinventors-are-pulling-away-from-the-pack

2. Courtesy of Onur Erdogan, formerly Estée Lauder, personal communication, 14/03/2019

3. McKinsey & Company; https://www.mckinsey.com/business-functions/digital-mckinsey/our-insights/the-case-for-digital-reinvention, https://www.mckinsey.com/~/media/McKinsey/Business%20Functions/McKinsey%20Digital/Our%20Insights/Digital%20McKinsey%20Insights%20Number%203/Digital-McKinsey-Insights-Issue-3-revised.ashx

4. Courtesy of Gieri Cathomas, Swisspath Health, personal communication, 16/08/2019

5. Courtesy of Urs Kissling, Embassy Jewel, personal communication, 09/01/2019

6. Courtesy of Jean-Charles Deconninck, Generix Group, personal communication, 22/03/2019

7. Courtesy of Dirk Linzmeier, OSRAM Continental, personal communication, 17/12/2018

8. Courtesy of Andreas Opelt, Saubermacher, personal communication, 23/10/2018

9. Courtesy of Safer Mourad, Saurer Group, personal communication, 14/01/2019

10. Courtesy of Patrick Koller, Faurecia, personal communication, 28/02/2019

11. Forbes; https://www.forbes.com/sites/mckinsey/2017/02/15/now-new-next-how-growth-champions-create-new-value/#f234ce61a81b

12. Courtesy of Bernd Reck, Sören Lauinger, Aesculap, personal communication, 19/12/2018

13. Courtesy of Harald Brodbeck, Horváth & Partners, personal communication, 17/01/0219

14. World Economic Forum; http://reports.weforum.org/digital-transformation/understanding-the-impact-of-digitalization-on-society/

15. World Economic Forum; http://reports.weforum.org/digital-transformation/understanding-the-impact-of-digitalization-on-society/

16. World Economic Forum; http://reports.weforum.org/digital-transformation/understanding-the-impact-of-digitalization-on-society/

17. Courtesy of Samy Jandali, BASF, personal communication, 23/01/2019

18. Courtesy of former executive manager, multinational conglomerate, personal communication, 23/01/2019

19. McKinsey & Company; https://www.mckinsey.com/mgi/overview/in-the-news/what-successful-digital-transformations-have-in-common

20. Courtesy of Jan Mrosik, Siemens, personal communication, 4/02/2019

21. McKinsey & Company; https://www.mckinsey.com/business-functions/digital-mckinsey/our-insights/how-digital-reinventors-are-pulling-away-from-the-pack
22. Courtesy of Julian Schubert, V-ZUG, personal communication, 22/03/2019
23. Forbes; https://www.forbes.com/sites/mckinsey/2017/09/25/the-three-biggest-misconceptions-about-a-digital-transformation-and-what-to-do-about-them/#2225d34f3278
24. Courtesy of Julian Schubert, V-ZUG, personal communication, 22/03/2019
25. Courtesy of senior manager (former), European bank, personal communication, 21/01/2019
26. McKinsey & Company; https://www.mckinsey.com/business-functions/digital-mckinsey/our-insights/how-digital-reinventors-are-pulling-away-from-the-pack
27. Rob Llewellyn; https://robllewellyn.com/great-digital-illusion/
28. Courtesy of Max Costantini, Mibelle Group, personal communication, 28/03/2019
29. Courtesy of Reiner Fageth, CEWE, personal communication, 20/11/2018

 CHAPTER 2. HOW TO MAKE YOUR STRATEGY, BUSINESS MODEL, AND DIGITAL INITIATIVES STOP FIGHTING EACH OTHER AND WORK TOGETHER

1. Gassmann, Oliver, Frankenberger, Karolin, and Csik, Michaela. *The Business Model Navigator: 55 Models That Will Revolutionise Your Business. Harlow: Pearson, 2014*
2. Deloitte; https://www2.deloitte.com/content/dam/Deloitte/fr/Documents/strategy/dup_strategy-not-technology-drives-digital-transformation.pdf
3. Courtesy of Thomas Pirlein, Müller Group, personal communication, 5/03/2019
4. Crainer, Stuart, and Dearlove, Des. "In search for strategy." In *Strategy@Work: From Design to Delivery*, Brightline Initiative and Thinkers50, 29–34. 2017. https://www.brightline.org/resources/thinkers50-strategy-at-work-book/
5. The Boston Consulting Group; https://www.bcg.com/publications/2015/double-game-of-digital-strategy.aspx, https://www.bcg.com/de-de/publications/2019/five-rules-digital-strategy.aspx
6. McKinsey & Company; https://www.mckinsey.com/business-functions/digital-mckinsey/our-insights/facing-up-to-digital-disruption-reinventing-the-core-with-bold-business-strategy
7. McKinsey & Company; https://www.mckinsey.com/business-functions/digital-mckinsey/our-insights/from-disrupted-to-disruptor-reinventing-your-business-by-transforming-the-core
8. Crainer, Stuart and Dearlove, Des. "In search for strategy." In *Strategy@Work: From Design to Delivery*, Brightline Initiative and Thinkers50, 29–34. 2017. https://www.brightline.org/resources/thinkers50-strategy-at-work-book/
9. The Boston Consulting Group; https://www.bcg.com/de-de/publications/2019/five-rules-digital-strategy.aspx
10. Courtesy of Safer Mourad, Saurer Group, personal communication, 14/01/2019
11. Vargas, Ricardo Vargas and Conforto, Edivandro. "Ten questions to help you turn strategy into reality." In *The Chief Strategy Officer Playbook*, Brightline Initiative and Thinkers50, 34–37, 2018; https://www.brightline.org/resources/thinkers50-cso-playbook/
12. The Boston Consulting Group; https://www.bcg.com/de-de/publications/2019/five-rules-digital-strategy.aspx
13. Vargas, Ricardo Vargas and Conforto, Edivandro. "Ten questions to help you turn strategy into reality." In *The Chief Strategy Officer Playbook*, Brightline Initiative and Thinkers50, 34-37, 2018; https://www.brightline.org/resources/thinkers50-cso-playbook/

14. McKinsey & Company; https://www.mckinsey.com/business-functions/digital-mckinsey/our-insights/facing-up-to-digital-disruption-reinventing-the-core-with-bold-business-strategy
15. Courtesy of Christian Schulz, Schindler, personal communication, 16/04/2019
16. Courtesy of Axel Schmidt and Dirk Ramhorst, WACKER Chemie AG, personal communication, 13/02/2019
17. Courtesy of Bernd Reck, Sören Lauinger, Aesculap, personal communication, 19/12/2018
18. Courtesy of senior executive, health care industry, personal communication, 19/12/2018
19. McKinsey & Company; https://www.mckinsey.com/business-functions/strategy-and-corporate-finance/our-insights/an-incumbents-guide-to-digital-disruption
20. Courtesy of Gisbert Rühl, Klöckner & Co, personal communication, 31/01/2019
21. McKinsey & Company; https://www.mckinsey.com/business-functions/strategy-and-corporate-finance/our-insights/an-incumbents-guide-to-digital-disruption
22. Courtesy of Thomas Gutzwiller, Platform Expert, personal communication, 3/05/2019 & 25/06/2019
23. Courtesy of Samy Jandali, BASF, personal communication, 23/01/2019
24. Courtesy of Markus Brokhof, formerly Alpiq, personal communication, 15/02/2019
25. Courtesy of Bernard Leong, formerly SingPost / now Amazon Web Services, personal communication, 8/02/2019
26. Courtesy of Markus Brokhof, formerly Alpiq, personal communication, 15/02/2019
27. Courtesy of Olaf Frank, Munich Re, personal communication, 11/02/2019
28. Courtesy of Stefan Stroh, Deutsche Bahn, personal communication, 28/01/2019
29. BASF uses the term "digitization" to describe the process of moving from analog to digital and the term "digitalization" to describe the use of digital technologies to move to a digital business.
30. Courtesy of Samy Jandali, BASF, personal communication, 23/01/2019
31. Courtesy of Michael Spiegel and Anna Neumeier, Deutsche Pfandbriefbank, personal communication, 18/01/2019
32. Carucci, Ron. "Why executives struggle to execute strategy." In *The Chief Strategy Officer Playbook*, Brightline Initiative and Thinkers50, 60–63, 2018; https://www.brightline.org/resources/thinkers50-cso-playbook/
33. *Harvard Business Review*; https://hbr.org/2012/05/managing-your-innovation-portfolio
34. *Harvard Business Review*; https://hbr.org/2012/05/managing-your-innovation-portfolio
35. The Boston Consulting Group; https://www.bcg.com/de-de/publications/2019/five-rules-digital-strategy.aspx
36. Courtesy of Olaf Frank, Munich Re, personal communication, 11/02/2019
37. Courtesy of senior executive, technology company, personal communication, 18/02/2019
38. Courtesy of Harald Brodbeck, Horváth & Partners, personal communication, 17/01/0219
39. This chapter makes use of and builds on content from Gassmann, Oliver, Frankenberger, Karolin, and Csik, Michaela. *The Business Model Navigator: 55 Models That Will Revolutionise Your Business*. Harlow: Pearson, 2014
40. *Harvard Business Review*; https://hbr.org/2002/05/why-business-models-matter
41. Demil, Benoit, and Lecocq, Xavier. "Business Model Evolution: In Search of Dynamic Consistency." *Long Range Planning* 43, (2010): 227–246; Osterwalder, Alexander, and Pigneur, Yves. *Business Model Generation: A Handbook for Visionaries, Game Changers and Challengers*. Hoboken: Wiley, 2010; Gassmann, Oliver, Frankenberger, Karolin, and Csik, Michaela. *The Business Model Navigator: 55 Models That Will Revolutionise Your Business*. Harlow: Pearson, 2014
42. Gassmann, Oliver, Frankenberger, Karolin, and Csik, Michaela. *The Business Model Navigator: 55 Models That Will Revolutionise Your Business*. Harlow: Pearson, 2014
43. The Boston Consulting Group; https://www.bcg.com/documents/file36456.pdf
44. Courtesy of Patrick Koller, Faurecia, personal communication, 28/02/2019
45. Gassmann, Oliver, Frankenberger, Karolin, and Csik, Michaela. *The Business Model Navigator: 55 Models That Will Revolutionise Your Business*. Harlow: Pearson, 2014
46. Osterwalder, Alexander, and Pigneur, Yves. *Business Model Generation: A Handbook for Visionaries, Game Changers and Challengers*. Hoboken: Wiley, 2010
47. Kim, W. Chan and Mauborgne, Renée. *Blue Ocean Strategy: How to Create Uncontested Market Space and Make the Competition Irrelevant*. Boston: Harvard Business School Press, 2015

48. Gassmann, Oliver, Frankenberger, Karolin, and Csik, Michaela. *The Business Model Navigator: 55 Models That Will Revolutionise Your Business*. Harlow: Pearson, 2014

49. Gassmann, Oliver, Frankenberger, Karolin, and Csik, Michaela. *The Business Model Navigator: 55 Models That Will Revolutionise Your Business*. Harlow: Pearson, 2014

50. Courtesy of Norman Willich and Alexander Maute, Eissmann, personal communication, 20/02/2019

51. Courtesy of Thorsten Müller, formerly Osram, personal communication, 27/11/2019

52. Gassmann, Oliver, Frankenberger, Karolin, and Csik, Michaela. *The Business Model Navigator: 55 Models That Will Revolutionise Your Business*. Harlow: Pearson, 2014

53. Gassmann, Oliver, Frankenberger, Karolin, and Csik, Michaela. *The Business Model Navigator: 55 Models That Will Revolutionise Your Business*. Harlow: Pearson, 2014

54. Courtesy of Gisbert Rühl, Klöckner & Co, personal communication, 31/01/2019

55. McKinsey & Company; https://www.mckinsey.com/business-functions/strategy-and-corporate-finance/our-insights/the-economic-essentials-of-digital-strategy

56. The Boston Consulting Group; https://www.bcg.com/publications/2015/double-game-of-digital-strategy.aspx

57. McKinsey & Company; https://www.mckinsey.com/business-functions/strategy-and-corporate-finance/our-insights/the-economic-essentials-of-digital-strategy

58. McKinsey & Company; https://www.mckinsey.com/business-functions/strategy-and-corporate-finance/our-insights/the-economic-essentials-of-digital-strategy

59. Courtesy of Christian Schulz, Schindler, personal communication, 16/04/2019

60. Courtesy of Eric Chaniot, Michelin, personal communication, 27/02/2019

61. Gassmann, Oliver, Frankenberger, Karolin, and Csik, Michaela. *The Business Model Navigator: 55 Models That Will Revolutionise Your Business*. Harlow: Pearson, 2014

62. Courtesy of Julian Schubert, V-ZUG, personal communication, 22/03/2019

63. Courtesy of Martin Watzlawek, REHAU Automotive, personal communication, 24/01/2019

64. Gassmann, Oliver, Frankenberger, Karolin, and Csik, Michaela. *The Business Model Navigator: 55 Models That Will Revolutionise Your Business*. Harlow: Pearson, 2014

65. BMI Lab; https://bmilab.com/resources

66. Gassmann, Oliver, Frankenberger, Karolin, and Csik, Michaela. *The Business Model Navigator: 55 Models That Will Revolutionise Your Business*. Harlow: Pearson, 2014

67. Courtesy of Ulrich Hermann, Heidelberger Druckmaschinen, personal communication, 07/12/2018

 PART 3. HOW TO DO IT

1. McKinsey & Company; https://www.mckinsey.com/business-functions/organization/our-insights/unlocking-success-in-digital-transformations

CHAPTER 3. ORGANIZATION: HOW TO DEVELOP A FLEXIBLE ORGANIZATION

1. Courtesy of Mirco Mäder, Kollibri / PostAuto, personal communication, 7/12/2018
2. Courtesy of Reiner Thede and Wolfgang Werz, Erbe, personal communication, 15/01/2019
3. Deloitte; https://www2.deloitte.com/content/dam/Deloitte/lu/Documents/about-deloitte/Inside/lu_inside12-full.pdf
4. *Harvard Business Review*; https://hbr.org/2019/03/digital-transformation-is-not-about-technology
5. McKinsey & Company; https://www.mckinsey.com/industries/electric-power-and-natural-gas/our-insights/traditional-company-new-businesses-the-pairing-that-can-ensure-an-incumbents-survival
6. Courtesy of Chief Digital Officer (former), chemical and consumer goods company, personal communication, 14/01/2019
7. Courtesy of Gisbert Rühl, Klöckner & Co, personal communication, 31/01/2019
8. Courtesy of Markus Brokhof, formerly Alpiq, personal communication, 15/02/2019
9. Courtesy of former CIO, fashion retailer, personal communication, 5/03/2019
10. Classification based on interview results and typologies introduced by third-parties (Wharton; https://knowledge.wharton.upenn.edu/article/do-you-need-a-chief-digital-officer/)
11. Wharton; https://knowledge.wharton.upenn.edu/article/do-you-need-a-chief-digital-officer/
12. Deloitte; https://www2.deloitte.com/content/dam/Deloitte/de/Documents/technology/Corporate_Accelerator_EN.pdf
13. Kohler, Thomas. "Corporate Accelerators: Building Bridges between Corporations and Startups." *Business Horizons* 59 (2016): 347–357
14. McKinsey & Company; https://www.mckinsey.com/business-functions/digital-mckinsey/our-insights/a-blueprint-for-successful-digital-transformations-for-automotive-suppliers
15. McKinsey & Company; https://www.mckinsey.com/industries/electric-power-and-natural-gas/our-insights/traditional-company-new-businesses-the-pairing-that-can-ensure-an-incumbents-survival
16. NESTA; https://media.nesta.org.uk/documents/incubation_for_growth_CqYbxVG.pdf; http://www.nesta.org.uk/publications/ good-incubation
17. Weiblein, Tobias and Chesbrough, Henry W. "Enganging with Startups to Enhance Corporate Innovation." *California Management Review* 57, No 2 (2014): 66–90
18. Courtesy of Stefan Stroh, Deutsche Bahn, personal communication, 28/01/2019
19. Deloitte; https://www2.deloitte.com/content/dam/Deloitte/lu/Documents/technology/lu_digitally-fit-organization.pdf; McKinsey & Company; https://www.mckinsey.com/business-functions/digital-mckinsey/our-insights/a-blueprint-for-successful-digital-transformations-for-automotive-suppliers; CIO; https://www.cio.com.au/article/626946/organisational-structures-digital-transformation-4-archetypes-emerge/; The Boston Consulting Group; https://www.bcg.com/publications/2017/technology-organizing-for-digital-future.aspx
20. Deloitte; https://www2.deloitte.com/content/dam/Deloitte/lu/Documents/about-deloitte/Inside/lu_inside12-full.pdf
21. CIO; https://www.cio.com.au/article/626946/organisational-structures-digital-transformation-4-archetypes-emerge/
22. The Boston Consulting Group; https://www.bcg.com/publications/2017/technology-organizing-for-digital-future.aspx
23. The Boston Consulting Group; https://www.bcg.com/publications/2017/technology-organizing-for-digital-future.aspx
24. Courtesy of automotive expert, automotive supplier, personal communication, 06/12/2018
25. McKinsey & Company; https://www.mckinsey.com/business-functions/digital-mckinsey/our-insights/a-blueprint-for-successful-digital-transformations-for-automotive-suppliers
26. The Boston Consulting Group; https://www.bcg.com/publications/2017/technology-organizing-for-digital-future.aspx
27. Courtesy of Michael Spiegel and Anna Neumeier, Deutsche Pfandbriefbank, personal communication, 18/01/2019
28. CIO; https://www.cio.com.au/article/626946/organisational-structures-digital-transformation-4-archetypes-emerge/
29. The Boston Consulting Group; https://www.bcg.com/publications/2017/technology-organizing-for-digital-future.aspx
30. Courtesy of executive manager, multinational conglomerate, personal communication, 23/01/2019
31. CIO; https://www.cio.com.au/article/626946/organisational-structures-digital-transformation-4-archetypes-emerge/

32. The Boston Consulting Group; https://www.bcg.com/publications/2017/technology-organizing-for-digital-future.aspx
33. Inc.; https://www.inc.com/bryan-adams/12-ways-to-encourage-more-free-thinking-and-innovation-into-any-business.html
34. The Boston Consulting Group; https://www.bcg.com/publications/2017/technology-organizing-for-digital-future.aspx
35. BASF uses the term "digitization" to describe the process of moving from analog to digital and the term "digitalization" to describe the use of digital technologies to move to a digital business.
36. Courtesy of Samy Jandali, BASF, personal communication, 23/01/2019
37. Rüdiger Mannherz, Michael Hepp, Walter, personal communication, 22/02/2019
38. Arthur D. Little; https://www.adlittle.com/sites/default/files/viewpoints/ADL_Definingthedigitalorganization_01.pdf
39. Bain & Company; https://www.bain.com/insights/digitalisierung-ist-chefsache-2018/
40. Courtesy of former executive manager, multinational conglomerate, personal communication, 23/01/2019
41. Courtesy of Philipp Wetzel, AMAG, personal communication, 6/05/2019
42. McKinsey & Company; https://www.mckinsey.com/business-functions/organization/our-insights/transformer-in-chief-the-new-chief-digital-officer
43. The Boston Consulting Group; https://www.bcg.com/publications/2017/technology-organizing-for-digital-future.aspx
44. The Boston Consulting Group; https://www.bcg.com/publications/2017/technology-organizing-for-digital-future.aspx
45. Daimler; https://www.daimler-mobility.com/en/company/news/joint-venture-closing/
46. Courtesy of Thomas Grübel, Govecs, personal communication, 28/01/2019
47. Courtesy of Chief Digital Officer (former), chemical and consumer goods company, personal communication, 14/01/2019
48. Courtesy of Olaf Frank, Munich Re, personal communication, 11/02/2019
49. Integrative Innovation; https://integrative-innovation.net/?p=2148
50. Courtesy of Bernd Reck and Sören Lauinger, Aesculap, personal communication, 19/12/2018
51. *Harvard Business Review*; https://hbr.org/2002/05/disruptive-change-when-trying-harder-is-part-of-the-problem
52. *Harvard Business Review*; https://hbr.org/2004/04/the-ambidextrous-organization
53. Courtesy of Florian Bankoley, Bosch, personal communication, 15/02/2019
54. Markides, Constantinos and Charitou, Constantinos D. "Competing with Dual Business Models: A Contingency Approach." *Academy of Management Executive* 18, No. 3 (2004): 22–36
55. Markides, Constantinos and Charitou, Constantinos D. "Competing with Dual Business Models: A Contingency Approach." *Academy of Management Executive* 18, No. 3 (2004): 22–36
56. Courtesy of Michael Spiegel and Anna Neumeier, Deutsche Pfandbriefbank, personal communication, 18/01/2019
57. Courtesy of Samy Jandali, BASF, personal communication, 23/01/2019
58. Courtesy of Markus Brokhof, formerly Alpiq, personal communication, 15/02/2019

CHAPTER 4. TECHNOLOGY: HOW TO USE TECHNOLOGY AS A DRIVER FOR THE TRANSFORMATION

1. Netflix; https://media.netflix.com/en/company-blog/completing-the-netflix-cloud-migration
2. Courtesy of Fabian Stenger, FlixMobility, personal communication, 20/02/2019
3. McKinsey & Company; https://www.mckinsey.com/featured-insights/future-of-work/tech-for-good-using-technology-to-smooth-disruption-and-improve-well-being, https://www.mckinsey.com/business-functions/digital-mckinsey/our-insights/disruptive-technologies
4. McKinsey & Company; https://www.mckinsey.com/business-functions/digital-mckinsey/our-insights/disruptive-technologies

5. Courtesy of Edouard Meylan, H. Moser & Cie., personal communication, 25/01/2019
6. Courtesy of Nicolas Verschelden, Anheuser-Busch InBev, personal communication, 18/12/2018
7. BBC; https://www.bbc.com/news/business-44871448
8. Verizon; https://www.verizon.com/about/our-company/5g/what-5g
9. McKinsey & Company; https://www.mckinsey.com/business-functions/digital-mckinsey/our-insights/disruptive-technologies
10. Managing Director, European bank, personal communication, 28/02/2019
11. McKinsey & Company; https://www.mckinsey.com/business-functions/digital-mckinsey/our-insights/disruptive-technologies
12. Courtesy of Christian Schulz, Schindler, personal communication, 16/04/2019
13. McKinsey & Company; https://www.mckinsey.com/business-functions/digital-mckinsey/our-insights/disruptive-technologies
14. The Boston Consulting Group; https://www.bcg.com/publications/2019/enterprise-applications-cloud-ready-prime-time.aspx; McKinsey & Company; https://www.mckinsey.com/business-functions/digital-mckinsey/our-insights/cloud-adoption-to-accelerate-it-modernization
15. Networkworld; https://www.networkworld.com/article/3224893/what-is-edge-computing-and-how-it-s-changing-the-network.html
16. McKinsey & Company; https://www.mckinsey.com/business-functions/digital-mckinsey/our-insights/disruptive-technologies
17. Siemens; https://www.plm.automation.siemens.com/global/de/products/manufacturing-planning/robotic-automation.html; https://new.siemens.com/global/en/markets/machinebuilding/robotics.html
18. Courtesy of Riccardo Giacometti, Hotel Atlantis by Giardino, personal communication 19/01/2019
19. Forbes; https://www.forbes.com/sites/robtoews/2019/11/04/questioning-the-long-term-importance-of-big-data-in-ai/#231724182177
20. Courtesy of Christian Schulz, Schindler, personal communication, 16/04/2019
21. Courtesy of Katharina Herrmann, ING, personal communication, 10/01/2019
22. McKinsey & Company; https://www.mckinsey.com/business-functions/digital-mckinsey/our-insights/disruptive-technologies
23. Courtesy of Patrick Koller, Faurecia, personal communication, 28/02/2019
24. McKinsey & Company; https://www.mckinsey.com/business-functions/operations/our-insights/digital-transformation-raising-supply-chain-performance-to-new-levels
25. McKinsey & Company; https://www.mckinsey.com/business-functions/operations/our-insights/digital-transformation-raising-supply-chain-performance-to-new-levels
26. McKinsey & Company; https://www.mckinsey.com/business-functions/marketing-and-sales/how-we-help-clients/digital-marketing
27. McKinsey & Company; https://www.mckinsey.com/~/media/McKinsey/Business%20Functions/McKinsey%20Digital/Our%20Insights/Digital%20McKinsey%20Insights%20Number%203/Digital-McKinsey-Insights-Issue-3-revised.ashx
28. KaaIoT Technologies; https://www.kaaproject.org/what-is-iot-platform; McKinsey & Company; https://www.mckinsey.com/business-functions/mckinsey-digital/our-insights/the-platform-play-how-to-operate-like-a-tech-company
29. Courtesy of Thomas Pirlein, Müller Group, personal communication, 5/03/2019
30. Courtesy of Bernd Reck and Sören Lauinger, Aesculap, personal communication, 19/12/2019
31. The Boston Consulting Group; https://www.bcg.com/publications/2019/next-frontier-digital-ai-transformations.aspx
32. Courtesy of Michael Spiegel and Anna Neumeier, Deutsche Pfandbriefbank, personal communication, 18/01/2019
33. Courtesy of Christian Schulz, Schindler, personal communication, 16/04/2019
34. Courtesy of Jan Mrosik, Siemens, personal communication, 4/02/2019
35. Courtesy of former senior executive, Jelmoli, personal communication, 09/01/2019
36. Arthur D. Little; https://www.adlittle.com/sites/default/files/viewpoints/ADL_Definingthedigitalorganization_01.pdf
37. WACKER uses the term "digitization" to describe the process of moving from analog to digital and the term "digitalization" to describe the use of digital technologies to move to a digital business.
38. Courtesy of Axel Schmidt and Dirk Ramhorst, WACKER Chemie AG, personal communication, 13/02/2019

39. The Boston Consulting Group; https://www.bcg.com/publications/2016/software-agile-digital-transformation-end-of-two-speed-it.aspx

40. McKinsey & Company; https://www.mckinsey.com/business-functions/digital-mckinsey/our-insights/a-two-speed-it-architecture-for-the-digital-enterprise

41. Meffert, Jürgen, and Swaminathan, Anand. *Digital @ Scale: The Playbook You Need to Transform Your Company*. Hoboken: Wiley, 2017

42. McKinsey & Company; https://www.mckinsey.com/business-functions/digital-mckinsey/our-insights/deploying-a-two-speed-architecture-at-scale

43. Courtesy of Bernard Leong, formerly SingPost / now Amazon Web Services, personal communication, 8/02/2019

44. The Boston Consulting Group; https://www.bcg.com/publications/2016/software-agile-digital-transformation-end-of-two-speed-it.aspx

45. The Boston Consulting Group; https://www.bcg.com/publications/2016/software-agile-digital-transformation-end-of-two-speed-it.aspx

46. Bain & Company; https://www.bain.com/insights/vishy-padmanabhan-why-two-speed-it-is-off-track-video/

47. The Boston Consulting Group; https://www.bcg.com/publications/2016/software-agile-digital-transformation-end-of-two-speed-it.aspx; Bain & Company; https://www.bain.com/insights/fast-and-faster-why-a-two-speed-it-model-is-offtrack/

48. Courtesy of Fabian Stenger, FlixMobility, personal communication, 20/02/2019

49. Courtesy of Konstantin Speidel, Allianz Global Investors, personal communication, 1/02/2019

50. Courtesy of Gisbert Rühl, Klöckner & Co, personal communication, 31/01/2019

51. Courtesy of Thomas Gutzwiller, Platform Expert, personal communication, 3/05/2019 & 25/06/2019

52. McKinsey & Company; https://www.mckinsey.com/business-functions/mckinsey-digital/our-insights/beyond-agile-reorganizing-it-for-faster-software-delivery

53. McKinsey & Company; https://www.mckinsey.com/business-functions/mckinsey-digital/our-insights/beyond-agile-reorganizing-it-for-faster-software-delivery

54. McKinsey & Company; https://www.mckinsey.com/business-functions/digital-mckinsey/our-insights/deploying-a-two-speed-architecture-at-scale; https://www.mckinsey.com/business-functions/digital-mckinsey/our-insights/bringing-agile-to-it-infrastructure-ing-netherlands-agile-transformation

55. Courtesy of Claus Fleischer, Bosch eBike Systems, personal communication, 12/11/2018

56. Courtesy of Michael Spiegel and Anna Neumeier, Deutsche Pfandbriefbank, personal communication, 18/01/2019

57. The People Space; https://www.thepeoplespace.com/ideas/articles/ability-adapt-new-technology-critical-future-career-success

58. McKinsey & Company; https://www.mckinsey.com/business-functions/mckinsey-digital/our-insights/the-cornerstones-of-large-scale-technology-transformation

59. Courtesy of former senior executive, BTPN / Jenius, personal communication, 13/11/2018

CHAPTER 5. PROCESSES: HOW TO GET STUFF DONE

1. Interaction Design Foundation; https://www.interaction-design.org/literature/topics/design-thinking; Gartner; https://www.gartner.com/en/documents/3941917/enterprise-architects-combine-design-thinking-lean-start

2. The Lean Startup; www.theleanstartup.com; Digitale Neuordnung; www.digitaleneuordnung.de

3. The Lean Startup; www.theleanstartup.com

4. The Lean Startup; www.thelearnstartup.com
5. twproject; https://twproject.com/blog/lean-agile-differences-similarities/
6. Bain & Company; https://www.bain.com/insights/agile-innovation
7. Bain & Company; https://www.bain.com/insights/agile-innovation
8. Digitale Neuordnung; www.digitaleneuordnung.de; Gartner; https://www.gartner.com/en/documents/3941917/enterprise-architects-combine-design-thinking-lean-start
9. Gregory Schmidt; http://www.gregoryschmidt.ca/writing/design-thinking-lean-startup-agile
10. Courtesy of Dirk Linzmeier, OSRAM Continental, personal communication, 17/12/2018
11. Courtesy of Luigi Pedrocchi, Mibelle Group, personal communication, 25/10/2018
12. Courtesy of Markus Brokhof, formerly Alpiq, personal communication, 15/02/2019
13. Integrative Innovation; https://integrative-innovation.net/?p=2148
14. Courtesy of David Hengartner, Swisscom, personal communication, 10/12/2018
15. Courtesy of Ian Roberts, Bühler, personal communication, 08/01/2018
16. Courtesy of senior executive, technology company, personal communication, 18/02/2019
17. Courtesy of Julian Schubert, V-ZUG, personal communication, 22/03/2019
18. Courtesy of Harald Brodbeck, Horváth & Partners, personal communication, 17/01/0219
19. Courtesy of Julian Schubert, V-ZUG, personal communication, 22/03/2019
20. Courtesy of Samy Jandali, BASF, personal communication, 23/01/2019
21. Courtesy of Deborah Sherry, formerly GE Digital / now AWS, personal communication, 23/01/2019
22. The Boston Consulting Group; https://www.bcg.com/de-de/publications/2019/five-rules-digital-strategy.aspx
23. The Boston Consulting Group; https://www.mckinsey.com/industries/financial-services/our-insights/a-roadmap-for-a-digital-transformation
24. Courtesy of Samy Jandali, BASF, personal communication, 23/01/2019
25. Courtesy of Otto Preiss, ABB, personal communication, 28/02/2019
26. The Boston Consulting Group; https://www.bcg.com/de-de/publications/2019/five-rules-digital-strategy.aspx
27. The Boston Consulting Group; https://www.bcg.com/de-de/publications/2019/five-rules-digital-strategy.aspx
28. Courtesy of Julian Schubert, V-ZUG, personal communication, 22/03/2019
29. Courtesy of Thorsten Müller, formerly Osram, personal communication, 27/11/2018
30. Courtesy of Bernd Reck and Sören Lauinger, Aesculap, personal communication, 19/12/2019
31. Courtesy of Chief Digital Officer, discount retailer, personal communication, 28/03/2019
32. Courtesy of Deborah Sherry, formerly GE Digital / now AWS, personal communication, 23/01/2019
33. McKinsey & Company; https://www.mckinsey.com/industries/electric-power-and-natural-gas/our-insights/traditional-company-new-businesses-the-pairing-that-can-ensure-an-incumbents-survival
34. Courtesy of Samy Jandali, BASF, personal communication, 23/01/2019
35. Courtesy of Konstantin Speidel, Allianz Global Investors, personal communication, 1/02/2019
36. Courtesy of Samy Jandali, BASF, personal communication, 23/01/2019
37. Courtesy of Harald Brodbeck, Horváth & Partners, personal communication, 17/01/0219
38. Courtesy of Reiner Fageth, CEWE, personal communication, 20/11/2018; Welt; https://www.welt.de/wirtschaft/article165098369/Das-Fotobuch-hat-uns-das-Ueberleben-gesichert.html; Com-Magazin; https://www.com-magazin.de/praxis/digitalisierung/erfolgsgeschichten-digitalisierung-1528949.html?page=5_im-gespraech-mit-dr.-reiner-fageth-cto-bei-cewe
39. McKinsey & Company; https://www.mckinsey.com/industries/electric-power-and-natural-gas/our-insights/traditional-company-new-businesses-the-pairing-that-can-ensure-an-incumbents-survival
40. Courtesy of Florian Bankoley, Bosch, personal communication, 15/02/2019
41. Courtesy of Samy Jandali, BASF, personal communication, 23/01/2019
42. Courtesy of Deborah Sherry, formerly GE Digital / now AWS, personal communication, 23/01/2019

43. McKinsey & Company; https://www.mckinsey.com/industries/electric-power-and-natural-gas/our-insights/traditional-company-new-businesses-the-pairing-that-can-ensure-an-incumbents-survival
44. McKinsey & Company; https://www.mckinsey.com/industries/electric-power-and-natural-gas/our-insights/traditional-company-new-businesses-the-pairing-that-can-ensure-an-incumbents-survival
45. Courtesy of Bernd Reck and Sören Lauinger, Aesculap, personal communication, 19/12/2019
46. Courtesy of Katharina Herrmann, ING, personal communication, 10/01/2019

CHAPTER 6. LEADERSHIP: WHAT TO LOOK FOR IN LEADERS AND HOW TO FIND THEM

1. Courtesy of Ian Roberts, Bühler, personal communication, 08/01/2018
2. Courtesy of Philipp Leutiger, LafargeHolcim, personal communication, 22/10/2018
3. Courtesy of automotive expert, automotive supplier, personal communication, 06/12/2018
4. Courtesy of Cristian Citu, World Economic Forum, personal communication, 21/12/2018
5. *MIT Sloan Management Review*; https://sloanreview.mit.edu/projects/coming-of-age-digitally/
6. *Harvard Business Review*; https://hbr.org/2019/01/managing-when-the-future-is-unclear
7. *Harvard Business Review*; https://hbr.org/2014/01/what-vuca-really-means-for-you; Forbes; https://www.forbes.com/sites/jeroenkraaijenbrink/2018/12/19/what-does-vuca-really-mean/#77a547ca17d6
8. *Harvard Business Review*; https://hbr.org/2016/06/do-managers-and-leaders-really-do-different-things
9. Korn Ferry Institute; https://www.kornferry.com/institute/leaders-for-a-digital-transformation
10. *Harvard Business Review*; https://hbr.org/2016/03/the-most-important-leadership-competencies-according-to-leaders-around-the-world, https://hbr.org/2018/10/the-6-fundamental-skills-every-leader-should-practice
11. Kohler, Thomas. "Corporate accelerators: Building bridges between corporations and startups." *Business Horizons* 59 (2016): 347–357
12. Courtesy of Carola Wahl, formerly AXA, personal communication, 14/12/2018
13. Courtesy of Otto Preiss, ABB, personal communication, 28/02/2019
14. Courtesy of senior executive, technology company, personal communication, 18/02/2019
15. Courtesy of Ian Roberts, Bühler, personal communication, 08/01/2019
16. Courtesy of Carola Wahl, formerly AXA, personal communication, 14/12/2018
17. Courtesy of Thorsten Lampe, Asellion, personal communication, 19/12/2019
18. Deloitte; https://www2.deloitte.com/content/dam/Deloitte/lu/Documents/technology/lu_digitally-fit-organization.pdf
19. Courtesy of Markus Streckeisen, SBB Cargo, personal communication, 10/12/2018
20. *Harvard Business Review*; https://hbr.org/2011/04/why-serial-entrepreneurs-dont-learn-from-failure; Egger, J.P. and Song, Lin. "Dealing with Failure: Serial Entrepreneurs and the Costs of Changing Industries Between Ventures." *Academy of Management Journal* 58, No 6. (2014): 1785–1803
21. Shaw, Kathryn and Lafontaine, Francine. "Serial Entrepreneurship: Learning by Doing?" *Journal of Labor Economics* 34, No. 2 (2016): 217–254
22. Courtesy of Martin Watzlawek, REHAU Automotive, personal communication, 24/01/2019
23. Courtesy of Gisbert Rühl, Klöckner & Co, personal communication, 31/01/2019
24. Courtesy of Onur Erdogan, formerly Estée Lauder, personal communication, 14/03/2019

25. Courtesy of Markus Streckeisen, SBB Cargo, personal communication, 10/12/2018
26. Courtesy of Martin Watzlawek, REHAU Automotive, personal communication, 24/01/2019
27. Courtesy of Otto Preiss, ABB, personal communication, 28/02/2019
28. Courtesy of Raphael Dölker, EnBW, personal communication, 05/12/2018
29. Courtesy of Martin Watzlawek, REHAU Automotive, personal communication, 24/01/2019
30. Courtesy of Falk Bothe, Volkswagen, personal communication, 14/11/2018
31. Courtesy of Andreas Sturm and Matthias Häne, Bank Cler, personal communication, 29/11/2018
32. Courtesy of Kurt Straub, Hyatt International, personal communication, 12/01/2019
33. Courtesy of Pietro Supino, TX Group, personal communication, 28/02/2019
34. Courtesy of Falk Bothe, Volkswagen, personal communication, 14/11/2018
35. Courtesy of Uli Huener, EnBW, personal communication, 05/12/2018
36. Courtesy of Jean-Charles Deconninck; Generix Group, personal communication, 22/03/2019
37. Courtesy of Chief Digital Officer, discount retailer, personal communication, 28/03/2019
38. Courtesy of Markus Schmidt, formerly at Bosch Automotive Electronics, 02/12/2019
39. Courtesy of Benedikt Schell and Tom Schneider, Mercedes-Benz Bank; personal communication, 25/02/2019
40. Courtesy of Stefan Wolf, ElringKlinger, personal communication, 21/01/2019
41. *Harvard Business Review;* https://hbr.org/2019/03/educating-the-next-generation-of-leaders
42. Korn Ferry Institute; https://www.kornferry.com/institute/leaders-for-a-digital-transformation
43. Korn Ferry Institute; https://www.kornferry.com/institute/leaders-for-a-digital-transformation
44. Courtesy of Otto Preiss, ABB, personal communication, 28/02/2019
45. Courtesy of Uli Huener and Raphael Dölker, EnBW, personal communication, 05/12/2018
46. Courtesy of Hermann Bach, Covestro, personal communication, 26/11/2018; Courtesy of Thorsten Lampe, Asellion, personal communication, 19/12/2019
47. Courtesy of Eric Chaniot, Michelin, personal communication, 27/02/2019

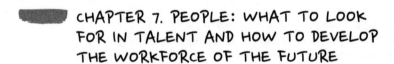

CHAPTER 7. PEOPLE: WHAT TO LOOK FOR IN TALENT AND HOW TO DEVELOP THE WORKFORCE OF THE FUTURE

1. The Boson Consulting Group; https://www.bcg.com/publications/2017/people-organization-technology-how-gain-develop-digital-talent-skills.aspx
2. Technical University of Munich and SAP. "Initiative for Digital Transformation Survey," 2017.
3. Organization for Economic Co-operation and Development; http://www.oecd.org/officialdocuments/publicdisplay documentpdf/?cote=DSTI%2FICCP%2FIIS(2015)10%2FFINAL&docLanguage=En
4. McKinsey & Company; https://www.mckinsey.com/featured-insights/future-of-work/skill-shift-automation-and-the-future-of-the-workforce
5. Courtesy of Benedikt Schell and Tom Schneider, Mercedes-Benz Bank; personal communication, 25/02/2019
6. Courtesy of Claus Fleischer, Bosch eBike Systems, personal communication, 12/11/2018
7. CNBC; https://www.cnbc.com/2019/03/05/how-millennials-and-gen-z-are-reshaping-the-future-of-the-workforce.html
8. Courtesy of Martin Watzlawek, REHAU Automotive, personal communication, 24/01/2019
9. Courtesy of Carola Wahl, formerly AXA, personal communication, 14/12/2018

10. Courtesy of former executive, Scandinavian bank, 22/01/2019
11. Courtesy of Bertrand Bodson, Novartis, personal communication, 18/01/2019
12. *Financial Times*; https://www.ft.com/content/7e25ed88-317f-11e8-b5bf-23cb17fd1498
13. Novartis; https://www.novartis.com/news/novartis-and-microsoft-announce-collaboration-transform-medicine-artificial-intelligence; Microsoft; https://news.microsoft.com/2019/10/01/novartis-and-microsoft-announce-collaboration-to-transform-medicine-with-artificial-intelligence/
14. Courtesy of Bertrand Bodson, Novartis, personal communication, 18/01/2019
15. Courtesy of Carola Wahl, formerly AXA, personal communication, 14/12/2018
16. Courtesy of former senior executive, BTPN / Jenius, personal communication, 19/11/2018
17. Courtesy of Patrick Marc Graf, luxury watches and jewelry retailer, personal communication, 10/01/2019
18. Courtesy of Mirco Mäder, Kollibri / PostAuto, personal communication, 07/12/2018
19. McKinsey & Company; https://www.mckinsey.com/~/media/McKinsey/Featured%20Insights/Future%20of%20Organizations/Skill%20shift%20Automation%20and%20the%20future%20of%20the%20workforce/MGI-Skill-Shift-Automation-and-future-of-the-workforce-May-2018.ashx
20. Courtesy of Sebastien Szczepaniak, Nestlé, personal communication, 01/02/2019
21. Courtesy of Gisbert Rühl, Klöckner & Co, personal communication, 31/01/2019
22. Courtesy of Stefan Stroh, Deutsche Bahn, personal communication, 28/01/2019
23. The Boston Consulting Group; https://www.bcg.com/publications/2017/people-organization-technology-how-gain-develop-digital-talent-skills.aspx
24. Samantha McLaren; https://business.linkedin.com/talent-solutions/blog/recruiting-tips/2018/5-innovative-ways-to-find-digitally-savvy-talent-when-its-in-short-supply
25. McKinsey & Company; https://www.mckinsey.com/~/media/McKinsey/Featured%20Insights/Future%20of%20Organizations/Skill%20shift%20Automation%20and%20the%20future%20of%20the%20workforce/MGI-Skill-Shift-Automation-and-future-of-the-workforce-May-2018.ashx
26. Courtesy of Norman Willich and Alexander Maute, Eissmann, personal communication
27. McKinsey & Company; https://www.mckinsey.com/featured-insights/employment-and-growth/independent-work-choice-necessity-and-the-gig-economy
28. Courtesy of Chief Digital Officer, globally leading food product corporation, personal communication, 07/11/2018
29. Courtesy of Raphael Dölker, EnBW, personal communication, 05/12/2018
30. Courtesy of Ian Roberts, Bühler, personal communication, 08/01/2019
31. McKinsey & Company; https://www.mckinsey.com/~/media/McKinsey/Featured%20Insights/Future%20of%20Organizations/Skill%20shift%20Automation%20and%20the%20future%20of%20the%20workforce/MGI-Skill-Shift-Automation-and-future-of-the-workforce-May-2018.ashx
32. McKinsey & Company; https://www.mckinsey.com/~/media/McKinsey/Featured%20Insights/Future%20of%20Organizations/Skill%20shift%20Automation%20and%20the%20future%20of%20the%20workforce/MGI-Skill-Shift-Automation-and-future-of-the-workforce-May-2018.ashx
33. McKinsey & Company; https://www.mckinsey.com/~/media/McKinsey/Featured%20Insights/Future%20of%20Organizations/Skill%20shift%20Automation%20and%20the%20future%20of%20the%20workforce/MGI-Skill-Shift-Automation-and-future-of-the-workforce-May-2018.ashx
34. IBM; https://www.ibm.com/services/learning/ites.wss/zz-en?pageType=page&c=N807151X80720G91; https://www.ibm.com/blogs/ibm-training/ibm-is-building-the-future-of-new-collar-jobs-with-digital-badges-published-in-evolllution/;
35. McKinsey & Company; https://www.mckinsey.com/featured-insights/future-of-work/retraining-and-reskilling-workers-in-the-age-of-automation

36. McKinsey & Company; https://www.mckinsey.com/~/media/McKinsey/Featured%20Insights/Future%20of% 20Organizations/Skill%20shift%20Automation%20and%20the%20future%20of%20the%20workforce/MGI-Skill-Shift-Automation-and-future-of-the-workforce-May-2018.ashx
37. Courtesy of Otto Preiss, ABB, personal communication, 28/02/2019
38. Courtesy of Raphael Dölker, EnBW, personal communication, 05/12/2018
39. Courtesy of Benedikt Schell and Tom Schneider, Mercedes-Benz Bank; personal communication, 25/02/2019
40. Courtesy of Andreas Sturm and Matthias Häne, Bank Cler, personal communication, 29/11/2018
41. Courtesy of Philipp Leutiger, LafargeHolcim, personal communication, 22/10/2018
42. Courtesy of Gisbert Rühl, Klöckner & Co, personal communication, 31/01/2019
43. Daniel H. Pink; https://www.danpink.com/drive./
44. Courtesy of Bastian Gerhard, formerly Zalando / now Alpiq, personal communication, 02/05/2019

CHAPTER 8. CULTURE: HOW TO GALVANIZE AN ORGANIZATION AND HELP YOUR PEOPLE PULL TOGETHER

1. Cameron, Kim S., Quinn, Robert. E. *Diagnosing and Changing Organizational Culture: Based on the Competing Values Framework.* San Francisco: Jossey-Bass, 2011; Gontard, Maximilian. *Unternehmenskultur und Organisationsklima.* München: Hampp, 2002; Hofstede, Geert. *Culture's Consequences: Comparing Values, Behaviors, Institutions, and Organizations Across Nations.* Thousand Oaks: Sage, 2001; Holleis, Wilfried. *Unternehmenskultur und moderne Psyche.* Frankfurt am Mein/ New York: Campus, 1987; Sackmann, Sonja. *Unternehmenskultur: Erkennen - Entwickeln – Verändern.* Wiesbaden: Springer Fachmedien, 2017; Schein, Edgar H. *Organizational Culture and Leadership.* Hoboken: Wiley, 2017
2. The Boston Consulting Group; https://www.bcg.com/de-de/publications/2018/not-digital-transformation-without-digital-culture.aspx
3. *Financial Times*; https://www.ft.com/content/f5f79cfc-8228-11e5-a01c-8650859a4767
4. *Harvard Business Review*; https://hbr.org/2018/01/the-culture-factor
5. Courtesy of Bernard Leong, formerly SingPost / now Amazon Web Services, personal communication, 08/02/2019
6. Courtesy of Eric Chaniot, Michelin, personal communication
7. Courtesy of Thomas Grübel, Govecs, personal communication, 28/01/2019
8. The Boston Consulting Group; https://www.bcg.com/de-de/publications/2018/not-digital-transformation-without-digital-culture.aspx
9. The Boston Consulting Group; https://www.bcg.com/de-de/publications/2018/not-digital-transformation-without-digital-culture.aspx
10. Courtesy of Thorsten Lampe, Asellion, personal communication, 19/12/2018
11. The Boston Consulting Group; https://www.bcg.com/de-de/publications/2018/not-digital-transformation-without-digital-culture.aspx
12. *Harvard Business Review*; https://hbr.org/2019/01/the-hard-truth-about-innovative-cultures
13. The Lean Startup; http://theleanstartup.com/
14. Courtesy of David Hengartner, Swisscom, personal communication, 10/12/2018
15. Courtesy of Ian Roberts, Bühler, personal communication, 08/01/2019

16. Courtesy of Mark Jacob, Dolder Hotel, personal communication, 23/01/2019
17. *Harvard Business Review*; https://hbr.org/2018/07/4-ways-to-create-a-learning-culture-on-your-team
18. *Harvard Business Review*; https://hbr.org/2018/07/4-ways-to-create-a-learning-culture-on-your-team
19. TechCrunch; https://techcrunch.com/2019/07/11/amazon-invests-700-million-to-retrain-a-third-of-its-u-s-workforce-by-2025/; Amazon; https://press.aboutamazon.com/news-releases/news-release-details/amazon-pledges-upskill-100000-us-employees-demand-jobs-2025
20. Zuri Kemp; https://blog.google/technology/ai/learn-google-ai-making-ml-education-available-everyone/; Google; https://ai.google/education/
21. McKinsey & Company; https://www.mckinsey.com/business-functions/organization/our-insights/building-the-workforce-of-tomorrow-today
22. McKinsey & Company; https://www.mckinsey.com/business-functions/strategy-and-corporate-finance/our-insights/the-strategy-and-corporate-finance-blog/digital-success-requires-a-digital-culture
23. McKinsey & Company; https://www.mckinsey.com/business-functions/strategy-and-corporate-finance/our-insights/the-strategy-and-corporate-finance-blog/digital-success-requires-a-digital-culture
24. Courtesy of Konstantin Speidel, Allianz Global Investors, personal communication, 01/02/2019
25. The Lean Startup; http://theleanstartup.com/
26. Courtesy of Ian Roberts, Bühler, personal communication, 08/01/2019
27. Courtesy of Deborah Sherry, formerly GE Digital / now AWS, personal communication, 23/01/2019
28. For an excellent account of how to make change stick, even when it's hard, we recommend *Switch* by the Heath Brothers.
29. *Harvard Business Review*; https://hbr.org/webinar/2018/12/leading-the-agile-organization, https://hbr.org/2018/05/agile-at-scale; The Boston Consulting Group; https://www.bcg.com/de-de/digital-bcg/agile/large-scale-agile-transformation.aspx; McKinsey & Company; https://www.mckinsey.com/business-functions/organization/our-insights/agility-it-rhymes-with-stability, https://www.mckinsey.com/business-functions/organization/our-insights/going-from-fragile-to-agile, https://www.mckinsey.com/business-functions/organization/our-insights/the-five-trademarks-of-agile-organizations
30. McKinsey & Company; https://www.mckinsey.com/business-functions/digital-mckinsey/our-insights/an-operating-model-for-company-wide-agile-development
31. Corporate Rebels; https://corporate-rebels.com/haier/
32. *Harvard Business Review*; https://hbr.org/webinar/2018/12/leading-the-agile-organization, https://hbr.org/2018/05/agile-at-scale; The Boston Consulting Group; https://www.bcg.com/de-de/digital-bcg/agile/large-scale-agile-transformation.aspx; McKinsey & Company; https://www.mckinsey.com/business-functions/organization/our-insights/agility-it-rhymes-with-stability, https://www.mckinsey.com/business-functions/organization/our-insights/going-from-fragile-to-agile, https://www.mckinsey.com/business-functions/organization/our-insights/the-five-trademarks-of-agile-organizations
33. Courtesy of Uli Huener, EnBW, personal communication, 05/12/2018
34. Courtesy of Thorsten Lampe, Asellion, personal communication, 19/12/2018
35. *Harvard Business Review*; https://hbr.org/2016/04/the-secret-history-of-agile-innovation
36. Hasso-Plattner-Institut; https://hpi-academy.de/en/design-thinking/what-is-design-thinking.html
37. *Harvard Business Review*; https://hbr.org/2017/11/what-managers-need-to-know-about-social-tools, https://hbr.org/ideacast/2018/02/make-tools-like-slack-work-for-your-company; Asana; https://asana.com/; Trello; https://trello.com/; Microsoft; https://products.office.com/en-us/microsoft-teams/group-chat-software, https://products.office.com/en-us/yammer/yammer-overview; Slack; https://slack.com/
38. Bain & Company; https://www.bain.com/insights/agile-innovation
39. The Boston Consulting Group; https://www.bcg.com/publications/2019/why-agile-works.aspx

40. Bain & Company; https://www.bain.com/insights/agile-innovation
41. The Boston Consulting Group; https://www.bcg.com/publications/2019/why-agile-works.aspx
42. The Boston Consulting Group; https://www.bcg.com/digital-bcg/agile/software-agile.aspx
43. The Boston Consulting Group; https://www.bcg.com/publications/2019/why-agile-works.aspx
44. Courtesy of Gisbert Rühl, Klöckner & Co, personal communication, 31/01/2019
45. Courtesy of Martin Watzlawek, REHAU Automotive, personal communication, 24/01/2019
46. Courtesy of Ian Roberts, Bühler, personal communication, 08/01/2019
47. Courtesy of Thorsten Lampe, Asellion, personal communication, 19/12/2018
48. Courtesy of Andreas Sturm and Matthias Häne, Bank Cler, personal communication, 29/11/2018
49. Courtesy of Thorsten Müller, formerly Osram, personal communication, 27/11/2018
50. Courtesy of Reiner Fageth, CEWE, personal communication, 20/11/2018
51. Courtesy of Andreas Opelt, Saubermacher, personal communication, 23/10/2018
52. Courtesy of Thomas Frésard, Contexta, personal communication, 02/05/2019
53. Courtesy of Philipp Wetzel, AMAG, personal communication, 06/05/2019
54. Courtesy of Chief Digital Officer, discount retailer, personal communication, 28/03/2019
55. Courtesy of Chief Digital Officer (former), chemical and consumer goods company, personal communication, 14/01/2019
56. Courtesy of Gisbert Rühl, Klöckner & Co, personal communication, 31/01/2019
57. Courtesy of Katharina Herrmann, ING, personal communication, 10/01/2019
58. Courtesy of Carola Wahl, formerly AXA, personal communication, 14/12/2018
59. Courtesy of Eric Chaniot, Michelin, personal communication, 27/02/2019
60. Courtesy of Bernard Leong, formerly SingPost / now Amazon Web Services, personal communication, 08/02/2019

CHAPTER 9. BECAUSE YOU'RE NOT DOING THIS FOR FUN BUT FOR RESULTS

1. Fortune; http://fortune.com/2014/09/25/why-startups-fail-according-to-their-founders/
2. Baghai, Mehrdad, Coley, Stephen, and White, David. *The Alchemy of Growth*. New York: Perseus Publishing, 1999
3. McKinsey & Company; https://www.mckinsey.com/business-functions/strategy-and-corporate-finance/our-insights/enduring-ideas-the-three-horizons-of-growth
4. *Harvard Business Review*, https://hbr.org/2019/02/mckinseys-three-horizons-model-defined-innovation-for-years-heres-why-it-no-longer-applies
5. Courtesy of Philipp Wetzel, AMAG, personal communication, 06/05/2019
6. Courtesy of Falk Bothe, Volkswagen, personal communication, 14/11/2018
7. Ries, Eric. *The Lean Start-up: How Today's Entrepreneurs Use Continuous Innovation to Create Radically Successful Businesses*. New York: Crown Publishing, 2011
8. World Economic Forum; http://reports.weforum.org/digital-transformation/wp-content/blogs.dir/94/mp/files/pages/files/digital-enterprise-narrative-final-january-2016.pdf
9. Courtesy of senior executive, technology company, personal communication, 18/02/2019
10. *Harvard Business Review*, https://hbr.org/2018/02/why-financial-statements-dont-work-for-digital-companies. New Yorker; https://www.newyorker.com/tech/annals-of-technology/

in-silicon-valley-now-its-almost-always-winner-takes-all; CNN; https://money.cnn.com/2013/11/07/technology/social/twitter-ipo-stock/index.html; Forbes; https://www.forbes.com/sites/parmyolson/2014/10/06/facebook-closes-19-billion-whatsapp-deal/#7d5f78a95c66; New York Times; https://www.nytimes.com/2018/01/24/business/ge-earnings.html

11. Courtesy of Falk Bothe, Volkswagen, personal communication, 14/11/2018
12. Venture Beat; https://venturebeat.com/2019/04/26/5-companies-are-testing-55-self-driving-cars-in-pittsburgh/
13. BMW; https://www.bmw.com/en/automotive-life/autonomous-driving.html
14. Courtesy of Olaf Frank, Munich Re, personal communication, 11/02/2019
15. Courtesy of Falk Bothe, Volkswagen, personal communication, 14/11/2018
16. Courtesy of Arnaud Zeitoun, BNP Paribas, personal communication, 05/12/2018
17. Lunney, John, Lueder, Sue, and O'Connor, Gary; https://rework.withgoogle.com/blog/postmortem-culture-how-you-can-learn-from-failure/
18. Forbes; https://www.forbes.com/sites/greatspeculations/2019/03/25/after-a-strong-performance-in-q3-2019-would-focus-on-digital-platform-drive-nikes-growth/#75ca2bab35e5; digirupt.io; https://digirupt.io/digital-transformation-helps-drive-nikes-earnings-run/
19. Forbes; https://www.forbes.com/sites/pamdanziger/2019/03/01/nike-the-worlds-most-valuable-fashion-brand-declares-2019-its-year-for-women/#acd106419d3e
20. Courtesy of Cristian Citu, World Economic Forum, personal communication, 21/12/2018; World Economic Forum; http://reports.weforum.org/digital-transformation/introducing-value-at-stake-a-new-analytical-tool-for-understanding-digitalization/, http://reports.weforum.org/digital-transformation/wp-content/blogs.dir/94/mp/files/pages/files/dti-executive-summary-20180510.pdf
21. Courtesy of former executive, Scandinavian bank, personal communication, 22/01/2019

CONCLUSION: REINVENT YOUR ORGANIZATION BY PUTTING THE PIECES TOGETHER

1. Courtesy of former senior executive, BTPN / Jenius, personal communication, November 19, 2018

Resources

This wouldn't be a proper how-to-guide if we didn't set you up for success as you embark on your own digital transformation. Besides waving you off with the host of cases you have seen, the best practices, and the pitfalls we have warned you about, we give you a map to navigate your digital transformation journey. No kidding, it's literally a map. Actually, multiple map-like tools.

For each of the elements of our Framework – Why, What, How, Where – there is a tool to use, not just stare at. Each aims to help you organize your thoughts around where you are in your own digital transformation, where you have come from, and how to proceed further. It helps you assess the status quo, map out your options, and prioritize next steps, following best practices from the book. You can use these tools to ponder strategies in your secret chambers, but they are best put to use if you run it as a joint exercise with your digital transformation team. Gathering everyone is not just helpful in pooling brain power to solve digital transformation problems, it's also necessary to establish a baseline of everything that's going on in your organization. Time and time again we have seen and heard that digital transformation efforts can be so numerous and dispersed around the organization that establishing a joint understanding of the current status is the first step in orchestrating efforts. This is best done as a team effort, as are all ensuing steps. Use the tools to guide you and your team's thinking along this process.

Blank versions are on our website (www.thedigitaltransformersdilemma .com) along with versions you can print (ideally in large scale) and use in a workshop format at your organization. There are also pre-filled versions, populated with examples from fictional companies, to illustrate ways to best think about working with these tools yourself.

The Why tool juxtaposes your reasons to optimize your core business with the potential for radically new, disruptive business ideas (see Figure 10.1).

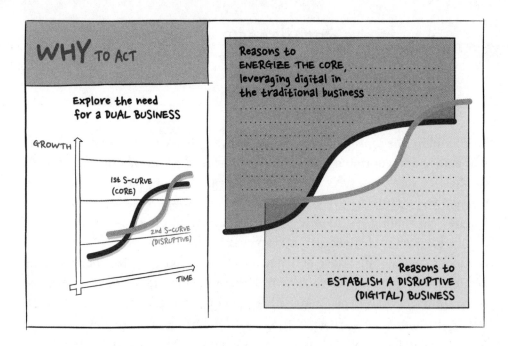

Figure 10.1 Why tool

Source: S-curve graph adapted from Gabriel Tarde. *The Laws of Imitation*. New York: Henry Holt and Company, 1903.

Gather your thoughts on post-its to determine 1st and 2nd S-curve digital transformation drivers and thus determine *your* reasons to act.

The What tool consists of three sub-parts (see Figure 10.2). First, it invites you to jot down your overarching strategy, the 1st S-curve strategy, your 2nd S-curve strategy, as well as connecting elements between the two. Second, it helps you organize your thoughts around your business models. Post-its in each of the four sections of the business model triangle map out your 1st and 2nd S-curve business models; connecting elements are those that both S-curves have in common and can thus be leveraged further. Third, it guides you in the visualization of your efforts as they relate to business models and technologies, helping you to prioritize them as well.

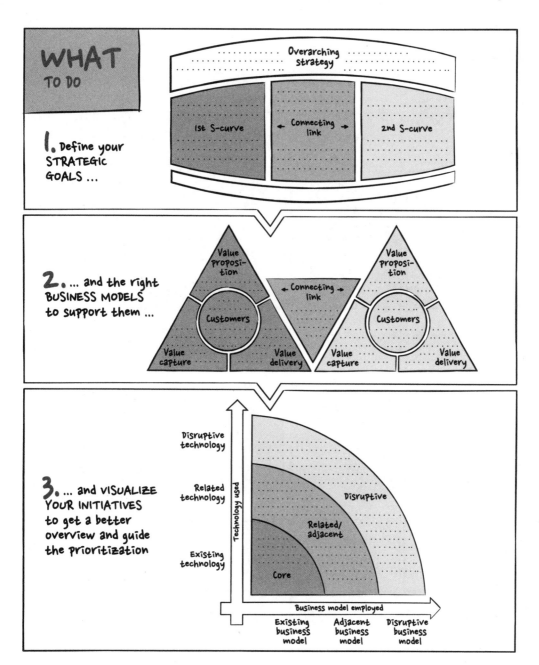

Figure 10.2 What tool

Source: Business model components adapted from Oliver Gassmann, Karolin Frankenberger, Michaela Csik. *The Business Model Navigator*. 1st Edition. ©2014. Reprinted by permission of Pearson Education.

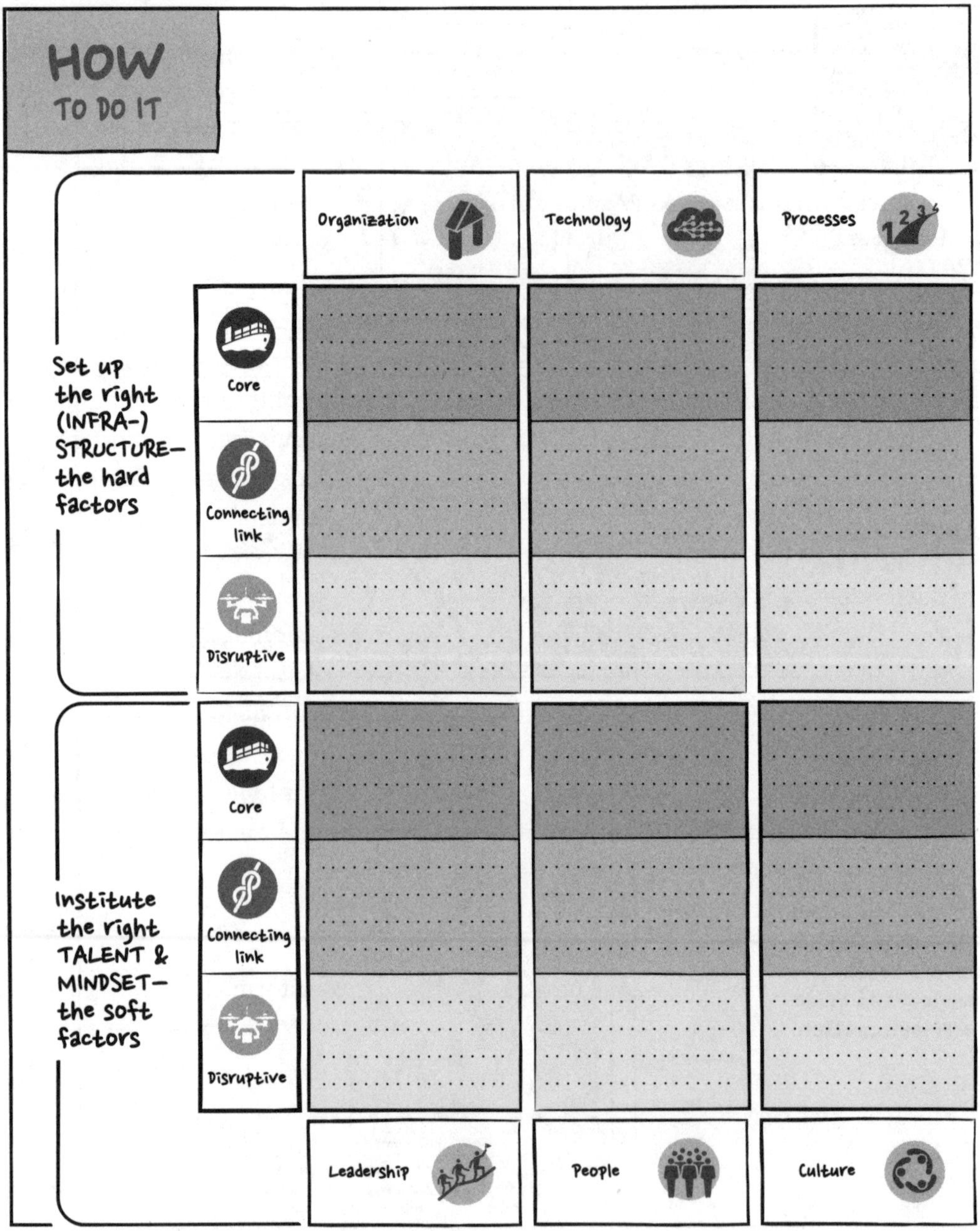

HOW
TO DO IT

		Organization	Technology	Processes
Set up the right (INFRA-) STRUCTURE— the hard factors	Core			
	Connecting link			
	Disruptive			
Institute the right TALENT & MINDSET— the soft factors	Core			
	Connecting link			
	Disruptive			
		Leadership	People	Culture

Figure 10.3 How tool

The How tool is the essence of this book (see Figure 10.3). For the six How dimensions, it lays out your 1st S-curve efforts, 2nd S-curve efforts, and the link between the two. This tool can be used to assess the status quo or to define an ambition level. Whether you use it as a backward-looking tool to assess what has already happened or a forward-looking tool to determine concrete next steps is up to you and will depend on the setting. We recommend doing both.

Because the How is so critically important, we've added a little extra for you here. While it's impossible to summarize the best practices listed at the end of each How chapter with just a few words, we did want to give that a try. So, we've boiled down the contents of the How dimensions into the most critical elements for each of them (see Figure 10.4). View this high-level summary as a picture taken from a great distance and as a discussion starter for your own endeavors rather than as a complete and comprehensive "answer sheet" to the empty tool.

Finally, the Where tool helps you define KPIs for your two S-curves (see Figure 10.5). Make sure to opt for a healthy mix of qualitative and quantitative KPIs suited to the respective S-curve (the first section of the tool) and then place those post-its along the S-curves according to when you would use them. You can do this exercise on a macro level (take stock of your holistic digital transformation KPIs on a company level) or micro level (assess the KPIs for individual strategic initiatives). Again, we recommend doing both.

For more resources and a host of other materials, please visit our website: www.thedigitaltransformersdilemma.com.

Nothing left for us to say other than, digitally transform away!

HOW to get the digital transformation done

		Organization Crafting a flexible organization conducive to both S-curves	**Technology** Using technology as a driver for the transformation	**Processes** Implementing the processual set-up to support both S-curves
(INFRA-) STRUCTURE	**Core**	Establish a **central digital unit** that takes control over the digital agenda, coordinates projects across business units and establishes external links	Build strong links between IT, business functions and operations and **position IT** as an important **partner** and integral part of the digital transformation	Adopt an **agile process set-up** to execute digital transformation initiatives and integrate employees from the core to ensure ownership and support
	Connecting link	Build effective **organizational links** between the two S-curves to unleash synergies, e.g., through central oversight and control	**Integrate legacy and new IT** by first establishing a 2-speed IT and then gradually extending agile principles to the back-end	Establish an integration manager or **gate-keeper** who aligns disparate 1st and 2nd S-curve processes
	Disruptive	**Separate** 2nd S-curve initiatives from your core business to gain more flexibility and freedom, and use a **balanced approach** between internal and external venturing	Examine how **combinations** of new **technologies** and business model innovation can unlock new value pools and implement a **focus group** for scouting and education	Define a new **rule book for the governance** of initiatives and adapt a **VC-like approach** for the evaluation of ideas and progress
TALENT & MINDSET	**Core**	Expose and **transition** 1st S-curve leaders increasingly toward **transformational leadership** styles, providing ample training and (reverse) mentoring	**Retrain or reallocate** existing employees around the company in an effort to invest in their long-term future at that firm and in their external job market viability	**Stay true to** deep-rooted, historic company **values** unless they are diametrically opposed to the new (digital) strategy, and slowly introduce new beliefs and behaviors
	Connecting link	Orchestrate **ongoing alignment** between 1st and 2nd S-curve leaders to allow for transparency, ensuring a non-judgmental leadership exchange environment	Make the exchange between 1st and 2nd S-curve employees seamless with **digital transformation teams penetrating the core**, and through employee rotations	Use **(senior) allies** across the organization to act as **agents of cultural change**, spreading the message and encouraging grassroots cultural movements
	Disruptive	**Source** 2nd S-curve transformational leaders who empower, inspire and motivate employees largely **internally**, e.g., through leadership campuses	**Recruit or rent** new workers with the requisite skills, experience, and mindset in an effort to quickly ramp up the needed skills base	Rely on **new mindsets, structures, and ways of working** to create a customer-centric, lifelong learning-oriented, failure-tolerating, agile organization
		Leadership Building leaders who drive transformational change	**People** Building the "right-skilled" digital transformation workforce of the future	**Culture** Altering beliefs and behaviors to yield a culture of change

Figure 10.4 How dimensions

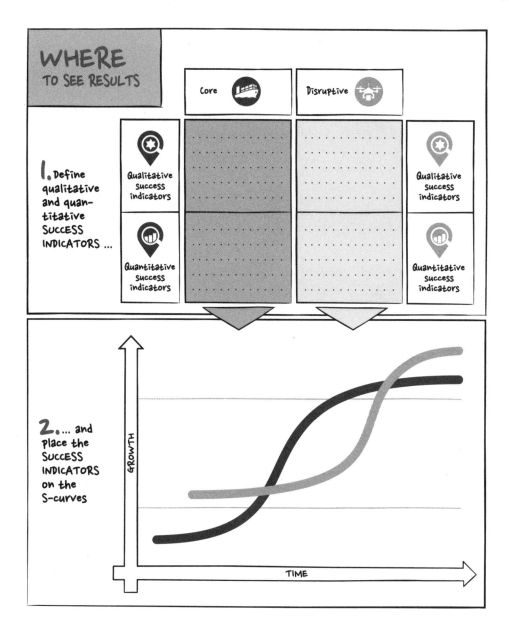

Figure 10.5 Where tool

Source: S-curve graph adapted from Gabriel Tarde. *The Laws of Imitation*. New York: Henry Holt and Company, 1903.

Acknowledgments

Although the front page of this book features four authors, the subsequent pages would have been empty without the cooperation of so many inspiring and accomplished individuals who have kindly devoted their time to speaking with us. This book is ripe with mini case studies and anecdotes from more than 100 globally leading companies and other entities whose executives have generously shared their insights, challenges, and best practices related to digital transformation with us. It was their candid stories that enabled us to derive our digital transformation framework and, very often, it was their own passion for the topic that spurred us on to work on this book even more excitedly. None of them would have needed to dedicate precious time on their calendars to four authors in search of answers but we are eternally grateful that they did. We thank them for their willingness to collaborate with us and we hope this book as a canvas for their own digital transformation journeys does justice to what they have accomplished and what they continue to strive for, all of which we deeply admire.

We would like to acknowledge as associated contributors to this book the following individuals, welcoming them to the extended authorship circle:

Alexander Maute; Director of IT & Business Services; Eissmann

Andreas Giesa; Head of eBusiness Consumer and Core Products & Solutions; Liebherr Hausgeräte

Andreas Opelt; Chief Market Officer; Saubermacher

Andreas Sturm; President of the Board of Directors (former); Bank Cler

Anna Neumeier; Associate Director Digitalization; Deutsche Pfandbriefbank AG

Anton Tremp; Local BU Manager for High Voltage Products; ABB Saudi Arabia

Arnaud Zeitoun; Deputy Chief Executive Officer in charge of Transformation; BNP Paribas Switzerland

Aurélie Picard; General Manager Vietnam/Laos/Cambodia/Myanmar; Ipsen Pharma

Axel Schmidt; Chief Digital Officer Frontend (former); WACKER Chemie AG

Bastian Gerhard; Managing Director; OysterLab; former Head of Innovation at Zalando

Benedikt Schell; Chairman of the Management Board; Mercedes-Benz Bank

Bernard Leong; Head of Post Office Network & Digital Services (former); SingPost

Bernd Reck; Head of Innovation; Aesculap

Bertrand Bodson; Chief Digital Officer; Novartis

Bruno Mercier; Chief Executive Officer and Executive Director (former); Sun Art Retail

Carola Wahl; Chief Transformation and Market Management Officer (former); AXA Switzerland

Christian Werb; Scrum Master (former); Liebherr Hausgeräte

Christian Schulz; Head of Operations; Schindler

Christof Stromberger; Managing Partner; Denovo

Claus Fleischer; Chief Executive Officer; Bosch eBike Systems

Cristian Citu; Digital Transformation Lead; World Economic Forum

David Hengartner; Head of Intrapreneurship; Swisscom

Davis Wu; Global Lead of Demand Planning and Analytics; Nestlé

Deborah Sherry; Chief Commercial Officer Europe, Russia & CIS (former); GE Digital

Dirk Linzmeier; Chief Executive Officer; OSRAM Continental

Dirk Ramhorst; Chief Digital Officer; WACKER Chemie AG

Edouard Meylan; Chief Executive Officer; H. Moser & Cie.

Eric Chaniot; Chief Digital Officer; Michelin

Fabian Stenger; Vice President Central and Eastern Europe; FlixMobility

Falk Bothe; Director of Digital Transformation Office; Volkswagen

Florian Bankoley; Vice President Corporate IT; Bosch

Gieri Cathomas; Managing Partner; Swisspath Health

Gisbert Rühl; Chief Executive Officer; Klöckner & Co

Glyn Williams; Vice President International (former); IDBS

Gregor Hofstätter-Pobst; Chief Financial Officer; UniCredit Bank Austria

Harald Brodbeck; Partner; Horváth & Partners

Hermann Bach; Head of Innovation Management & Commercial Services; Covestro

Ian Roberts; Chief Technology Officer; Bühler

Jan Mrosik; Chief Operating Officer Siemens Digital Industries; Siemens

Acknowledgments

Jean-Charles Deconninck; President of the Board of Directors; Generix Group

Julian Schubert; Managing Director V-ZUG Services AG; Head of Leasing V-ZUG AG; V-ZUG AG

Katharina Herrmann; Global Head of Platforms and Beyond Banking; ING

Konstantin Speidel; Vice President Digital Transformation; Allianz Global Investors

Kurt Straub; Vice President Operations Middle East, Africa and South West Asia; Hyatt International

Leonhard Muigg; Business Development Digital Enterprise / Industry 4.0; Siemens Austria

Luigi Pedrocchi; Group Chief Executive Officer; Mibelle Group

Mark Jacob; Managing Director; Dolder Hotel

Marko Kavcic; Digital Advisory Business Development Manager; Microsoft Slovenia

Markus Brokhof; Head of Digital & Commerce (former); Alpiq

Markus Köpfli; Head Digital Business Services; Mettler-Toledo International

Markus Reithwiesner; Chief Executive Officer; Haufe Group

Markus Streckeisen; Chief Transformation Officer & Head of Sales; SBB Cargo

Martin Watzlawek; Head of Strategy & Innovation; REHAU Automotive

Matthias Häne; Head of Strategy and Digital Transformation (former); Bank Cler

Max Costantini; Chief Strategy Officer; Mibelle Group, part of the Swiss MIGROS group

Michael Hepp; Vice President Digital Transformation; Walter

Michael Spiegel; Head of Digitalisation; Deutsche Pfandbriefbank AG & Chief Executive Officer; CAPVERIANT GmbH

Michael Weiss; Head of HR Development; Kommunalkredit Austria

Mirco Mäder; Project Manager (former); Kollibri / PostAuto

Nadine Borter; Owner and Head of Project Management; Contexta

Nicolas Verschelden; Head of Digital Innovation (former); Anheuser-Busch InBev

Norman Willich; Chief Financial Officer (former); Eissmann

Olaf Frank; Head of Business Technology; MunichRe

Onur Erdogan; General Manager (former); Estée Lauder Switzerland

Otto Preiss; Chief Operating Officer Digital; ABB

Owen Bethell; Global Issue and Communications Manager, Public Affairs; Nestlé

Patrick Koller; Chief Executive Officer; Faurecia

Patrick Marc Graf; Chief Commercial Officer; luxury watches and jewelry retailer

Philipp Leutiger; Chief Digital Officer; LafargeHolcim

Philipp Wetzel; Managing Director AMAG Innovation & Venture Lab; AMAG

Pietro Supino; Publisher and Chairman; TX Group

Piotr Jasiński; Senior Digital Manager; Carlsberg Group

Raphael Dölker; Co-Head of Digital Office; EnBW

Reiner Fageth; Chief Technology Officer, Head of R&D; CEWE

Reiner Thede; President & Co-Chief Executive Officer; Erbe Elektromedizin

Riccardo Giacometti; General Manager; Hotel Atlantis by Giardino

Rüdiger Mannherz; Vice President Finance & IT; Walter

Safer Mourad; Vice President Saurer Technology Centre; Saurer Group

Samy Jandali; Vice President Digital Business Empowerment; BASF

Sandra Ficht; Head of Digital Banking; Capgemini Invent

Sebastian Skalic; Agile Coach (former); ING DiBa Austria

Sebastien Szczepaniak; Vice President eBusiness; Nestlé

Sören Lauinger; Vice President Intrapreneurship & Co-creation; Aesculap

Stefan Stroh; Chief Digital Officer; Deutsche Bahn

Stefan Wolf; Chief Executive Officer; ElringKlinger

Stuart Bashford; Digital Officer; Bühler

Thomas Frésard; Chief Executive Officer; Contexta

Thomas Grübel; Chief Executive Officer; Govecs

Thomas Gutzwiller; Professor for Executive Education, Transformation Expert and Independent Board Member

Thomas Pirlein; Chief Information Officer; Müller Group

Thorsten Lampe; Chief Executive Officer; Covestro / Asellion

Thorsten Müller; Group Senior Vice President of Innovation (former); Osram

Tom Schneider; Chief Transformation Officer; Mercedes-Benz Bank

Uli Huener; Chief Innovation Officer; EnBW

Ulrich Hermann; Chief Digital Officer; Heidelberger Druckmaschinen

Urs Kissling; Chief Executive Officer; Embassy Jewel

Wilko Stark; Member of the Board Procurement and Supplier Quality (former); Mercedes Benz Cars / Daimler

Wolfgang Werz; Vice President Information Technology; Erbe Elektromedizin

Acknowledgments

Automotive expert; automotive supplier

Chief Digital Officer, discount retailer

Chief Digital Officer (former); international chemical and consumer goods company

Chief Digital Officer; globally leading food product corporation

Chief Information Officer (former); European fashion retailer

Communications executive; international financial institution

Director; European national central bank

Executive (former); Scandinavian bank

Head of Digital Office; European national central bank

Head of Digital Transformation Office; international financial institution

Head of Strategy; European national central bank

Innovation manager; international financial institution

Managing Director; European bank

Patrick Marc Graf; Chief Commercial Officer; luxury jewelry retailer

Senior executive (former); BTPN

Senior executive (former); European bank

Senior executive (former); Jelmoli

Senior executive (former); US media and entertainment corporation

Senior executive; diversified conglomerate

Senior executive; diversified retailer

Senior executive; luxury hotel chain

Senior executive, technology company

Senior strategy manager; international financial institution

Besides these associated contributors, to whom we owe the very existence of this book, we are similarly indebted to a number of digital transformation experts and other colleagues who have kindly reviewed early versions of our framework and other contents of this book. It is their opinion and challenging of our initial ideas that often stimulated the necessary pondering to sharpen our thoughts. The lives and calendars of this group of people are just as packed as those of the distinguished contributors we mentioned earlier, and we cannot thank them enough for the time they have kindly given us. They include, but are not limited to, Participants of the BMI Lab Think Tank Focus Group Seminar 10, attendees of all our keynote speeches, board presentations, and workshops, and other speaking engagements (including the 2019 Global Peter Drucker Forum, the 2019 Thinkers50 Conference, the 2019 NZZ X.Days, and the 2019 World Tourism Forum – just to name a few), and the students and executives whom we teach, with whom we often engage in lively discussions, and whose feedback we value enormously (including, but not limited to, St. Gallen EMBA, MBA, graduate, and undergraduate students).

We appreciate the remarks and questions from our connections in the LinkedIn community, visitors of our book website (www.thedigitaltransformersdilemma.com), and anybody else who laid their eyes on early excerpts of our work and took up a dialogue with us.

Also, we want to sincerely thank our fellow researchers and academics for their thoughtful comments, remarks, and advice on how to further refine and expand original drafts of the book.

An array of additional contributors was involved in creating this book. We are grateful to our graphic designer, Malte Belau, for demonstrating unfettered dedication to interpreting and implementing even our weirdest wishes; our research associate, Kira Prosi, for supporting with data analysis; and HSG students Tom Bauer, Milena Hasler, Elisa Frost, and Khaled Shaker for building upon our theorizing and continuing in that spirit, contributing their own research insights to our book.

Finally, we are beyond grateful to our editors at Wiley, Richard Narramore and Julie Kerr, for believing in our potential and providing excellent feedback; the graphic designers for a great cover that so exactly captures the spirit of our book; and the entire team at Wiley, including but not limited to Vicki Adang and Victoria Anllo, as well as Debbie Schindler and Jayalakshmi Erkathil Thevarkandi (and everyone else who helped with typesetting, copyediting, production, marketing and everything else), for the fantastic cooperation in making this happen.

About the Authors

KAROLIN FRANKENBERGER

is a full professor in strategy and innovation at the University of St. Gallen, Switzerland, where she is also Director of the Institute of Management and Strategy and the Academic Director of the Executive MBA. Prior to her academic career, Karolin worked for seven years at McKinsey & Company. Owing to her award-winning research, which focuses on (digital) business transformation, business model innovation, ecosystems and circular economy, she has recently been named Thinker of the Month by Thinkers50, the world's foremost resource for sharing leading management ideas of our age. Her publications appear regularly in top-tier academic and practitioner-oriented journals and her book, *The Business Model Navigator* is known as a standard reference in business model innovation literature. Karolin has founded a spin-off, is an internationally renowned keynote speaker and supports company leaders from numerous industries worldwide in their strategy and innovation challenges. She holds a PhD with highest distinction from the University of St. Gallen and was a visiting PhD student at Harvard Business School and the University of Connecticut. She and her husband are parents of two children.

HANNAH MAYER

is a PhD Fellow at Harvard Business School and part of the Laboratory for Innovation Science at Harvard, where she does research on digital transformation and AI-powered business models. Her research interests also extend to (digital) business ecosystems and platforms – an area she explored as part of her doctoral studies, which she completed at the University of St. Gallen (Switzerland). She frequently publishes thought-leading insights from the digitization, innovation and technology spaces in leading media outlets, such as Forbes.com and Harvard Business Review. Prior to her academic career, Hannah was a management consultant at a leading international management consulting firm, where she specialized in digital transformation, digital skill building and digital marketing projects within the tech sector and other industries, and across various geographies. Previously, she spent two years at Google as a Digital Strategist, helping media agencies optimize their digital strategies. In addition to her PhD, Hannah holds masters degrees from Queen's University (Canada) and the Vienna University of Economics and Business (Austria).

ANDREAS REITER

is currently a PhD student at Karolin's Chair at the University of St. Gallen/HSG, specializing in digital transformation and (digital) business ecosystems. His prior academic career saw him graduate with honors in business administration from the Vienna University of Economics and Business (Austria) and London Business School (UK). His professional experience includes two years at a globally leading management consulting firm, where he focused on digital transformation projects and the set-up of digital business models for incumbents in the financial services industry.

MARKUS SCHMIDT

is the CEO and founder of QSID Digital Advisory, a consulting boutique dedicated to supporting medium-sized and family-owned companies in their strategy, leadership and digital transformation challenges. This role was preceded by a long experience leading globalization and digital transformation efforts at Valeo and Bosch, most recently as Executive Vice President at Bosch Automotive Electronics. His many years of leaderhship experience at Bosch gave Markus deep insights into the opportunities and challenges of digital transformation for industrial companies. He now draws on these as a coach and advisor to C-level executives in digital transformation implementation matters, as a keynote speaker at industry events, and as a lecturer at multiple universities. Markus also serves on the board of Fashion 3 of Mulliez Group and XTECH Invest/Clayens NP Group. He and his wife, Claudia, are parents of two children.

Index